Living Tangier

CONTEMPORARY ETHNOGRAPHY

Kirin Narayan and Alma Gottlieb, Series Editors

LIVING TANGIER

Migration, Race,
and Illegality
in a Moroccan City

Abdelmajid Hannoum

PENN

UNIVERSITY OF PENNSYLVANIA PRESS

PHILADELPHIA

Published by
University of Pennsylvania Press
Philadelphia, Pennsylvania 19104-4112
www.upenn.edu/pennpress

Printed in the United States of America on acid-free paper
1 3 5 7 9 10 8 6 4 2

A Cataloging-in-Publication record is available from the
Library of Congress
ISBN 978-0-8122-5172-2
LCCN 2019020159

For Gabriel Asfar

Contents

Introduction

I have old memories of Tangier. I experienced the city first in the early 1980s. I was on my way to France, and Tangier was the gateway to that fascinating world that the youth of my generation dreamed of as we heard incredible stories of wealth, freedom, love, and rights. Tangier, as I could see it from the train that crossed part of downtown all the way to the port, looked modest, poor even, and only the beach, located in the downtown itself, distinguished it as an interesting city. The train used to cross the Corniche and enter the port, stopping right at the ferry gate. By the time it arrived in Tangier, the train had become a currency market, with men offering to sell foreign bills, especially the French franc and the Spanish peseta. The city, by then, had a reputation for hosting contraband, dealers of all types, and sex workers and druggies. Not without foundation, these stereotypes are still widespread, and not only among Moroccans. But what Tangier did not have at the time is its reputation as host to migrants from almost every corner of Africa, including, of course, Morocco. These travelers stay for a while as they prepare for their crossing or, as some say, "burning" (*lahrig*) to Europe.

Since the early 1990s, the southern Mediterranean has emerged as a hub for migration, "legal" and "illegal." Here, a large number of West Africans and young Moroccans, including minors, make daily attempts to cross to Europe. The city of Tangier, because of its close proximity to Spain—only 14 kilometers—is one of the main gateways for this movement. It has also become a magnet for middle- and working-class Europeans seeking a more comfortable life. In this book, I use Tangier as an ethnographic site and focus on its three largest migrant populations: Moroccans, West Africans, and Europeans. All these communities meet in the city and share its space, albeit unequally.

The migration of Africans to Europe is not, of course, new: it is as old as European migration to Africa.[1] In modern times, colonialism gave rise to perhaps one of the most significant human flows from Europe to the rest of the world, even as it also engendered a wholesale migration to Europe. Many of us are familiar with the colonial regime of mobility, that is, the patterned movement of Europeans to the rest of the globe. Now, and starting in the 1990s, a *post*colonial global regime of mobility has arisen. These flows are not spontaneous; as Saskia Sassen writes, "Migrations do not just happen; they are produced. And migrations do not involve just any possible combination of countries, they are patterned."[2] There is indeed a pattern of flows from Africa to Europe and from Europe to Africa that is neither recent nor unfamiliar. The history of this pattern is told numerous times in narratives about the colonial adventure.

In his novel *Heart of Darkness*, Joseph Conrad captures the movement of the "white" man traveling to the colonies as part of the colonial machinery that was operating in full force in Africa. However, Conrad does not mention that migrants were also moving in the other direction. Africans were heading to Europe to be soldiers, laborers, students. This "reverse" movement is articulated in Tayeb Saleh's novel *Season of Migration to the North*.[3] The movement of the period—both from the metropole to the colony, and the reverse—was intense, regulated, and organized mainly by the colonial state. This colonial regime of mobility consisted of importing human labor and manned gunpowder, especially during and after World War I and World War II, and sending settlers, colonialists, soldiers, and all types of colonial agents to the colonies.[4]

The postcolonial regime of mobility is patterned differently, even though its genealogy is rooted in the colonial flows that marked the world especially from the sixteenth to the nineteenth century, when most of the globe was ruled by a handful of European countries. Immediately after their colonies' independence, these former colonial powers initiated a process of postcolonial migration, motivated in large part by the need to reconstruct Europe after the destruction and tragedies of two world wars.[5] Yet, by the early 1990s, the call to halt migration was backed by an array of laws and rules. In 1993, the French minister of interior affairs, Charles Pasqua, respected and feared for his tough stand on immigrants and all other "outlaws," called for zero immigration and implemented draconian laws to stop it, including the restriction of French citizenship: children of resident immigrant parents were no longer automatically granted citizenship but could apply for it when they reached age eighteen. Ironically, migration, legal and illegal, was not halted; if anything, it intensified. Neither laws nor walls stopped this process.

From the media discourse and also from the vast literature on migration, one cannot but conclude that migration is a challenge faced mainly by Europe and North America. It seems that Europe is besieged by migrants and refugees, whereas the rest of the world, including Africa, does nothing but send its youth to Europe. What is often overlooked is the fact that, especially since the 1990s, migration has intensified from Europe to the rest of the world, including to Africa and to Latin America. As I demonstrate in Chapter 5, Morocco is now a coveted destination for European migrants. The city of Tangier has become a magnet for middle-class Europeans who find the cost of life increasingly high in their countries of origin. This European mobility to the South is rarely described as migration, let alone immigration, and is often presented as evidence of the global mobility that allows people to move in a fast world. This mobility seems to highlight the very idea of Kantian cosmopolitanism, a key cornerstone of the discourse on globalization.[6] Yet, I describe this movement as migration in and of itself, motivated by a desire to search for a new life. In a good number of cases, it can be explained by economic factors as well as by cultural ones. I seek, then, to understand its processes, dynamics, and the transformative power of the city and, by implication, Moroccan society by and large.

Once a marginal postcolonial city,[7] Tangier has indeed emerged in the past ten or so years as a major, global city of the southern Mediterranean. In a relatively short time, it has been transformed, under the reign of King Mohammed VI (beginning in 1999), from a provincial and poor municipality to the second-largest economy in Morocco—second only to Casablanca.

Colonial Events and Postcolonial Imagination

Tangier has had a rich, complex, and long relationship with Europe, perhaps more than any other city in the southern Mediterranean. Even its early modern history is intricately linked with the politics of European nations.[8] Ruled by the Spanish from 1581 to 1643, it was brought again under Portugal by a popular uprising in support of King John IV. The British received it from the Portuguese as a dowry—offered by the Portuguese queen, Catherine of Braganza, to Charles II.[9] The early colonialism of the British thrived there, with the creation of the Levant and Barbary companies, long before the creation of the East India Company.[10] For the British, the acquisition of this town, a strategic spot on the Mediterranean, became "a reassuring sign of national power and unity."[11]

Amid an ambitious project to remake the then-town into a port, under the British, Tangier became the target of attacks from surrounding Moroccan tribes. This sustained and never-waning armed opposition, along with a Spain wary to see Great Britain gain a foothold in the Mediterranean, forced the British to withdraw in 1684.[12] Even though it "made up for the loss" by taking over Gibraltar in 1713,[13] Great Britain "made it a fixed policy to prevent any other European Power from seizing Tangier."[14] It was also willing to do whatever it took to prevent any other European power from taking control of Moroccan territory.[15]

Morocco was then independent, though still coveted by European powers, with Great Britain playing the role of a friend eager to safeguard its sovereignty.[16] Tangier, along with all the Moroccan coastal cities, was no stranger to Europeans, nor were Europeans a stranger to it. Trade and diplomatic activities continued unabated. Historian Jean-Louis Miège considers it "the most European city of Morocco"[17] because of its important commercial and diplomatic relations with Europe, especially France, Great Britain, Portugal, and Italy. The European population was estimated at 965 of a total local population estimated to be between 6,000 and 9,000.[18] Miège also documents how the city was an attractive destination for European political refugees, those who fled during the French revolution and during the Napoleon wars, French and Italians, from different social backgrounds— people "with no means" and high officers of the French army.[19] Also, the Jewish population of Tangier, most of it comprising Iberian Jews, was already Europeanized and mixed well with Muslims. "Tangier became known as the place where Jews walked freely in the streets, dressed like Europeans, displaying a newfound sense of self-worth different from Jews elsewhere in Morocco," Susan Miller notes.[20] Yet, despite the ongoing presence of Europeans and European culture, Tangier still—and strangely—appears foreign and hostile in its depictions penned by European and American visitors, characteristics perhaps exaggerated to align with contemporary readers' expectations of travel literature in general and of the so-called Orient in particular.[21] Consider the testimony of Edmondo de Amicis, a writer who visited in 1875 as part of an Italian delegation headed to Fes, then the capital of Hasan I (r. 1873–94):

Three hours later, and the very name of our Continent sounds strange; Christian signifies enemy, and our civilization is unknown, or feared, or scoffed at. Everything, from the very foundations of society to the most trifling details of private life, is metamorphosed, and all indication of the close proximity of Europe has completely disappeared. We suddenly find ourselves in an unknown land, without ties of any kind, and with everything to learn. To be sure the European coast is still visible from the shore, but in our hearts there is a consciousness of immeasurable distance, as though that narrow strip of water were an ocean, those blue, distant hills a delusion.[22]

Also in the mid-nineteenth century, another visiting writer, Mark Twain, stays true to the stereotype of the intrepid European traveler in desolate foreign lands. To him, Tangier conveys utter strangeness: "We wanted something thoroughly and uncompromisingly foreign—foreign from top to bottom—foreign from center to circumference—foreign inside and outside and all around—nothing anywhere about to dilute its foreignness—nothing to remind us of any other people or any other land under the sun, and lo in Tangier we have found it."[23]

Twain sees the city as "a weary prison";[24] here, his "innocents abroad" find themselves in "the completest exile."[25] He quips, "I would seriously recommend to the government of the United States that when a man commits a crime so heinous that the law provides no adequate punishment for it, they make him Consul-General to Tangier."[26]

Twain also, in the same context, writes, "Tangier is a foreign land if ever there was one, and the true spirit of it can never be found in any book save The Arabian Nights. Here are no white men visible, yet swarms of humanity are all about us. Here is a packed and jammed city enclosed in a massive stone wall which is more than a thousand years old."[27]

On a visit in 1845, Alexandre Dumas, the renowned French writer, describes Tangier as "dark and silent as a tomb,"[28] a place of 7,000 people living in a land wholly foreign and beastly hostile: "'How strange it is,' I thought to myself, 'you are perfectly at home anywhere in Europe, but if you cross this narrow stretch of water to Africa, you are at once conscious of a fundamental change. This morning you left a friendly country, but tonight you are in a hostile land. Those fires you see were lit by men of a race alien to your own, who regard you as their enemy, though you have done them no harm. . . . Once you set your foot in that land, even if you evade the wild beasts, how shall you escape the enmity of man?"[29]

In the nineteenth century, Tangier reemerged as a point of European contention after the 1880 Conference of Madrid.[30] Disagreements between Great Britain and France were first settled by the Entente Cordiale, signed on April 8, 1904, which allowed Great Britain to secure its interests in Egypt and free passage to Gibraltar (with the understanding that the other European powers would not erect any fortifications on the Moroccan coast) and guaranteed France a free hand in Moroccan politics if it could reach an understanding with Spain on the matter.[31] This set the diplomatic stage for Spain, by virtue of its geographical proximity to Morocco, and France, by virtue of its occupation of Algeria, to negotiate Morocco's status. An agreement between the two powers was reached on October 3, 1904, when they secretly divided Morocco. This agreement immediately stirred discord among European powers, especially Germany, which felt ignored and left out.[32] Further diplomatic maneuverings led to another set of agreements at the Algeciras Conference (April 7, 1906). This was intended to resolve the first Moroccan crisis between colonial powers and paved the way[33] for the establishment of a French protectorate in Morocco on March 30, 1912, and a Spanish one in November of the same year. France took the largest share, leaving the northern Rif region to Spain, which had been in possession of the Spanish Sahara to the west since 1884. Tangier became the focus of diplomatic tension between France and Spain, as well as between these two and Great Britain. Whereas the French argued that Tangier was under Morocco's sultan and thus should be part of their protectorate, the Spanish argued that Tangier was in the Rif and therefore should fall under their jurisdiction. Great Britain, meanwhile, hoped to make Tangier an international zone, on the model of Shanghai.[34]

The end of World War I changed the dynamics of Europe's political maneuvers in Tangier. With Germany eliminated and Italy making its own claims, an agreement between France, Spain, and Great Britain was reached in Paris on December 18, 1923, and Tangier became a so-called international zone.[35] Yet the French remained clearly privileged in Tangier,[36] since their protectorate stretched across the rest of Morocco. This French privilege may still be strongly felt in the city today.

In the years during which it was an international zone (1923–56), Tangier was subject to the colonial machinations of several European powers, who ruled it through a municipal council. Tangier thus, along with Casablanca, experienced the full force of colonialism. But while Casablanca was characterized by what Paul Rabinow calls "techno cosmopolitanism,[37] Tangier was marked rather by "diplomat/capitalist cosmopolitanism." As an international zone, Tangier had become part of "Europe," with its capitalist system, network of banks, European population, and its colonial dynamics of spying, trading, negotiating, and even dating and intermarrying. The city that just a century ago had looked foreign to European travelers and diplomats had now become an annex to the metropole. By the mid-twentieth century, Paul Bowles dared to compare its capitalist spirit to that of New York City: "Tangier is more New York than New York. . . . Then you must see how alike the two places are. The life revolves wholly about the making of money. Practically everyone is dishonest. In New York you have Wall Street, here you have the Bourse. . . . In New York you have the slick financiers, here the money changers. In New York you have your racketeers. Here you have your smugglers. And you have every nationality and no civic pride."[38]

However, while capitalism thrived in the city, the local population suffered distress and saw their condition worsen under international status. Graham Stuart believes that "this condition was due partly to the lack of natural resources in the International Zone, but even more to the heavy fixed charges imposed by the Statute."[39] The Jewish population also suffered Nazi propaganda, especially in the international zone, that damaged the Muslim-Jewish entente that was supposed to constitute a common Muslim and Jewish front against racism and anti-Semitism.[40] Notwithstanding, the city's European immigrants enjoyed the good life.[41] Like its sister cities in the southern Mediterranean under colonial rule, Tangier, too, was made of two parts well described by Frantz Fanon: the town of the natives, poor and wretched, on the one hand, and the town of the Europeans, prosperous and blessed, on the other.[42] Mohamed Choukri, who ran away from his village to become a street kid in the city, would later describe it in these terms: "When I arrived, there were two Tangiers: the colonialist and international Tangier and the Arabic Tangier, made of misery and ignorance. At these times, to eat, I combed the garbage cans. The European ones preferably, because they were richer."[43]

Throughout Tangier's time as an international zone, the European town remained firmly attached to the capitalist network of Europe and the United States. While the city rapidly transformed into an important theater of geopolitical maneuverings, it became an attractive destination for those bourgeois who found themselves marginalized in Europe. Tangier also offered anonymity and protection to gay men of means, or the so-called remittance men, as I have heard them described,[44] not to mention an abundance of sexual pleasure, exotic and cheap.[45] However, the miserable city alluded to by Choukri continued to exist on the margins of the modern world that had conquered it and increased the suffering of most of its local population, reduced to the status of noncitizens in their own city.

Independence in 1956 did not change the condition of this population. Having suffered colonial rule, they now had to suffer its postcolonial effects—powerful and pervasive. During the rule of King Hassan II, the relatively few Europeans and Americans who stayed on continued to enjoy the city that privileged them. Colonial rule was of recent date and Tangier remained a point of convergence, a magnet for rich men and women from the Western world, including many celebrities. The native town, the Casbah and the medina, not to mention the shantytowns randomly built at the outskirts by migrants from rural areas, remained on the margins of the nation-state and continued to be, as in the colonial period, "a place of ill fame, peopled by men of evil repute," to borrow again from Fanon.[46]

For Hassan II, Tangier, along with the entire region of the Rif, was the soft belly of his rule. The Rif had a different colonial experience from the rest of Morocco. It had been occupied by Spain and had sustained a staunch armed struggle against its colonizer, which, at one point, it was able to defeat, in the Battle of Anwal on July 22, 1921, establishing the Republic of the Rif (1923–26), free and victorious, headed by the Rif's heroic figure Abdelkrim al-Khattabi.[47] Seen by and large as more loyal to the memory of Abdelkrim than to the Alaouite monarch (whether Mohammed V or his son Hassan II), the region of the Rif was neglected, and was even brutally repressed in 1958 under the rule of Mohammed V (and again in the 1980s, when it protested the rise of food prices in what are called the bread riots).[48] Then came more neglect and marginalization. Tangier shared the lot of the Rif. The situation looked as colonial as before. As Jean Genet reported to Mohamed Choukri, "The situation here is very unstable. Everything reeks of poverty and misery. The foreigners are the only ones here who live like human beings."[49]

For much of the local population, as for many Moroccans, especially from rural areas, migration to Germany, the Netherlands, and Belgium during the 1960s and 1970s became the alternative pathway to a better life.[50] Their migration was at the time desired and even sought after by European nations. European firms and companies came to rural Morocco in search of human labor, offering "contracts" to recruit laborers for European factories.

The contract laborers' migration helped create an urban middle class. Also, and importantly, it created a culture of migration, meaning an entire vision of migration as the road to wealth, as the road to a new way of life, and a modern one to be sure. This vision engendered a set of practices henceforth recognized as migrant practices: clothes, cars, gifts, remittances to family members, summer weddings, and various other displays of having "made it." By the late 1970s, European factories no longer needed to recruit laborers; the laborers knew the way, and often undertook it. This was a time when several European countries, including France, did not even require a visa of visitors from Morocco. Moroccan cities, especially Tangier, the main gate to Europe, transformed drastically during the summer, when many of these migrants returned to visit their families. Cars with registration plates from almost every country in Europe—especially France, the Netherlands, and Germany—could be seen not only traversing but also filling up the city. This scene can still be seen today with the important difference that most of those who visit are no longer migrants but European citizens of Moroccan ancestry, some with several generations' roots in Europe. In short, the labor contract period was transformative, engendering a small urban middle class and a large Moroccan diaspora that impacts the dynamics not only of Moroccan society but also of European societies. The contract period also created and propagated the myth of migration as a salvation—as expressed by a Moroccan idiom, *ghâb wa jâb*, the migrant "left and brought back [good things]."

Tangier is the offspring of modernity; like many of the cities in Africa,[51] it is a colonial creation, for colonialism effected a complete spatial revolution in the city, and not only a cultural and economic one. As a revolution, colonialism created a new space—as revolutions always do.[52] The old Tangier, the precolonial one, consisting mainly of the medina, became, during the city's life as an international zone, peripheral—architecturally, culturally, and politically. Even today it has to be defined in relation to the new space, as tradition is defined by modernity. The *centre ville* or *ville nouvelle* (the center of the city, or the new city), made of modern buildings constructed by the Spanish, the Italians, and the French, with a central boulevard, wide and open, has become the heart of the cultural and economic life of the city. In addition to its buildings, there are the names—such as Boulevard Pasteur, Rue du Mexique, Rue Vasquez, Place de France, Rue d'Angleterre. These names are still in use today, even for those boulevards formally renamed to announce independence (Pasteur was renamed Mohammed V; Vasquez was renamed Khaled Ben al-Walid).

In postcolonial times and especially since the early 1990s, the Casbah and, to a certain extent, the medina have also been reinvented as Europeanized neighborhoods.[53] Like many African cities, Tangier is divided into the old city and the new city, the Arab city and the European city. But the Western imagination, surprisingly, is captured only by the first and rarely, if ever, by the second, of its own creation. Put differently, the colonial, now postcolonial, myth of Tangier is made of images from the old city. These images have long spoken to European "expats" and visitors. They have been elaborated throughout the decades by artists and writers such as Eugène Delacroix, Henri Matisse, Mark Twain, Paul Bowles, and Roland Barthes. These images can be found in Western works of literature, art, and film and are often reproduced in global print media such as the *New York Times* and *Le Monde*.

There are several Tangiers, as there are several representations of Tangier created by its local population, or by its bourgeoisie, or its outsiders—its migrants, whether Moroccan or West African. There are also different representations of Tangier within Morocco itself, including in fiction, in songs, and in folktales.[54] Different names and nicknames—Tangier, Tangiers, Tanja, Tingis, Tanger, *'Arûs al-shammâl* (the bride of the north)—are used in different representations and in different contexts. But the image of Tangier that seems to dominate and transcend Moroccan borders is the colonial image—what I am calling the myth of Tangier. This myth consists of various images of the city as a traditional city, an Oriental one for sure: exotic, seductive, sensuously deviant, treacherous, cruel, but also open and welcoming in unpredictable ways. Images of its modernity are not part of the myth. For instance, the urban youth that constitute most of the local population are not part of the image of the city. The city appears to be not an empty space but a space of and for Europeans only. Moroccans in general, young or old, are absent except in the form of a reference to a "maid" or "servant"[55] or as "wealthy Moroccans" in the midst of "bronzed European families and ladies."[56] Even the West African population, now a visible component of the city, does not draw the attention of the visiting reporter. They have their place only in narratives of tragedy, images and stories of deaths at sea.

The myth of Tangier is made also of a specific representation of space. The centre ville is absent save for Café de Paris and Hotel Continental, both of which were frequented in the past by European and American celebrities, many of them writers and artists. The Boulevard Mohammed V, the heart of the city for Moroccans, their meeting place, is often absent in these writings. So is the most urban, most global part of the city, the Corniche, with its chains of American, French, and Italian restaurants and luxury hotels.

They are not part of the image of Tangier. It is as if their portrayal would unsettle the myth and would make Tangier appear almost as ordinary as any other city. Instead, Tangier exists as composed by European works of literature and art, known and obscure. This Tangier has triumphed over time. Indeed, it is unchanging in its otherness, its difference. In the print media of the new millennium, Tangier appears exotic, backward, and "dreaming of Europe."[57] Words such as "eccentricity," "wonder," "unusual magic," "mystery" are used to paint the city.[58] The Tangier described in, say, the *New York Times* in the year 2010 is made of narrow streets, the Casbah, Café Hafa, of colors, objects, and a few shadows of Moroccans—a journalist sees "someone in a tangerine-colored *djellaba* walking past a mint-green door with a pistachio set of tiles and it seems so natural."[59] A woman, veiled, passes by. All this is in the background, composing the Orientalist mise-en-scène for daring expats from Britain, the United States, and Europe: "Deep in the Casbah and high on the slopes of Veille Montagne, you find these people [expats], these elegant, exotic plants who fill their days with lunch parties and gossip. They may be the harmless denizens of an old idea, doing it with style, living beyond their means but strictly within their taste. It is a painted city where ripe vegetables and aged spies litter the souks, where men of hidden consequence can always find a drink. Most of all, Tangier is a city where attention to detail is undivided, a place where you meet people just crazy for beauty."[60]

Rooted in colonial creation, and elaborated by several icons of Western literature, this image still "defies the length of time," as Joseph Conrad would say.[61] Its continuity is guaranteed even by "native" writers such as Tahar Ben Jelloun and Mohamed Choukri.[62] It is also secured by an ongoing cultural production. For instance, a relatively recent article in *Le Monde* evokes the Arabian Nights, cites Twain and Delacroix, and drops a series of names that populate the Western imaginary about Tangier: Truman Capote, Jack Kerouac, Tennessee Williams, Paul Morand, Roland Barthes, Jean Genet, Marguerite Yourcenar, Paul Bowles.[63] There is a discursive subconscious that surfaces in present-day reporting about the city and continues to be repeated in Western literature, major and minor.[64]

"Perception is the absolute knowledge of the philosopher," Maurice Merleau-Ponty once wrote.[65] He had in mind a specific philosophy, a new one, the phenomenology that was established with Edmund Husserl as a radical critique of knowledge, that is, as an intellectual practice that subordinates discourse to perception. Given that perception is the main but not absolute knowledge of the anthropologist, one can surely say that anthropology[66]—a discipline more "promiscuous, inconstant, and ill defined"[67] than any other in social science—has inherited, especially with interpretive and postmodern anthropology, the phenomenological tradition Merleau-Ponty alludes to.[68] Perception, or what is commonly called participant observation, makes ethnographic practices appear as a sort of practicing phenomenology, or at least a discipline where perception plays an important role in the making of knowledge.

About Tangier and its migrants, perception is then the main, but not the absolute, knowledge of the anthropologist. History, especially a critical history that interrogates the present, is also, to a certain extent, the other source of this book: colonial and postcolonial histories of Tangier, of Moroccan perceptions of darker bodies, of race and racism in the former colony that is Morocco, of class and education, and so on. The chapters of the book, then, discretely express a commitment to history as an important mode of sociological analysis to rethink the present.

This book shies away from the myth of Tangier, deconstructed in this introduction, and instead explores the lives of those who appear often only as the objects of sensational literature and media reporting: the migrants, both the African and the European ones as well. More specifically, it is an examination of human flows to and from the city, and the politics of these flows within and outside the nation-state. In other words, the book looks at migration in its intersection with race and the law in order to not only highlight the global dynamics of the city, but also the city's dynamics in relation to global politics as they pertain to migration, racial thinking, and legality. The book endeavors to contribute to the debate on these questions not only across disciplines, but also across geographical areas. The goal here is to look at the dynamics of migration at the border between Africa and Europe as well as within an African nation itself.

Migration, Race, and Illegality

Within the larger field of Middle Eastern studies,[69] research on migration is nascent. With few exceptions, the migratory flows within Arab societies and across Africa and Europe have not received the attention they so much deserve. Yet, one of the most major transformations that can be noticed in Middle Eastern societies is precisely the intense migratory movements of the past twenty years or so. I hope, with this book, to contribute to the fields of both migration and urban anthropology by examining how, on the Mediterranean border, in the city of Tangier, migration is entangled with European Union (EU) law and Moroccan racial perceptions and practices.

The study of migration, as Abdelmalek Sayad noted decades ago, in the 1970s, is mainly the study of *im*migration, that is, the study of migrants in their host country—in Sayad's case, France. He noted the absence of research on the sending country, that is, the study of emigration, and the ways it affects those who undertake the journey.[70] With few exceptions, the situation remains the same.[71] Despite the fact that the countries of the so-called Maghreb, and not only Morocco, have been transformed by becoming receiving countries, migration has not drawn much scholarly attention compared with the journalistic reporting that often makes a sensation out of it, especially at the moments of large-scale tragedies that are too frequent on the shores of the Mediterranean.

The present study, as has been noted, looks at not only migrant movements to Europe but also, comparatively, migrant movements to Africa itself, to the city of Tangier. The aim is to show that migration is not one-dimensional or straightforward. By studying its multidimensionality, this study touches on larger issues as well. By comparing the situations of West Africans and Europeans in the city, for instance, this book brings the issue of race in Moroccan society to the fore. Through the situations outlined here, I show how Moroccan society thinks about itself and how it thinks about difference(s).

It should be noted, at the outset, that race and racism are inherent to modernity.[72] For race and racial thinking form the cultural foundation not only of colonialism but of modernity itself, as Hannah Arendt powerfully argued.[73] Since the region we commonly call the Maghreb has known and was itself transformed by colonial modernity, race was also that import that came with the project of modernity. In the case of Tangier, for instance, Susan Miller notes in passing that racism entered the city in the nineteenth century, before the colonial project but definitively with the modern project of the first European community to settle in the city.[74]

In 1951, Claude Lévi-Strauss published a pamphlet on race that ruffled many feathers. He argued, in the tradition of Franz Boas, that race has no scientific value and instead argued in favor of the concept of culture, which is always hybrid, the product of ongoing contributions of human groups near and far. Later, Michel Foucault, his colleague at the Collège de France, lamented the absence of race in France, an absence that masks inequalities.[75] What Foucault had in mind was race as a social construct, as a category, not race as a biological reality. In anthropology today, race is considered nonexistent (meaning biologically) and thus without scientific value.[76] However, what does not exist biologically may well exist socially. The existence of racism in modern human societies does indeed betray the existence of race—a certain view that constructs an "other" based on skin color and/or some perceived moral and biological difference. Even if anthropology liberated itself from racial thinking, the societies that anthropologists work in may practice racial difference and express racist views that are themselves cultural practices. Anthropologists who ignore this can no longer be on the avant-garde of race studies.[77]

As Magali Bessone notes, "The reality of race resides not only in anthropology or biology, but in the socio-historical relations produced by practices that are founded on race." By saying that "race" is real, she means that "the concept pertains to the ontology of social science where categories have a reality which is not the reality of natural science."[78] Therefore, race remains a critical analytical category central to anthropological and critical minority studies.[79]

Interrogating the racism that permeates a society cannot be possible without interrogating race as a social construct. As Paul Gilroy put it, "Races are political collectivities not ahistorical essences."[80] Colonialism itself introduced the concept to the countries of the Maghreb.[81] Early on in their encounters with the populations of the region, especially in Algeria, colonial authors observed the existence of several "races" that soon disappeared from the colonial discourse to preserve only the racial dichotomy of Arabs versus Berbers that postcolonial discourse, even in its nationalist form, has kept.[82] Noting that races exist in these narratives does not mean that local populations saw themselves through racial lenses, but rather that racial categories became demarcated with the advent of modernity. Precolonial, local categories of difference and even identity were not racial but depended on other differences, such as religious affiliation,[83] tribal genealogy, regional location, even city identification, among others.[84] As Lévi-Strauss pointed out long ago when discussing the racial theory of Arthur de Gobineau,[85] it is not that Gobineau saw people as constituting races, but rather that he put the idea of degeneration at the core of racial theory.[86]

The present study examines the issue of race in Moroccan society both in terms of "blackness" as well as "whiteness." But what do these two concepts mean in this context, and what they do refer to, in concrete terms? In other words, what does it mean to be white in Morocco (which is part of a larger cultural landscape we call Arab societies)? What does it mean to be black? How are these constructed? By whom?

First, let us stress the fact, again following Paul Gilroy, that for a variety of historical reasons, no general theory of race and racial relations can be sustained.[87] Gilroy further argues that races "are imagined—socially and politically constructed—and the contingent processes from which they emerge may be tied to equally uneven patterns of class formation to which they, in turn, contribute."[88] Indeed, there is a variety of concepts of race as seen in the "social expressions" we label racist.[89] If we consider racialized expressions to be a field of discourse, as David Goldberg suggests, then anyone familiar with Moroccan society and, by extension, Arab societies must also be familiar with a plethora of racial expressions (beliefs, epithets, slurs, jokes)[90] used in a variety of contexts that are clearly indicative of racial thinking. The case of West Africans leaves no doubt that race and racism are important issues in Moroccan society (made explicit by an entire field of racial expressions, as I explore in Chapter 4). However, there are surely others that may be masked under other denominations. Other names, slurs, epithets, especially those that refer to regional origin, may be indicative of ethnic expressions in that, as Fredrik Barth argues about ethnicity, they refer to boundaries within society itself.[91] However, scholars of race and racism have persuasively noted that "ethnic connotations" pertain to race and that "race sometimes takes on significance in terms of ethnicity."[92] Therefore, several ethnic groups in Morocco are also racial, and one finds around them an entire field of racial expressions.

As a postcolonial society, Morocco experienced, with full force, the politics of race in the colonial period, when its society was ruled by a white power (i.e., France). After colonialism, the racial ideology has remained very much present in the country via its languages, its values, and an entire economy of visual images of race. The racial thinking that was at the core of colonialism and that separated the world of the colonized and the colonizer, symbolically as well as physically,[93] could not have possibly disappeared without leaving a trace. On the contrary, race and racism, in their modern conceptions, have become part of the Moroccan imagination.

For instance, blackness and whiteness in Moroccan society are colonial categories that have passed with the project of modernity, in which whiteness is a matter not only of skin color (even though it is also that) but also, and particularly, of its originating from a center of colonial power: Europe.[94] Blackness and whiteness are the most common categories for what constitutes the "positive" and "negative" other in Moroccan society. Whiteness (European and American), because of colonial experience and its postcolonial legacies, denotes superiority, power, and beauty. For instance, Moroccans with fair skin are classified not necessarily by their color but according to other denominations that are at the interstice between what can be construed as ethnicity (such as Fassi or Jebli)[95] and what can be understood as racial—that is, part of a racial discourse that somehow classifies, categorizes, but also marks as positive or negative certain groups of people. By contrast, blackness constitutes the negative other, inferior and of lower status.[96] Several other racial dominations lie ambiguously, almost hidden, between these two racial categories. These are not necessarily the colonial ones opposing Arabs to Berbers, nor the postcolonial ones differentiating Arabs and Amazighs. These remain categories embedded in the discourse of cultural and political organizations that are reproduced often uncritically by scholars. These are rarely differentiations or categories of the everyday. Most of the time, and not only in deep Morocco, people would define themselves as Shalh, or Rifi, or Gharbaoui, and so forth. And there are fields of racial expressions even between groups defined from a certain perspective as Amazigh. A Shalh may as well express slurs, epithets, and all sorts of racial expressions against a Sussi or a Rifi or a Jebli, who may express similar racial expressions against the Shalh. Similarly, while one may be categorized as "Arab" in a political discourse, in everyday life, one can be identified and self-identified as Hayani, Hawzi, Dukkali, and so forth. And there are racial expressions among these groups the way there are among groups identified by Amazigh associations as Arabs. In other words, Moroccan societies are not stratified by the categories of Arabs and Amazigh, but rather by a number of other categories whose grammar has not yet been written precisely because race studies are quasi-absent in the field of Maghrebi studies (and by and large Middle Eastern studies).

For decades, in both Morocco and France, race as a category has been invisible from public discourse even though racism has been rampant. The invisibility of race in the political and legal discourse seems almost strategic, since it is all the more difficult to tackle racism (the way the absence of discussion about gender or class makes it difficult to recognize sexism and class and social divisions). Such misrecognition makes it difficult to address issues of inequality based on race (or class or gender). Yet again, racism still exists even though, precisely because of the quasi-absence of racial categories, it is hidden or rather "disguised." There is still no racial language in the law in Morocco (or in France),[97] and the public discourse seems, at first sight, indifferent to it as well. But this is just because, often, racism has been appearing as something else; hence its invisibility. The discursive invisibility of race must have been inherited from France itself, which continues to elide race from its legal and political discourse despite tremendous racial practices and discrimination against populations from the colonies that were once categorized as races.[98] This does not seem to be new since Fanon wrote a long time ago that "racism no longer dares to appear without disguise . . . it is unsure of itself." Maybe it is this disguise that has constituted its very force, the secret of its effectiveness, and the motor behind its longevity.

In Morocco, one of the immediate consequences of the presence of West African migrants is precisely the lifting of the veil on rampant racism against them. However, if racism exists against West Africans, it is because it has been at work against others inside Moroccan society. This is why the question of race needs to be opened not only in relation to what the media call the "sub-Saharan Africans" but also to Europeans (whites) in their relations to Moroccans, and vice versa, as well as to those Moroccans perceived as "others" by virtue of their looks, accents, and of course social status or lack thereof.[99] In other words, we need to recognize the existence of "political collectivities," as Paul Gilroy calls them, in order to tackle questions of inequality and citizenship. When I discuss blackness in the present study, I do so not in terms of historical slavery but rather in the new terms of the black migrant—that is, illegality and outsideness. Likewise, when discussing "whiteness," I consider its articulations in the French society of colonial times as well as in its present moment. Moroccans may have only a faint memory of slavery, but they have a vivid memory of colonialism that colors their views of Europeans, West Africans, and of course themselves.

In short, my ambition in this book is to open up the discussion of race in Moroccan society and history, and also to link this discussion to issues of race in France, Great Britain, and the United States, especially in relation to migration. Whether in Europe, in the United States, or now even within Africa itself, migration is undoubtedly racialized. In Morocco, it is, too. Migration is associated with Moroccans, and illegal migration is synonymous with sub-Saharan Africans, despite the presence of an increasing number of European migrants in the country.

A 2003 law now regulates the movement and presence of "foreigners" but really targets the "sub-Saharan Africans" present in Morocco. Several recent studies examine its coherence, the conditions of its formulation, and its effectiveness (or lack thereof) in halting migration. Some of them also pay attention to the racist dimension of this law—the fact that it is produced specifically to control, exclude, and restrain the movements of a black population.[100] Legality has undoubtedly become an important dimension of the study of migration.[101] For the concept of migration itself seems to be a product of the law and the state that produces the law. Illegality is the flip-flop of legality.

Anthropologists have paid significant attention to the concept of illegality in their examination of migration and drawn attention to its political construction, and thus to the very politics promoted by the state.[102] Drawing mainly from Michel Foucault and his contention that "the existence of legal prohibition creates around it a field of illegalist practices,"[103] scholars of migration have looked at how the law on migration has created what we call the "illegal migrant" and how illegal practices themselves are used, as Foucault himself argued, and controlled by means that are themselves illegal in order to achieve "illicit gains."[104]

Despite, or rather precisely because of, the laws and treaties of nation-states, the geography of migration has expanded in this age of globalization. Morocco, once a country of emigration, is now a country of "illegal immigration." Indeed, I argue that EU policies have created a new category of "illegality" outside EU borders. Morocco has then become, in the past ten years or so, one of the main countries to host "illegal" migrants to and from Europe. This is an important development that shows the globalization of the "illegality" once confined to the borders of the nation-state in Europe. However, the topic of how these illegal practices are controlled by illegal means and how they generate "illicit gains" is beyond the scope of this study. Who controls illegal migration in the region? By what means? For what gains? These are the questions that this study hopes to open and that I hope to pursue in the future.

Here I examine how "race" participates in the making of "illegality." I especially pay close attention to how West Africans manage the laws that make them "illegal" as well as daily racism in the city. I juxtapose the experience of West African migrants with the experience of European migrants in the city of Tangier, and examine how legality/illegality is produced by racial perceptions as well as the colonial histories that have in part shaped these perceptions. This study endeavors to examine the dynamics at the borders between Africa and Europe as well as within Moroccan society and thus help break a tradition that makes migration studies a matter of relevance only to the Western world—Europe and North America.[105]

The Shape of the Book

Migration in the region, between its parts, within the continent, and from Africa to Europe is by no means new. It is just that a new pattern has emerged since the 1990s. This book addresses this relatively new pattern of migration traversing the Mediterranean shores. More specifically, it considers what makes Tangier one of the most attractive cities for migrants preparing to cross to Europe. Many live in the city for several years before they cross, and many others return after exiting, or get stuck in the city for longer than they expect. Migrants not only live in the city, but they also *live the city*—they experience it, they encounter its people, engage its culture, walk its streets, and participate in its events.

My aim is twofold: on the one hand, the book is a study of African "illegal" migration to Europe and European "legal" migration to Morocco. On the other, it is a study of how a city has changed and been transformed by the flows of migrants from both Europe and Africa. It is a study of two main regimes of mobility—one African, the other European.[106] Because the ethnographic site is the city of Tangier, the book is also an examination of how Moroccan society has been affected by the flows of migrants from Africa and from Europe. In other words, the book is as much a study of transnational migration as it is a study of Moroccan society in the so-called age of globalization.

My fieldwork in the city was marked, from beginning to end, by a major postcolonial event: the so-called Arab Spring that was triggered in January 2011 only a few weeks after my arrival to Tangier on December 24, 2010. Soon Morocco was affected by this major event that swept Arab countries. In Morocco, too, a movement of young (and not-so-young) people quickly came together to demand political reforms. I saw this as an important event that cannot be separated from the internal racism seen in Moroccan society. A revolution against this racism framed locally in terms of *hogra* was part and parcel of the so-called Arab Spring. Therefore, the first chapter provides the political and cultural contexts necessary to understand the system of the hogra that migrants in Tangier suffer, as well as the general political condition of the phenomenon of migration in Moroccan society. It also provides the background for the rest of the book by showing, through a series of protests in the city, the political culture of the city and, by extension, of Morocco itself. Hogra is a form of cultural violence specific to the Maghreb region. It can be defined in a variety of ways depending on the setting and the actors involved. Generally, hogra consists of visible and invisible violent practices—name calling, insults, slurs, denial of taxi or restaurant services, discriminatory practices in hiring and the provision of services, and so on. These practices are extremely harmful because they deprive people of the basic rights of citizenship (the right to dignity, safety, decent livelihoods, and so forth). Throughout the chapters, I come back to the concept to analyze it contextually.

In the first chapter, I also show that European migrants were unconcerned with the protests. The political unrest was moderate, and people on the streets did not ask for a radical change. If anything, by demanding a constitutional monarchy in which the king reigns but does not rule, the February 20 movement remained royalist. The events, too, did not concern the West Africans, many of whom were fleeing or avoiding carnage in Libya. Local politics were not part of their worries. Their focus was crossing to Europe. Anything else was a distraction, especially if it did not affect their everyday lives. By comparison with Libya, Morocco looked safe and still advantageous for crossing. Meanwhile, for the Moroccan youth set on migrating to Europe, the harraga, the political protest brought no hope: "one thief goes, another thief comes" (*yamchi chaffàr, yji chaffàr*). Having already lost hope in Morocco, the harraga entertain another hope, in Europe.

In their introduction to an edited volume of essays on children, Nancy Scheper-Hughes and Carolyn Sargent lament the absence of children's voices in ethnographic writings: "Children's voices are conspicuously absent in most ethnographic writing, where young people seem to behave like good little Victorians, neither seen nor heard. By and large children appear in ethnographic texts the way cattle make their appearance in Evans-Pritchard's classic, *The Nuer*—as forming an essential backdrop to everyday life, but mute and unable to teach us anything significant about society and culture."[107]

Chapter 2 consists of an examination of the harraga children who gather around the port, waiting to cross to Europe by sliding under, on, or into trucks waiting for a ferry to Spain. They constitute a visible population in Tangier, especially in and around the port area. Who are these children?

What do they want? How do they live? Why are they here? What motivates them to leave home, live on the street, and risk death? What are their goals and their dreams?

I further examine, in Chapter 3, how Moroccan society itself has produced the harraga. Using insights from Georges Bataille, Karl Marx, and Giorgio Agamben, I argue that Moroccan society has produced an excess of human labor that it can now not only neglect but also even "let die." Yet, the predicament of the harraga, most of them children and young adults, is a complex one. In their activity of "burning," that is, crossing, to Europe, they not only demonstrate an exceptional resilience in coping with extraordinary conditions, but also are motivated and guided by universal impulses toward freedom. The chapter describes the structural violence that Moroccan children and youth are caught up in and demonstrates how their activity, deemed illegal, is itself an exercise of freedom—freedom from the system of hogra and freedom to find a better life.

Chapter 4 looks at West African migrants in Morocco and in Tangier specifically, where preparations for crossing to Spain are undertaken. I examine the trajectory of the migrants, their status as "illegal" newcomers in the city, and the rationale that justifies their activity—deemed illegal by the EU and by Morocco but considered legitimate by the migrants themselves. I also discuss the new form of "illegality" that has transformed Morocco into not only a country of immigration but also a so-called transit state. The migrant in Tangier is a transnational and transitional being. I focus on the dynamics of racial difference in a self-identified "white" city and explore the everyday cultural violence the migrant is subjected to.

Since migration emerged as an international subject of study, it has become too closely associated with state policies, with labor, policing, and governmentality,[108] and because of that, I contend, it often espouses its own categories. Indeed, migration has been racialized. It is often a movement from South to North, and, depending on the host nation-state, the prototype of the "immigrant" is the Pakistani, the Maghrebi, the Turk, the Mexican, or the sub-Saharan African, as with the case at hand. However, flows of humans in the opposite direction, from North to South, have also, mutatis mutandis, increased since the 1990s, in the era of globalization. But these flows are rarely referred to as immigration and thus in fact rarely studied unless they are evoked to make a point about globalization and its key concept of cosmopolitanism. In Chapter 5, I examine the conditions, motivations, and goals of middle-class and working-class Europeans who migrate to Tangier.

I interrogate why European residents of the city are not called or considered migrants but instead referred to as expats or cosmopolitans. As with West Africans, the concept of race as an analytical category is essential in understanding the living conditions of these migrants, who, in comparison with the conditions of West Africans, are awash with rights and privileges. It should be made clear, however, that even as I excluded from this study those privileged Europeans who reside in the city seasonally, I also excluded the privileged West Africans who do the same. Indeed, there is in Tangier people of that global class who enjoy the privileges and rights of flexible citizenship. Surely, the racial dynamics among this class play out differently. The populations I speak of are comparable; both are working-class and middle-class migrants. Here, too, I look again at the race question by contrasting the experience of Europeans with those West Africans who are often stuck in the city while hoping to cross "illegally" to Europe. Last, I examine how Moroccan perceptions of Europeans (whites) and West Africans (blacks) shape the experience of these two populations in the city and thus within society itself.

At age nineteen, I migrated from Morocco to France as a student to join my father, who had emigrated a decade earlier. Overwhelmed by my experience of intense racism in the town of Perpignan, the hub of the then-emerging National Front, I immediately returned to Morocco. The rather short stay marked me in such a way as to spur me to return a few years later, albeit apprehensively. I went to Paris, where I chose to pursue graduate studies, rather than to Perpignan. In the epilogue, I use my personal story to reflect on the condition of migration in the 1980s and compare it with the conditions of migration I discussed in the preceding chapters. The idea here is to juxtapose two experiences: mine, and that of the young Moroccans (including minors) whom I had recently researched. I conclude by asking whether the migrant can ever return home. Drawing on the work of Hannah Arendt, Edward Said, Tayeb Saleh, Amin Maalouf, and Dany Laferrière, I reflect on my personal trajectory as well as the trajectories of family members, friends, and the many people who migrated to Europe in the 1970s and 1980s, to examine how migration transforms the self and creates hybrid subjects with no belonging and no "home." For home is often lost in the experience of migration. Thus, I conclude by examining the concept of the "exile of time," borrowed from Laferrière, and how it differs from the "exile of space." The conclusion also juxtaposes postindependence migratory conditions in Morocco with postcolonial ones. It explains, in clear terms, how the dynamics of migration have changed in Moroccan society from a legal labor source, sought after and mainly coming from the countryside, to an urban, young, "illegal" migration (and sequestration).

The book, then, ventures into some new territories. For this same reason, it proceeds cautiously. Its goal is not necessarily to provide definitive answers but rather to present new questions that might help both reconfigure migration as a postcolonial phenomenon (that needs to be liberated from policy studies) and interrogate how Moroccan society responds to new cultural processes involving waves of migration from Europe as well as from western Africa.

Notes on the Fieldwork

This book is based on extensive fieldwork I conducted in Tangier every summer from 2008 to 2016, and also for the full year from December 2010 to January 2012. The book is thus the result of twenty-four months of fieldwork. My approach to the field was mostly what Clifford Geertz calls "deep hanging out" with three migrant populations: Moroccans, West Africans, and Europeans. I conducted individual and group interviews and engaged in long conversations with members of these three communities. I also observed and participated in their events and activities. This long fieldwork resulted in real friendships with several young Moroccan migrants, West Africans, and Europeans. My choice of these communities was motivated by the fact that they constitute the most (and only) visible migrants in the city. Arab migrants, such as the Syrians, who constitute the largest group, tend to blend with the Moroccan population. Tangier hosts several communities from many parts of the world, including from Taiwan, Indonesia, and India, but these are quite small.

It seems that nothing could be easier for a Moroccan than conducting fieldwork in Morocco, ensuring easy and constant access to contacts and interviews in one's native language. True, "being from there" facilitated certain aspects of the fieldwork, but it also made others more complicated, sometimes in unexpected ways. First, with the Moroccan harraga, there was always a stage of deep suspicion that could be long or short, depending on the person, the circumstances, and maybe even my skill in dissipating the doubt. I had to convince them, not just by words or by showing them papers, that I was not an undercover police officer, a spy for the government, or even a journalist who would get them arrested or expose them in local newspapers. They needed to have that sense of trust that only intuition can provide. Second, even when the trust was gained, the social world of these youth is not mine. I left the country in 1985, before most of them were born. Their ages ranged between six and twenty-eight years, with only two of them thirty-four years old. They were a different generation. They were also all male. Women harraga do not exist, even though one may hear from a woman that she wishes to "burn." The port area and the Moroccan streets at night are more dangerous places for women than men. Burning requires hanging out in the streets and in the port for months and even years. Women of course do migrate, too, but by different means such as marriage (real or fake); they never hang out in the port randomly, as male migrants do, in search of an opportunity to cross.

In any case, with these harraga, speaking their "language" and understanding their motives, explications, and sometimes even jokes was not a self-evident task. There is nothing more dangerous for research, I believe, than the sense that we understand something we do not understand. An awareness of one's ignorance is the sine qua non of acquiring knowledge. Familiarity and, in this case, my Moroccan bond with these harraga made me at the beginning believe I could understand if only I listened. To enter their social world was a humbling experience that required patience and perseverance.

Within the city, there were different sites for this research. Moroccan harraga, children and young adults alike, hung out mostly in the port area of downtown Tangier. They ate leftovers donated to them by the fish restaurants in the area. There were those who picked up the food themselves, from the restaurants' garbage cans. There were also those who could eat in one of the cheap restaurants in the medina, paying with money earned from begging. They slept on the fishermen's nets or on piles of cardboard boxes next to the port's mosque. Some of them slept under carts or even on top of them. Nights were time for relaxation and entertainment. They played cards, told stories, or just chatted. In the large area of the port itself, there were around five hundred harraga. This number increased during the summer. But even in the middle of winter, one could still see a couple hundred harraga hanging out there. With time, the port area, including its inside, became as familiar to me as it was to them. I conducted sixty in-depth interviews with male harraga in 2011 and 2012 in addition to thirty interviews I conducted during the summers of 2008, 2009, and 2010. Most of the interviews lasted a couple of hours. During the month of Ramadan 2011, I spent almost every night at the port conversing with ten harraga from around 10 p.m. until 4 a.m. Eight harraga became my confidants, and thanks to them, I was able to enter their social world. In the early months of January and February, I used a tape recorder, but I quickly noticed that it took away the spontaneity of the conversations.

The harraga (youth and children alike) are almost as familiar to me as family members. I speak their language, meaning their own brand of Moroccan. They are shantytown kids, and so was I. Their milieu was once mine, and it constitutes my home (both in my memory and in the physical space I still call home despite years of exile resulting from a decision to leave). Moroccan shantytowns are alike: no water, no electricity, no hope, no prospects; only an extraordinary effort, and a real coup of luck, can get you out of there. My father, too, was a shantytown kid. I heard his stories many times, especially as he aged. At age thirty-eight, when he had nine children, he was able to leave his hometown, Meknès, for France—Perpignan. He came back only years later, rather prosperous even by French standards of the time. Very loyal to his roots, and a son of the people, he maintained an unbelievable loyalty to the shantytown such that, despite his increasing prosperity, he kept us in it even as he bought a house in a more prosperous neighborhood, a house with water, electricity, and all the necessary amenities. I inherited this loyalty, not because I am deeply attached to that neighborhood, with its bad reputation, known even beyond the city, but because I am attached to its people, to memories that shaped my childhood and remain with me. My contact with the harraga was then as natural as my contacts with the children of my neighborhood. I recognized the signs of their misery as they must have recognized that I was a member of the family despite the fact that a coup of destiny, initiated by a father's act of migration, so drastically changed the course of my life. Their narratives were familiar to me; I still hear them whenever I visit Morocco. Often I am asked, "Can you take me with you?" "How?" I ask, "I do not own the key to the country." "*Ghîr shûf ki diîr li-nâ*" (you can find a way to help us), I am told; my negation does not seem to convince anyone.

Yet, despite the shared roots, in the field, I had to find strategies to connect. When hanging out in the port, I dressed in plain sportswear, sandals, and a T-shirt, not very different from many of the harraga themselves. This was not because I wanted to make the effort to show that I belonged to their world (for I surely did not, even if I still recognized it) but rather to be able to function in such a dirty space, teeming with bugs and vermin. I was infected with a skin disease for several weeks as a result of sitting on fishermen's nets night after night. It is true that my means were also of great help. The fact that I could help them with money, with advice, and even with information about that "other world" that I came from cemented the connection, and that, in turn, facilitated interviews, dialogues, and conversations. I should also acknowledge that my friend and initially my research assistant, Chakib, was instrumental in introducing me to the world of the harraga. Chakib was young, a twenty-six-year-old man, from Tangier itself. Not only did he introduce me to the harraga's world, but Chakib also introduced me to the culture of Tangier. For Tangier is a different city for a Moroccan from elsewhere. It has its own way, its own language, and its own cultural practices. In navigating these, Chakib was my guide.

With West Africans, the situation was different. A stranger to them, as they were to me, by virtue of the fact that I was perceived as a local Moroccan, there were still connections. All of them first approached me on Boulevard Mohammed V or while I was sitting in a café, and would ask for *sadaqa* (alms) using rudimentary Moroccan phrases, accompanied by gestures to be understood. From the outset, the relation I established with them was a monetary one. The sadaqa might be returned in words, that is, in stories, especially when requested. But not always. Some of the migrants, especially women, would intuitively know that their words had value and ask for a payment upfront, putting a high price on them. Often, I was asked to pay their rent, an amount between $50 and $70 a month. Even when I bargained down the price, my interview experiences with these women were often disappointing as they would confide very little. Because of the gender dynamics, it was also not possible to hang out longer or invite them to a café or a restaurant, as I often did with men. "Deep hanging out"[109] with West African men was possible but not with the women, who very much kept to themselves. I met several West African migrants who told me that they were accompanied by their wives. The woman stayed at home whereas the man went out on the street, making a living and searching for ways to cross to Europe. I was able to gather information about these women but from the perspective of their male companions.

West Africans lead lives separate from the Moroccans in general and from the Moroccan harraga in particular. They do not gather inside the port, as the Moroccans do. They usually hang out on the benches of the Corniche. They also frequent Khadra at the entrance of the medina from the port side, a popular café, with a big screen projecting Hollywood films amid the intense smoke of cigarettes and hashish. There are several Senegalese outside the café at a crossroad between the old medina and the port area through Boulevard Mohammed VI. One can see these Senegalese men selling art objects and knock-off sunglasses and luxury watches. The second site where I conducted research is a popular neighborhood called Masnana, a twenty-minute drive from downtown Tangier. Masnana is home to many West Africans, who rent rooms with other West African migrants (often from the same country) or are given garages for free or for a small fee (around 500 dirhams a month, the equivalent of $50). They hang out in an open field that looks like a park with an open stadium where they can watch soccer games between Moroccans from different neighborhoods.

"You speak English well," my interlocutors from Nigeria or Liberia would say, showing surprise that a Moroccan spoke English. The surprise often triggered curiosity and more exchange with migrants from anglophone countries. With those from francophone countries, there was also the connection of language, combined with the connection of religious affiliation—Islam—which often facilitated our dialogue. Of course, not all of them were Muslims. Many also pretended to be. We had to find bases upon which to establish a contract of trust for the exchange of information and provision of help. The frequent greetings of "Salam," "*Hamdou* Allah" (praise be to Allah!), and "*khouya*" (brother) were meant to facilitate these encounters. Yet, my interlocutors also could connect with me as an African. Often, they would say, "We in Africa" and "We Africans," which created that "rapport" that George Marcus speaks about as important and necessary in fieldwork.[110]

From 2008 to 2016 (including yearlong fieldwork in 2011–12), I interviewed over eighty West African migrants. These interviews took place in cafés and shops or on a street corner in one of the neighborhoods I mention in Chapter 4. Each interview took from two to four hours. I could rely on a handful of interlocutors I met regularly during the entirety of 2011. They were still in Tangier in the summer 2016 when I last conducted interviews. I was only interested in those who came to Tangier to cross to Europe. I also used a snowball technique to recruit my interviewees and study participants.

The phenomenon of so-called illegal crossing remains a fundamentally male activity for both harraga and West Africans[111] mainly because migration, as I explain in Chapter 4, is a family project, and usually it is the men who undertake it to help those left behind. There are also other factors such as the high risk of rape on migratory routes and the extraordinary hardship and physical endurance required. Few women take up the challenge—with or without a male companion. As I have noted, the handful of women I encountered were often more discreet and more cautious, gave less information, and asked for a higher payment for the interview. All of them were accompanied by their husband and had children. Only one, Sandra, a twenty-three-year-old woman, was by herself because her husband had been deported by the Spanish to Nigeria. She stayed in Tangier hoping one day she would cross.

In Europe, this population is often referred to as sub-Saharan Africans. Moroccan francophone media use the same name. However, in Morocco during the entirety of my fieldwork, all those who I encountered were from West Africa. I believe that those from central and eastern Africa usually take the Libyan, the Tunisian, or the Egyptian roads, not the Moroccan one—or at least rarely.[112] The fact that all my interlocutors were from West Africa led me to abandon the more general label of "sub-Saharan African."[113]

The biggest challenge of my fieldwork, at least initially, was with the European community. My "Moroccanness" seemed to be the problem. Postcolonial relations tend to make connections between Moroccans and the French awfully complicated—whether in France or in Morocco. I discuss some of these complications in Chapter 5. Suffice it to say that at first it was difficult to conduct research in this community. The level of mistrust was high, and as I learned later from those who became friends, they had been told to be very cautious with Moroccans. As with most fieldwork experiences, fortunate moments of breakthrough are often accidental. By pure coincidence, I rented an apartment downtown, in a neighborhood called Hayy al-Shayâtîn with many bars, discothèques, and cafés attended by sex workers—hence its name (the Quarter of Devils). Two stores away from my building, there was a new French bookstore called Les Insolites. It turned out to be a major meeting place for Europeans. The owner, a young French woman, organized weekly or biweekly cultural events—usually a reading by an author, French or francophone, and sometimes art exhibits, usually by a French or a francophone artist. The events were open to the public, though most of the attendees were Europeans with a small number of Frenchified Moroccans. Even though I introduced myself to the owner, talked to her about my research, and was included in the email list of invitees, distance was a rule between me and the Europeans. The American way of introducing oneself (by mentioning your name and trying to shake hands) seemed bizarre. One needs to be introduced by someone trusted, not introduce oneself. My dif-

ficulties in meeting European migrants drastically eased when I met Elena
Prentice in the same bookstore. She was an American and director of the
Tangier American Legation Institute for Moroccan Studies (TALIM) who
had been living in the city for twenty-five years. Thanks to her incredible
warmth and generosity, my day-to-day life in the city became more produc-
tive. My interactions with Europeans became easy, and several of these connections were the results of a dinner or a gathering prepared by Elena. I
continued to frequent the bookstore, also regularly frequented by Elena.
Here, too, there was snowballing. I was introduced to others, and eventually
I became part of a social network.

There are 7,000 registered French men and women in Tangier and 3,000
Spaniards. There are a few hundred Italians and dozens of British men and
women. I conducted over forty interviews with French, Italian, and Spanish
men and women. The majority of my interviews were in French. I also had
a handful of key interlocutors who, with time, became friends. Also, with
time, I became part of this social group and participated in their cultural
and social events.

Conducting ethnography about migration and illegality could not leave
me indifferent to what was happening around me. My fieldwork was marked
from beginning to end by the protests and political unrest that were part of
the Arab Spring that started in Tunisia just as I returned to Tangier in December 2010. This is the most important political event to happen in the
city since its independence in 1956. I participated in every event of this revolution that seriously worried the *makhzen*, the political elite, as they saw
governments, leaders, and regimes fall in Tunisia, Egypt, Yemen, and Libya—
some of them tragically. I decided to include this experience because it explains in large part, if only indirectly, the conditions of the Moroccan youth
and children trying to leave the country at the risk of death. I also include
it because it offers background to the entire book: this ethnographic narrative is itself a historical narrative of the then present of the city.

For reasons that should be clear by now and will surely be clearer in the
chapters to follow, my interviews and conversations with Moroccan harraga
were in Moroccan Arabic. With West Africans, they were conducted in French
with those from francophone Africa (such as Mali, Senegal, or Cameroon)
and in English with those from anglophone Africa (such as Nigeria or
Ghana). With the French, the interviews and conversations were naturally in
French. Interviews and conversations with people from Spanish-, Portuguese-,

or English-speaking countries were conducted in English. I took notes while I was interviewing these people. My early interviews, from January 2012 to March 2012, were also recorded.

The digital age in which we live has drastically changed the ways fieldwork is now conducted. The influx of information from virtually every corner of the globe at the drop of a hat is incredible. One can follow developments in the field through videos posted on social media as well as through direct, speedy, and easy communication with interlocutors in the field. Several of the people I interviewed are now my friends on Facebook. With others, I could regularly communicate via Skype, WhatsApp, and Facebook. Several friends and interlocutors continued, through social media, to update me about the protests in the Rif I discuss in Chapter 1.

I changed all the names of my interlocutors to protect their identity. Whenever it was possible, I also altered any indication of profession or activity or nationality that may reveal who they are. As much as I could, I followed the Middle East Studies Association (MESA) system for transliterating Arabic except in cases where that was impossible because of the peculiarities of the phonetics of Moroccan Arabic. An alternative sound was given to make the transliteration as accurate as possible. Also, all translations in this book are mine unless otherwise indicated. I use the standardized, English names of Moroccan cities, towns, and regions. And of course, any shortcomings in this book are my sole responsibility.

Chapter 1

Revolution

A moment of uncertainty always characterizes a new
beginning.
            —Michel de Certeau

I started working on the subject of migrants in 2008, when I spent my first
summer in Tangier testing the field and conducting my first interviews with
the Moroccan youth, or *harraga*, hoping to cross the Mediterranean to Spain.
I came back in the summer of 2009 and again in the summer of 2010 to
conduct more interviews and establish contacts in preparation for a longer
period of more extensive and intensive fieldwork. On December 25, 2010, I
returned to Tangier for one year to continue my work on African and European flows of migrants to the city. The port and its environs were, as I left
them in August 2010, full of young Moroccans, many of them underage,
and hundreds of West Africans. The kids were lying down on fishermen's
nets, smoking or napping, or standing in front of fish restaurants, waiting
for leftovers. Several of the Africans were selling items such as fake luxury
watches, skin creams, sunglasses, cell phones, African crafts. These men were
mainly, if not exclusively, Senegalese. Others, many of them Nigerians, were
begging in the streets. I had not expected such things to change. These new
"wretched of the earth" had been here for over a decade, and they would
remain so long as the global conditions that created the phenomenon of
"illegal" migration persisted.
    It was at this time that a small event of almost no political importance
occurred: a young Tunisian man burned himself to death in reaction to

police repression and humiliation. Briefly covered by Al Jazeera, this incident immediately took on unexpected significance. Small, peaceful, and well-behaved protests by professional associations, students and intellectuals, and even ordinary citizens followed. These quickly grew nationwide. I followed the protests on Al Jazeera and wrote in my field journal that, considering the police state of Tunisian president Ben Ali, they would go nowhere.

President Ben Ali's last speech on January 13, 2011, in which he promised real reforms (as he shook with fear), became the object of discussion among people I ran into. This was the same Ben Ali I had seen on the Boulevard Mohammed V in Tangier parading with the then-new Moroccan king, Mohammed VI (r. 1999–present), in June 2001. At the time, he had looked absent-minded, cold, and confident. It was difficult for me to reconcile that picture of him with the one on television, and not because of the years that had passed. This must have been the first time the Arab people had seen a scared president. That in itself was a sign that something important was about to happen. Soon the news that he had fled was broadcast sensationally through the voice of a Tunisian lawyer in the street, defying the curfew and shouting at the top of his lungs, "Ben Ali *hrab*! Ben Ali *hrab*!" (Ben Ali, run! Ben Ali, run!).

This event had an immediate impact on Tangier. In the strategic Square of Nations (Sahat al Umam, or Place des Nations) at the heart of Tangier, young protesters gathered, chanting slogans of congratulations to the Tunisian people and waving communist and Moroccan flags. Later, I came to learn that a communist, antiglobalization, yet national movement had been active in the city for some time. This protest was both a celebration of the Tunisian revolution and an unmistakable sign that the wave of revolution had reached the city.

The protests of the antiglobalization youth continued every day. And the Egyptian protesters' descent on Tahrir Square in Cairo, which followed the Tunisian revolution, gave this small movement more momentum. They now gathered daily at the Square of Nations not only in solidarity with the Egyptians but also to show that they were part of the wave of change that had hit the region. They raised Egyptian, Tunisian, and Moroccan flags, along with photos of Che Guevara and communist flags. Though the protesters themselves were mostly young, their speaker was a middle-aged man. Speaking into a microphone, he expressed support of the Arab cause, interrupted from time to time by applause and V-for-victory signs from the crowd. Young women were noticeably present.

Figure 1. Antiglobalization movement celebrating the victory of the Tunisian people at the Square of Nations in downtown Tangier. Photograph by the author.

The speaker was probably in his mid-forties but looked younger. He had a stern face, salt-and-pepper hair, and a southern accent (he was most likely from Marrakesh). He started talking about the political situation—denouncing corruption in the country, lamenting the poverty of the people, and drawing attention to the enormous wealth of the nation and Tangier's auspicious location between the Atlantic Ocean and the Mediterranean Sea. Yet, he declared, its people were unemployed and impoverished because corruption was rampant. "Two seas, two seas, O creatures of God," he continued, "but even sardines are expensive. The citizens in the *dâkhil* [inland area] buy them for thirty dirhams a kilogram, and the state sells them for two dirhams to corporations."

A few weeks later, on February 11, 2011, when Egyptian president Hosni Mubarak stepped down, the same group descended on the same square. The contagion was unmistakable: just as the Egyptian revolution had been preceded by thousands of small protests since the creation of the Kefaya movement in late 2004, the Moroccan youth knew that their protests were also a preliminary step toward a new beginning—or beginnings. Hence, they persisted despite their small number.

In this chapter, I provide an ethnographic account of the revolution in Morocco and how it manifested itself in the city. Considering this political moment in the history of Morocco sheds light on not only the phenomenon of the harraga (discussed in more detail in Chapters 2–3) but also on mobility from both West Africa (Chapter 4) and Europe, specifically France and Spain (Chapter 5).

Against the *Hogra*

A few days after the fall of Mubarak, a YouTube video suddenly appeared online and went viral. It showed several seemingly middle-class Moroccan men and women. Some were in their twenties, others were in their late teens, and one woman was in her late fifties, all calling for a general protest on February 20, 2011, to end the state of *hogra* (injustice and corruption) in the country.[1] The video itself seemed to me a revolution in the country—for a group of Moroccan citizens to publicly denounce injustice and corruption was a new and audacious event. But to do that *and* call for general political protest took it one step further, creating a rupture in the state of Moroccan politics. Protests now were no longer the work of unemployed graduates who did their sit-ins in front of the parliament or city halls, nor were they the work of a small movement with a specific ideology—they now included the citizenry.

Before February 20, all political space was monopolized by the regime and the political parties. Indeed, I remember back to the 1980s, when politics was a dangerous matter altogether. "Do not talk about the king," one used to hear from parents and even friends, "they will cut your tongue," or "Do not talk politics; you will go to prison." Now citizens had entered the political domain, thanks to the wave of change triggered by a young man who had burned himself to death against the hogra and by the countless small protests of communists, Islamists, and the unemployed. There was even a public protest calling for gay rights in the city of Meknès. These small protests were not revolutionary, just claims of specific rights: employment rights, housing rights, sexual rights. In that regard, they benefited the regime, as they gave it a democratic face. After February 20, politics lost its aura of exclusivity and fear. The revolution destroyed idols, the least of which was the sanctity of the king. The protestors asked for a constitutional monarchy—that is, a king without power, a sine qua non condition for empowering the people and lifting the hogra, since then citizens would rule through their true representatives.

Hogra is a concept unique to the Maghreb region. It does not translate to only injustice. It is a concept that was first made the battle cry of the Kabyle protest in Algeria in July 2001. Not only does hogra refer to marginalization, but it also implies disdain and condescension. It is an attitude of the state toward a segment of its population that enjoys few if any rights, whose dignity can be violated with impunity. It is the discriminatory face of the state. It is also an attitude of the people trapped inside a pecking order, with the elite at the top and the unemployed poor at the bottom and "outsiders" beyond the margins. It is children on the street, tossing pebbles and ethnic slurs at a sudden stranger. Hogra is contextual; a victim would recognize it as such, the way an Moroccan observer would also recognize that this or that person has been subjected to hogra. This is to say that other forms of cultural violence are not hogra and are not labeled as such (*ghalba* and *dsara*, among others[2]).

In the context of the Moroccan protests, hogra means, among other things, the absence of the state of law, of the rights of the privileged, of accountability; nepotism; and the unemployment that has deeply affected large sections of the middle class and entire sections of the lower classes. Hogra approximates colonial times, when Europeans and natives were separated and only a few, privileged, upper-class natives could move between the two groups. Yet, if the colonial administration used and even modernized hogra, it cannot be credited with or blamed for its invention. Hogra constituted the symbolic order of precolonial politics.[3] It has continued in postcolonial Morocco with all the changes introduced by colonial culture that touched all aspects of Moroccan culture, including its spatial organization. It is the state of affairs that sociologist Janet Abu-Lughod called urban apartheid in Rabat.[4] But apartheid was a legal concept, a law that separated people by skin color; thus, one could see it and possibly contest it. Hogra is invisible, except for those who live it. While others perceive it as unfriendliness or plain meanness— that is, as apolitical—it is inscribed in the class structure in Morocco and the entire region of the Maghreb. After colonialism, that is, since 1956, the hogra has manifested itself in a clear-cut separation of space. The *mahgûr* (the victim of hogra), once contained in the old Casbah of the natives that Fanon speaks of,[5] lives on in the shantytowns and suburbs (*brarak* and *dawahi*) added to create housing for rural migrants searching for work.[6]

Hogra is a daily condition for those who are not protected by the state, who are abused by the very law that claims justice for all. Hogra is structural in Morocco—that is, it operates vertically, from top to bottom, but also horizontally, from one citizen to another. Hogra shows itself in small daily acts in the streets—when a driver does not heed a stop sign and still curses you for trying to cross in front of him. It also shows itself in government administration—when you stand in line and others pass in front of you, or when you are asked for bribes to get something as basic as a birth or residence certificate. It shows itself in ordinary interactions with a citizen eager to display his status and class by putting others down, either verbally or with an attitude of contempt and disdain. Finally, it shows itself in the structure of the family—when a son, usually jobless, becomes an object of contempt for his siblings and even his parents, or when a brother bullies a younger brother or a sister.

The video that announced the birth of the February movement referred to the state of hogra. In it, youth and a middle-aged woman denounce hogra and urge the viewer to take to the streets against it. They speak Moroccan with different accents, and one speaks Tamazight (Berber), giving the movement an "authentic" national character. The change was drastic indeed. The mahgûr had finally spoken. In a postcolonial, dictatorial regime that exerted the hogra with impunity, that made the hogra its law and way of life, speaking itself was revolutionary—it was not a sign of power; it was power itself. Or as Michel de Certeau put it, in the context of the May 1968 protests in France,[7] "It is impossible to capture speech and to keep it without a capture of power. To want to speak oneself is to be committed to *make* history."[8]

The call to protest was against not poverty, but poverty as a consequence of the hogra. And the call to protest the hogra was a call against the very foundation of Moroccan politics and the Moroccan state, the *makhzen*, accused of being the perpetrator of hogra, that is, the *haggar*. This was clear from the movement's posters: "Stupid makhzen, this is a revolution for dignity, not for food" (*ayuha al makhazan al balid, hadhihi thawrat al kibriyâ' la al radhâ'*).

The Moroccan press reported the formation of the February 20 movement, which meant that the makhzen had taken note of this unpredictable and even unthinkable uprising. Counterattacks were immediately organized and launched with great force. The protestors in the video, it was reported, were members of the Polisario;[9] other stories said they were Algerians seeking to destabilize the regime. Photos and videos were distributed showing one of them in the arms of the president of the Polisario: "she was his wife," one poster said. A second member was accused of being a Christian and was shown in a church.

Figure 2. In a December protest of the February movement, a banner reads,
"Makhzen, Haggar, Get Out!" Photograph by the author.

Tactics of this type were an obvious ploy to find an external enemy on
whom to blame the agitation. However, this was an act of hogra itself.
When Moroccan politics could not rule by force, it ruled by scandal, that is,
by defamation. This strategy is not unique to Morocco—it is a salient char-
acteristic of all modern politics. Thanks to the new world order of social
media—Facebook, YouTube, Twitter—the makhzen could respond to the
uprising without being subject to physical retaliation. But debunking the
state's defamation by showing that the people in the video were real Moroccans (most of them high school students) through the same channels was
just as easy. The call for protest had succeeded, and the efforts to stop it had
failed.

On February 17, I found a Facebook page that was being used to exchange information on the movement. By then, 24,000 mostly anonymous
people were members. The number increased to 64,000 in only a few weeks
and to 72,000 a year later.[10] The site itself was greatly hampered by postings
from what members called the makhzen of the Internet, the dogs of the
makhzen, or, often, the *baltajiya* (thugs)—a new word borrowed from
the Egyptian revolutionary lexicon.

Yet, the harraga, adults and children alike, were absent from these protests—not surprisingly. Not that they were uninterested or uninformed. Or even that, vulnerable as they are, they were too afraid to protest and thus confront the system that had reduced them to harraga. The harraga do not shy away from political topics. The political situation came up often in my talks with them. In fact, the topic of *lahrig* ("burning" or crossing to Europe sans papers) is highly political not only because of the legality issues but also, more important, because the *harrag* is perhaps the most tangible evidence of the failure of the state, its inability to protect its children and youth, and its subordination to EU laws that do not necessarily serve its best interest and force it in many cases to violate the human rights charters it has signed.[11] Lahrig itself is a strong form of protest against the policies of marginalization and state neglect.

Unlike the youth of the protests, the majority of them middle class, who dream of an egalitarian society where they may ask for dignity and social justice, the harraga are mostly from the poorest areas; they aspire to no hope from within the country. Hope is only possible when it offers real possibilities of improvement in the very material condition of the hopeful. Otherwise, it is a morbid pathology. The harrag lost his hope in the country, or maybe he was born without it. The harrag may also be the hope of a family too destitute to hope for anything else. The hope of the parents, especially for their later years, if they ever reach them, is to rely on the child, and the child may now be a harrag. Intuitively and by experience, the harrag knows there is no hope in the country. If there were, he would not be the hope of his family. The revolution was not his.

The revolution in the country, as well as in the rest of the Arab world, was a revolution of hope for hope.[12] But not for the harraga, long abused by the system and exposed to daily expressions of hogra from fellow countrymen. Studies of the recent revolutions in the Arab world have focused exclusively on those who participated in them (the revolutionaries, the counterrevolutionaries) but not on those who did not participate, such as the harraga.

They put no hope in any reform and know that if such reforms were to happen, they would be untouched by them. *"Yamshi chaffâr wa yji chaffâr"* (one thief will replace another), I heard a boy say on more than one occasion. The crux of the matter, the revolution, despite its supposed lack of ideology and leadership, seemed to be the concern of only the middle class, those with hope of changing their lot. The harrag, as I explain in Chapter 2, has already been sacrificed. With limited schooling, from a broken family, and belonging to a segment of a society that does not even qualify as a class, any change, even a radical revolution, will not save the harrag from a fate that was already sealed, maybe before his birth. Whenever I brought up the topic, the responses were similar. Tayeb, the oldest harrag I met, whose stories I narrate in Chapters 2 and 3, told me, "Why should I care about the February 20 movement? What I care about is my problems here. You see my February 20 movement?"—and he pointed to the fishermen's nets we were sitting on.

Yet, the harraga were not indifferent to the events shaking up the Arab world. They would make small comments, most often on what was distant and yet somehow close. "We are with the people of Libya," a twenty-three-year-old harrag told me when the regime of Gaddafi collapsed. Before his death, jokes about some of the phrases Gaddafi used in his last public speech seemed to amuse them (as they amused many all over the region and beyond). He threatened to chase the rebels *zenga, zenga* (street by street), and he called them *jurdhan* (rats). They laughed each time they used his phrases, in or out of context. And they commented on tragic events, such as Gaddafi's brutal murder.

"We have pity for him, by God [*bqa fina wallah*]. The sons of whores, they just butchered him with no mercy, while he was asking for it," Tayeb told me, still with the usual smile on his face.

Tayeb was convinced Jews were behind all of it.

"How?" I asked.

"So as to introduce chaos [*fasâd*] and destroy Islam. That is what they did in Iraq. Did you see what they did in Iraq? They destroyed it. They [the Iraqis] are now fighting [between each other]. It is worse than in the time of Saddam."

While Tayeb used the highly anti-Semitic narrative that sees the Jews behind the Libyan revolution, the huge masses of the February 20 movement celebrated the end of Gaddafi as evident in their chant, "Gaddafi is gone, gone. It is your turn O Bashar!" For many I spoke with, including organizers, the revolution was the work of the people as it was the work of youth like them in every part of the Middle East. Despite the existence of negative views about Jews in Moroccan society,[13] Tayeb's explanation struck my other interlocutors as "stupid." For instance, when I reported Tayeb's statement to Abdillah, who worked as a guard of a building (concierge) and who had mixed feelings about the protests in Morocco, he responded, "This guy [Tayeb] is dumb [*mkallakh*], what do the Jews have to do with it? The guy [Gaddafi] fucked up with his people [*qawwadha m'a sha'bu*], instead of finding a solution with them, instead of taking care of them, and look after their well-being, he bombed them. Plus, the intervention was international; he [Tayeb] speaks rubbish [*ghir yahrabakh*]."

The harraga expressed sympathy for the tragic end of Gaddafi, yet they also made jokes not about him but about the context. A young man, twenty-seven years old, from Boujad—well-built, looking clean and healthy—came and greeted everybody, me included, calling me *ustâdh* (professor). He said he wanted to take a nap, and he put some pieces of cardboard on the ground. Then he said, imitating the threatening words of Gaddafi when protesters against him took to the street and he urged his supporters, "*Ilâ al amâm daqqat sâ'at al 'amal*" (Go forward, time for work!). I joked and told him that his life is better than Gaddafi's (who was still alive and battling the "rebels"). He agreed and said, "Gaddafi cannot afford to nap like me, here in the air. I can. I have nothing to fear unless there is a tornado."

Life at the port looked different from life in the city—it seemed apolitical on the surface. However, the very existence of the harraga points to a tragic political problem. Their presence, their marginalization in today's world, is part of a global trend, the global marginalization of youth, that may be, according to Jean and John Comaroff, "a structural consequence of neoliberal capitalism."[14] Neoliberal policies were indeed accelerated with the reign of Mohammed VI. These policies, touching all sectors, especially the vital ones such as education and labor, have contributed to the emergence of phenomena such as youth unemployment and youth migration.

No, there were no sign of protests at the port. It was a space of free movement of people and animals in close proximity: harraga, fishermen, stray cats and dogs, and a few police officers, indifferent to their surroundings. Or so it seemed to me. But beneath the surface, life at the port was as political as outside of it and in many ways even more so because the space of the port is almost like a camp[15] in that it is a space of let go and let die.

Peaceful Protests and Urban Violence

Sunday, February 20: I woke up sick with a cold but managed to catch the protest just in time, as I lived downtown on a small street just behind the Boulevard of Tangier. The crowd seemed modest—several hundred—and made up of the same antiglobalization protesters who had been active every weekend, even before the beginning of what came to be called the Arab

Spring. It was 10 a.m., and by 11 a.m., thousands upon thousands of people could be seen coming from the top of the boulevard. Traffic was entirely blocked. In an hour or less, the entire two- or three-mile length of the boulevard was packed, and it was impossible for me to see anything but my immediate surroundings.

I noticed the police were strangely absent. But several young men confided to me that undercover police were everywhere. I was also told that they had received strict orders not to intervene, no matter what the protesters did or said—for the worst thing the makhzen could do was to try to suppress the protest, a fatal mistake made by both Ben Ali of Tunisia and Mubarak of Egypt.

The last time I had participated in a Moroccan protest was in 1983, during the ruthless reign of Hasan II, when I was a college student in Fes. Then, the police had brutally dispersed us, badly beat up those who could not run fast enough, and arrested known activist students. One night in November, they stormed the campus, entering dorms to arrest known activists and beat up others. The protests of the Arab revolutions looked different. I was surprised to see this liberated, fearless young force in the street. Compared with the Egyptian and Tunisian protests, the Moroccan slogans were not radical. Whereas the Egyptian and Tunisian protesters shouted *Irhal!* (*Dégagé*, or "Get out") and "People want the fall of the regime!" the Moroccans shouted for the end of dictatorship, the end of corruption, and the end of hogra. Small groups of people formed here and there. I stood next to one, listening to a woman in her early forties speaking a bit shyly about the need to end the state of hogra. "We want no war with anybody," she said. "All we want is justice, equality, and the end of hogra in our country."

The nationalist tone was unmistakable. She, like others, spoke about the greatness of the country and denounced in the harshest terms the corrupters who stole its wealth and impoverished Moroccans with impunity. The king was not mentioned, but the kingdom was. The banners called for a constitutional monarchy (*malakiya dustûriya*). The king's best friend, Fouad Ali El Himma, was denounced as the epitome of corruption. Several teenagers enjoyed the show and acted the part of revolutionaries, posing like Che Guevara for some photographers, including me.

I found myself in this ocean of young people without once remembering that I had already passed my youth in France and the United States. I felt entirely one of them, for their cause was also mine. I had always felt that my exile was not voluntary—it was forced upon me, as it was upon thousands of others. Ten percent of Moroccans live in exile, according to state statistics. I, too, had left the country in my early twenties, running away from the hogra, and when I wanted to return in the mid-1990s, it was because of the hogra that I was unable to find a job. My advanced graduate education in both France and the United States was not enough to get me a position at a Moroccan university, not even in one that had just opened, and was still almost totally empty. My pedigree as a shantytown kid could not be overlooked.

"How did you get to Princeton?" the dean of one of the universities I applied to asked me. He was familiar with the American educational system and the hierarchy of its universities and colleges.

"I applied," I answered almost naively, but would have come up with the same answer if I had wanted to be clever.

"We are looking to hire, give us time to contact your references."

They never contacted my references. They contacted my acquaintances in Rabat instead, I learned later, surely to know about my social background.

My presence, then, among the protesters, was not only because of my profession, as a participant observer, but also because I was a citizen of that country and deeply concerned about its politics.

As the movement prepared to descend on the streets, Moroccan officials and the Moroccan press continuously repeated that Morocco was an exception among the Arab countries, that the king had created a revolution when he succeeded his father in 1999. Morocco, they all said, was already a democracy, and one could only conclude that the protesters in both Tunisia and Egypt were doing nothing but following the path of the young king.

True, the Moroccan situation was different from that of Tunisia and Egypt, though not in the ways being advertised. Morocco had among the highest rates of illiteracy in Africa and the Arab world—over 45 percent, even counting those who were minimally schooled. State propaganda had been effective in convincing the people of the legitimacy of the regime and the absence of any alternative. Instead of ruling by fear and violence, as his father had, the new king ruled with love and masked the violence. He was often seen visiting patients in hospitals, kissing the handicapped, and driving his own car in the streets. Yet, if force and terror cannot rule absolutely and guarantee total submission, neither can love. The proof was precisely in the large number of protests in the Moroccan cities. In a medium-size city such as Tangier, the number of protesters exceeded 100,000. Yet, this was just the beginning; the fear of the unknown, of politics, and, of course, of

Figure 3. Forcing the door of a currency exchange with a stop sign.
Photograph by the author.

the police still gripped many Moroccans, preventing most from joining the protests.

At 4 p.m., exhausted beyond limit due to my cold, I decided to leave for a nap, which lasted two hours or so. At 6 p.m., I heard a noise from my apartment that I thought came from the protest. When I got outside, I found that the boulevard was the object of intense violence. Thick smoke was coming from everywhere. Banks, stores, and boutiques were being vandalized. I stood in the middle of the boulevard amid young people who were busy destroying a cell-phone store called INWI, reputed to belong to the king himself. No slogans were shouted, as in the protests—these were just acts of sheer violence. The leader of the group, his face masked, walked slowly and with great confidence, carrying a stop sign and totally indifferent to his surroundings. He started ramming the sign against the glass door of the store, harder and harder. The glass broke, but the door barely opened. Then he went on, forcing other doors with the same weapon. Several other kids finally forced INWI's door open and picked up cell phones and other electronic items.

I was taking photos, but no one noticed me. Everybody was busy either destroying things or taking items and running away. Several people just watched with speechless shock. I then saw a group of kids on the other side of the street, in the dark, gathering around something, and was told that they were struggling to open a coffer of cash they had stolen from the bank.

"If they see you, they will take your camera," another onlooker warned me. "They just destroyed someone's camera."

I put the camera back in my pocket and continued walking.

I asked someone, "Why aren't the police here?"

"The police start working only after 8:30," he said.

I found that strange. It was close to 8:30 p.m. and the kids were fearlessly destroying the bank. When they managed to break the door, they rushed in. Others were struggling to break the ATM machine. The strange absence of the police continued to baffle me.

All the stores were closed and targeted by the kids. Their number was relatively small, barely two dozen.

"Were these part of the protests?" I asked.

"No, these came after the end of the protests. They were at a soccer game and poured into the boulevard after six when all the protests were over," someone told me.

The protests ended at 4:30. But where were the police? The country had always been a police state. If a fight started, even in the middle of the night, an undercover police officer, or even a uniformed one, showed up almost immediately. Later, a police officer's wife told me that the police were given orders not to interfere with the protests, but when her husband and several of his colleagues reached the violent scene at 9 p.m., they observed that the kids who were destroying the city were talking to some people in a car. When the police went to check who was in the car, it sped away. The woman suggested that the people in the car might have been members of the makhzen (government officials).

At 9 p.m., however, a small squadron of special forces, two hundred or so, looking more like soldiers than police officers, was lined up with batons and shields. The sight of them scared me and I wanted to go back to my apartment, but I saw people walking down the boulevard and decided to do the same. I then realized that the entire boulevard was badly damaged. A burning car was in the middle of the street, filling the air with acrid smoke. Several banks, including the Arab Bank and Popular Bank, were totally de-

Figure 4. The boulevard burned. Photograph by the author.

stroyed, including all the ATM machines. The kids were all gone. The special forces squadron was on alert. Their chief caught a teenage boy who was skateboarding, hit him a couple of times, and dragged him while the boy screamed that he had not participated in the protests. A few minutes later, the boy was released and I saw him running up the boulevard. I wished he would go home.

The special forces squadron stood on one side, clearly ready to intervene—but I wondered against whom. The boulevard was entirely empty, dark, and filled with suffocating smoke. On the other side there was only a group of curious onlookers, including me, watching carefully and ready to run at the slightest movement from the squadron.

"Go home," the chief told us. "His Majesty told us not to beat you. We have not touched any one of you. Just go home."

That did not sound reassuring to me. I interpreted it as a threat and did not entirely believe that the day would be free from violence. I walked back home, looking behind me continuously, and when I was far enough away from the squadron, I took more photos of the damaged city. As I was walking down the street, a Frenchman was walking down it, too. Unlike most of us, he seemed unafraid; he smiled at me, and shook his head in a sign of disapproval. The European community had little to fear from the protests, which seemed to be an internal affair, not radical enough to make them worry.

One day in early June 2011, I met a European lady for an interview. She was joined by a friend for an unplanned lunch. The conversation immediately turned to the scandal of Dominique Strauss-Kahn, who a month earlier had been accused of sexual assault in a Sofitel Hotel in New York City. The older of the two ladies, in her early sixties, asked, "And why did he want to sleep with a black woman, did he know that they all have AIDS?"

Then she answered her own question: "Maybe he did that purposely. He may not have wanted to become president of France, and I heard that was his wife's plan for him?"

Many Europeans I met in Tangier expressed an indifference to local politics that was, I thought, consistent with their overall indifference to Moroccan culture. In any event, that same night, photos of and messages about the burned city were circulated on Facebook. The next day, a Facebook page was created that was called "*Reconstruire notre ville*" (Rebuild our city), but the messages posted were mostly versions of the slogan "Long Live the King!" I tried to participate in a discussion about what had happened the previous day. I realized that my interlocutors were clearly members of the makhzen who wanted to blame the February 20 movement for the violence and intimidate anyone who tried to argue otherwise.

That same weekend, the antiglobalization movement had its weekly gathering in the Square of Nations. The same middle-aged leader spoke: "The protesters did not do that; they dispersed at 5. At 6:30, the vandalism started and was the work of people of the makhzen seeking to boycott the protests, so that they can say all we want is destruction, that we are violent, so as to discredit us, and make people scared of us. Yes, they arrested several kids who were not the vandals; they were just poor kids from the neighborhood who knew nothing and made the mistake of stealing things when the doors of the stores were destroyed."

When I asked Chakib, my research assistant—a man in his mid-twenties whom I had known for several years—why he did not participate, he said, "I do not agree with those people; they do not protest, they break everything. They also attack the symbol of the state. That is not a protest."

Chakib, with his limited schooling, admitted that the hogra was rampant, but implied the king should be above criticism. Despite my testimony that the movement had nothing to do with the vandalism, he still believed it did.

The movement was thus represented as a group of destroyers (*mukhar-ribîn*) and antiroyalists. Though the movement did not ask for the departure of the king, the way the Egyptians and the Tunisians did of their respective presidents, it still was perceived by the average Moroccan as an antiroyalist movement. In other words, the protestors became the enemies of the symbol of the state, as Chakib told me, and opponents of the rule by love; they deserved to be ruled by the stick (*ma khâshum ghir la'sâ*).

From *Centre Ville* to the Suburbs

A few weeks later, on March 9, the king made a speech announcing constitutional reforms and early elections. In the following days, several of the newspapers announced in their headlines, "The King Created a Revolution." As always, cars running down the boulevard displayed posters of the king along with Moroccan flags. A group of youth created a Facebook page called the March 9th Movement.[16] All the taxis I could see in centre ville—the downtown area, containing the entire stretch of the Boulevard Mohammed V (or, simply, the Boulevard) from the Square of the Lazy to the beach area called the Corniche—had "Yes" signs posted on their rear windows. I was also told that the imams were advocating for the new constitution in mosques, especially during Friday prayers, which always included prayers for the king as the Commander of the Faithful, his official title. In the streets and even in coffee shops, copies of the new constitution were distributed as handouts by people.

The tireless campaign of the makhzen, however, could not stop the protests. The youth of the February movement believed that the king did not meet the minimum requirement of constitutional monarchy, a sine qua non condition for the founding of a real democracy, without which the hogra would continue.

On March 20, at 1:15 p.m., I went to a protest planned in Bni Makada, a popular neighborhood of the city. It was crowded—a lot of young people, mostly from the middle or lower classes with a noticeable presence of women, shouting slogans:

My rights, my rights, my rights
They are in my blood and in my veins
I will never give them up even if they execute me!

The most recurrent slogan was from a famous poem by the young Tunisian Abu al Qasim al-Shabi (1909–34), chanted in the struggles against colonial occupation in the Arab world. It was chanted in all the Arab revolutions from Tunis to Cairo, from Casablanca to Tangier, to Tripoli and Benghazi:

If one day people decide to live
Destiny will no doubt respond
Night will no doubt dissipate
Chains will no doubt break.

Islamists who were members of Justice and Charity, an outlawed movement, were present in large numbers but stood at the rear of the march. Bearded men, veiled women in *niqâb*, and others only in *hijâb* held signs: "No God but God," "Majesty Belongs Only to God," and "the Quran is the Solution."

I felt this was a different march—openly ideological and clearly Islamist. I felt out of place; my secular prejudice and my clothes did not fit the scene. I took a few photos and then moved to the front, where all the organizers were grouped. In later protests, the slogans of the movement had changed. While they still shouted, "Majesty Belongs Only to God," the signs that said "the Quran is the Solution" had disappeared. They also had several banners denouncing the law of terrorism, and called for the freeing of prisoners whose photos they displayed.

Since the day of vandalism, the protests departed from Bni Makada and did not occur even once in the Square of Nations. Bni Makada is a suburb, once a shantytown that became part of the city as it expanded. In an effort to eliminate shantytowns, city planners gave people permission to build apartments and traditional Moroccan houses, with two and even three stories, and with water and electricity. Though the neighborhood may have erased most traces of its poor history from the streets, the people still bore it. The population of Bni Makada has the reputation of being conservative and religious. While young men and women in jeans are not absent, one sees mostly veiled women and bearded men wearing loose clothes.

In April, I made a brief visit to the United States and so was unable to attend the protests. But I followed them on Facebook and YouTube. It was clear that centre ville (downtown) and especially the Square of Nations were no longer the protests' epicenters. Squares were highly strategic sites for the social revolutions of the Arab world. It was in Tahrir Square that the Egyptian protests had escalated into a revolution, and it was also in Change Square that the Yemenis forced the president to abdicate. Small wonder, then, that the state prevented the protesters from using the Square of Nations.

The protests had turned violent, as I could see from the videos posted on the movement's webpage. Several veiled women were attacked by the police. A man was cornered in a small street and was beaten up so badly he could no longer move. The police cornered a group of veiled women who were defiantly shouting, "No God but God," as several young men taunted the police, calling them "*haggara* of women" (bullies of women). Seeing the carnage and brutal oppression, I felt lucky I was not around to witness it.

I came back to Morocco by the end of April. The climate of revolution could still be felt as strongly as when I left. More protests were planned for May, I was told. On Sunday of the first week of May, I took a taxi to Bni Makada, feeling apprehensive. I was told the protests were next door to Cinema Tarek, but they were supposed to take place in Change Square. When I got there, the entire square was occupied by special forces—more than just a police force but not quite an army. Unable to enter the square, a crowd of several thousand gathered in different places around it and started chanting slogans.

The referendum for the new constitution was planned for July 1. The makhzen quickly changed the dynamics of the movement itself, if only temporarily. Instead of continuing to call for a constitutional monarchy and the lifting of the state of the hogra, the movement focused on an anti-constitution campaign. The rules of the game then changed. The makhzen descended on the boulevard as the protestors occupied the square in Bni Makada. The Moroccan press, all aligned with the regime to differing degrees, spoke about the Moroccan exception, as had Egyptian and Libyan officials before them. The protests, however, continued every Sunday. Protestors occasionally denounced corrupt people by name, for example, Fouad Ali El Himma, the king's confidant and adviser, and several members of the Fassi family reputed to monopolize state positions and engage in corruption—even as the people starved and struggled.

At this time, I realized that while the streets, and especially the Boulevard, seemed calm and even harmonious—as elegantly dressed young men and women strolled by, some trying to get the attention of others—cyberspace told another story, one of extreme conflict and tension. The camps were clear: members of the youth movement commented on the situation, circulating

Figure 5. Special forces "antiriot" police, occupying the Square of Change
in Bni Makada. Photograph by the author.

videos about the protests and denouncing corruption; others circulated
speeches given by opponents of the regime as well as a speech by the former king Hasan II calling people "rabble rousers" and threatening in street
language "to descend and beat the hell out of them" (*nackli dâr babahum*).
The supporters of the regime frequently responded with, "Long Live the
King" and "No to the Polisario, No to the Algerians," implying that the
agitation was the creation of Morocco's enemies. I received three messages
in my Facebook box from people I did not know: one accusing me of being
a fundamentalist, the other of being a homosexual who was defending the
right of "men to marry each other," and a third asserting I was not a Moroccan. This was not surprising—the entire movement was now accused
of being a heteroclite group of fundamentalists, homosexuals, and Ramadan eaters.[17]

Race was also expressed during these exchanges. Fassi families were specifically pointed out as the ones controlling everything. One post listed all
the names of those who held important positions in the government, mentioning that the twenty-three-year-old daughter of a minister, Mohamed El
Yazgh, was already the director of the Royal Palace. The post stated that in

the same Royal Palace, Fassi "are everywhere like parasitic plants" (*nabâtât tufayliya*). Another post responded, "How can you complain against French racism, when you express racism against the Fassi?" That did not deter more posts to comment on the power of the Fassi and their hegemonic position in the country. A post referred to their Andalusian origin and pointed out that they were not Fassi but Andalusians, with families that were Jewish or of Jewish origins. This was meant to imply not only that they were foreign to the country, without commitment to the rest of its population, but also that they constituted a danger to it. The statement also conveys the anti-Semitic view that Morocco is run by the Jews (disguised as Fassi).

At one point, the exchange seemed to be opposing the *awlâd sha'b* (children of the people) not to the makhzen but specifically to the Fassi, reputed to be sons and daughters of privilege, born with silver spoons. And even when the opposition specified the makhzen, the Fassi were always assumed to constitute an important part of it—as they are in Moroccan popular understanding of politics. However, the movement seemed to homogenize and even mask the fact that among the *awlâd sha'b*, there are serious inequalities, and some are so unequal as to have no hope from any revolution. Their hope is Europe.

Tangier is not a city whose residents particularly likes the current regime. It has, more than other cities, memories of the brutal years of King Hassan II, and its colonial history can be summed up in what is called the War of Rif—first sparked by Abdelkrim al-Khattabi in 1921, crushed mercilessly by a coalition of the French and Spanish armies using napalm, and revived in 1926 by the infamous Marshal Petain, then a famous hero of World War I.[18] Close to Spain, the dialect spoken in Tangier is distinct and mixed with Spanish. When I came here as a teenage boy, I did not always understand what I heard—not only because of the frequent Spanish words but also because of the distinct accent. The city feels closer to Spain than to Morocco, probably because it has shared more with that country and continues to do so. Also, taking on a Spanish color is probably the city's way of turning its back on the regime.

But in these times of revolution, the city had rediscovered its Moroccan heritage and its political ardor. Most participants in the political protests were young, middle or even lower middle class, and unemployed. Women of all ages were present, but stood near the back. Many wore a niqâb that covered their bodies; others just used a hijâb and dressed conservatively. They were the followers of the Justice and Charity movement led by an elderly man, a former

Figure 6. A protest in Bni Makada. The participation of women, many from the
Justice and Charity movement, was noteworthy. Photograph by the author.

Sufi who had transformed himself into a charismatic political leader.[19] Many
Moroccans (with secular leanings or more mainstream Muslim sensibilities)
fail to see his charisma and understand his appeal. However, the elements of
his Sufi-like figure—old, small, humble—and his simple speech about piety
and sharia resonate with his followers. I noticed that women were well represented and that their slogans were more radical: "Majesty Belongs only to
God," which targeted the king himself—his Majesty, as he must always be
called. I came to know then that several women had been incarcerated in relation to a bombing in Casablanca and a subsequent law against terrorism.[20]

    As the date of the referendum for the new constitution neared, tension
in the city became more visible. Propaganda work by supporters of the state
increased. Small parades were held, and thousands of white leaflets were
thrown into the streets, distributed to people, and posted on taxis, on buses,
and across the boulevard. White, everybody knew, was the color of the king
(or the Palace, or the regime—which I came to understand were all one thing
with different names). In the 1970s, amid the so-called elections, parties were
asked to pick a color, as most people were illiterate and it was easier for them

to vote for a blue, green, yellow, or even a pink party. But no party could choose white—it was the exclusive color used in referendum when the king, the Palace, or the regime decided to pass a law.

In mid-July, the press reported that the new constitution was voted in by 97.58 percent. The result, disappointing as it was, was not entirely unpredictable. The movement had no trust in the regime and claimed they had seen vans taking voters—mostly women and rural people—to voting locations. They said some people were forced, others bribed, and still others intimidated.

The king's speech and the so-called new constitution were seen as tricks to stop the protests and dissipate the anger in the streets. Such a ruse, however, only gave momentum to the movement. Protests took place as often as twice a week from mid-June on. The antiglobalization movement continued to make elections the center of its discourse. Both sides, the movement and the state, vigorously propagated their cause. For the movement, the constitution, once again given from above, was not any different from the old one. For the makhzen and the press, the constitution was a great event in the history of the country. They said the country had entered an era of democracy similar to that of France and the United Kingdom (even though the United Kingdom has no written constitution). Others, who had less taste for exaggeration, said that the constitution had put the country definitively on the road to democracy. But the youth mocked the change. The new constitution said that the king had relinquished all his powers to the chief of the government, formerly called the prime minister, but in reality, he still had all the power to approve, disapprove, or even dismiss the head of the government. The powers, the legislature, and the executive were still in the hands of the king. Nevertheless, now that the constitution was approved, elections were set for November 25.

The following protest, also on Sunday, was in June and happened to correspond with the month of Ramadan. The square was still occupied by special forces. One could see uniformed police officers everywhere in the neighborhood. Some of them were comfortably sitting in cafés, watching the scene. Thousands of protesters came in from all directions, many of them carrying food to break their fast. The presence of the police made it impossible for them to gather. Finally, the crowd moved to a smaller square, chanting the usual slogans. They gathered in small groups of four and five, and as soon as they heard the *azan* (call to prayer), they started sharing food with one another. Some of them complained about the lack of organization. In less than an hour, however, the crowd started to disperse and soon the square was totally empty.

Tangier becomes a different city during the summer—it changes face, or maybe it reveals its true face. It becomes more cosmopolitan under the summer wave of tourists and visitors, both Europeans and Moroccans. The sounds of the city change: more cars with foreign plates are seen and heard, and one also hears all sorts of European languages spoken, usually by young Moroccans coming in from various parts of Europe. Yet, even in the midst of summer, preparation for the elections intensified. The newspapers followed the speech and actions of political party leaders and speculated about winners and losers. Most, if not all, continued to talk about the revolution created by the king. The space of the city was monopolized by the makhzen. The Boulevard was filled with posters calling the citizens to "exert their constitutional right to vote." Small minivans in different squares across the city broadcasted taped speeches about democracy, the rights of citizens, and elections made possible by the king.

The February 20 movement did not have access to the same space. It created its own—it marched from Bni Makada to the Boulevard, a five-hour march that started at 4 p.m. and ended at 9 p.m. It became as active as before, if not even more. What was at stake was of tremendous importance. The protestors called the people to boycott the elections and reiterated their demands on Facebook and in several marches. As the time of the elections neared, the intensity grew. The rate of participation would measure who was more popular—the regime or the movement.

On the morning of October 20, Al Jazeera announced the arrest of a wounded Gaddafi. The news was confirmed by an insurgent leader, once a jihadist in Afghanistan with Al Qaeda and now a fighter with NATO. Less than an hour later, Gaddafi was shown on television begging for mercy. It sickened me, despite my initial support for the Libyan revolution. I walked that same day, as always, down the Boulevard to see a protest of over a hundred people—it was the same antiglobalization group. Flags of Tunisia, Egypt, and now Libya and Syria were being waved, and the protesters were shouting, "Gaddafi is gone, gone. It is your turn, O Bashar!"

Gaddafi had been perceived by the existing Arab regimes as the rampart, the strong man who could stop the unpredictable wave of revolutions sweeping one regime after another. An older Moroccan friend of mine, also active in the February movement in Meknès, told me, "When Gaddafi started bombing his people with jets and missiles, members of the makhzen told us: sons of whores [*wlâd laqhâb*], this is what we will do to you if you ever think about a revolution."

The tragic end of Gaddafi sent a message to the regimes in the region— this is what could happen to you if you decide to use force. Feeling empowered by the event, one organizer in a June protest shouted to the crowd, "Here we are, makhzen, here we are; I dare you to touch any one of us, I dare you touch any one of us."

A week before the elections, on Sunday, November 20, Tangier witnessed the biggest protests ever. Participants carried a coffin representing the elections, as well as Syrian and Libyan flags. They chanted the same slogan: "Gaddafi is gone, gone. It is your turn, O Bashar!"

They were addressing Syria's Bashar Assad, now openly in war with his people. The special forces were watching carefully, ready with their batons and shields. One could still walk near them, as I did. They were young and darker skinned than the natives of Tangier; in fact, I was surprised that they were all dark skinned. They looked like rural youth. They were not looking at any one in particular—just staring straight ahead. I wondered what they were thinking, on the shore of this ocean of people. I looked again at a few of them, thinking that they had families to support; this was only a job to them. When I asked a young person next to me about them, he said, "Most of these men are children of the adoption houses. They have no families. The makhzen recruits them as security forces; that is why they have total allegiance to the makhzen."

One of the young people in the minivan addressed the protesters: "Look what the makhzen has for you, sticks [*zrâwat*], soldiers, oppression. That is what the makhzan has for us. We tell them: O makhzen, O haggar, O coward, we do not accept any hogra; go liberate Ceuta and Melila [two Moroccan northern cities still occupied by Spain]."

Some of the slogans explicitly referred to the harraga:

Come donkey, come vote,
Then go die in a boat.

Others picked national events, such as the highly publicized visit of the performer Shakira to the Mawazzine festival for the price of $1 million:[21]

They gave Shakira one million to play,
Unemployment is in every home today.

Figure 7. The coffin of the elections. Photograph by the author.

Figure 8. Syrian and Libyan flags flew along with Moroccan flags in a September protest after the killing of Gaddafi. Photograph by the author.

And they repeated over and again: "Two seas, two seas, and our country is in misery."

I felt I stood out in the crowd, especially when the protests moved to Bni Makada. Once I was followed by several kids (the oldest of them not even eighteen) who kept laughing at me and from time to time pushed one of their own toward me, screaming, "Spy, spy!" I looked different not only because of my clothes but also because I held a digital Canon camera and was strategizing about what photos to take next. I also had eyeglasses that made me look like an intellectual from the 1960s or a spy from the 2010s. Annoyed, I managed to lose them as I caught up with the leadership of the movement. I engaged in a conversation with a couple of organizers, partly to interview them and partly to show the teenagers, just in case they were still following me, that I, too, was in the revolutionary camp.

Hicham, one of the young organizers, in his mid-twenties, told me, "We have a problem—we do not have the support of the intellectuals." Undoubtedly, only a few intellectuals supported them, usually those not dependent on the makhzen. Unlike in Tunisia and Egypt, Moroccan intelligentsia have been close to the regime, and closer since the coming to power of Mohammed V. Historically middle and upper middle class, they were employees of the state and very often members of a political party—either the Socialist Party for the middle class or the Istiqlal (a right-wing party) for the upper class.[22] But there were also those associated with communism or one of the numerous political parties that appeared and disappeared overnight.

When I publicly asked a respected political scientist and intellectual about the protests after he finished a lecture on the Arab Spring in Tangier in December 2011, he said, smiling dismissively, "I would not support the Justice and Charity [movement]."

I was surprised that he had reduced the February 20 movement to Justice and Charity, but continued listening as he went on to explain how the concept of *fasâd* that the protestors attacked in their slogans did not mean corruption but moral turpitude, and thus the movement's claim was entirely religious.

On November 25, the day of the elections, members of the movement were watching the elections everywhere on screens. At 10 a.m., they reported that participation was low, 10 percent, and even lower at 12 p.m. However, by the end of the day, the press started to reveal higher percentages and explained that it was only in the afternoon that citizens came in to vote. The rate of participation was announced as 45 percent in the country and 47 percent in Tangier.

I asked Hicham, whom I had befriended by then, "Was there fraud in these elections? I mean, can they lie or make up that number?"

He said, "No, not really. The numbers must be the same or close. But those who registered were 13 million people out of 22 million eligible citizens. Only 5 million 850 thousand voted, which means the rate of actual participation was 26 percent and not 45 percent as the government falsely announced."

"What is it now?" I asked him.

"Well, the protests are continuous. This is a stage among stages [*mahatta min al mahattât*]."

However, I still wondered why 13 million people had bothered to register. When I inquired, I was told that the elections were supervised and even organized by the infamous Ministry of the Interior (the same ministry used to organize political repression and fraudulent elections in the 1970s and 1980s). They could register whomever they wanted, even people who might have died long ago. Indeed, I read several messages on Facebook telling such stories. One woman from Meknès had discovered her long-dead father on a list of registered voters. I wondered if I was registered in Meknès, my hometown, without my knowledge, though there was no way for me to know for sure. Whether such accusations were true or not is difficult to say, but one thing was for sure: the stakes for the regime were alarmingly high; anything was possible.

In the aftermath of the elections, protestors were asked to escalate. And an escalation did indeed happen—at least in numbers and slogans. The protests seemed much larger. Organizers estimated that over 200,000 people took part in one rally on Sunday, December 4. The slogans became more daring. The king's father, Hasan II, was mentioned by name, maybe for the first time.

> Elections are the same
> As under Hasan II's reign.

The prime minister, Abbas El Fassi, was also mentioned by name, as his entire family was believed to have monopolized key political and economic positions. The message to him was rather threatening:

Figure 9. A banner of the December protest: "The February 20th Movement against Injustice and Corruption: The Struggle Continues." Photograph by the author.

From Tangier to Meknès
We will put you on trial, O Abbas.

A young leader in a minivan addressed the crowd: "Did you vote?"

"No," said the crowd in unison.

"Did anyone in this crowd vote?"

"No," said the crowd again in one voice.

"Where did they then come up with the idea that 47 percent of the people of Tangier voted?"

The crowd shouted, "Elections are the same as under Hasan II's reign!" (*al intikhabât hiya, hiya! Wa tariqa hasaniya!*).

On a Sunday evening, December 14, the small antiglobalization movement gathered again in the Square of the Lazy. The same middle-aged man with a southern accent said, "We have to be proud of this city, of our city. This city has been the first city in the entire country to massively protest. We have the highest percentage of protesters. We are sending the message

Figure 10. A December rally—the largest ever since the beginning of the protests
in February 2011. It filled the Boulevard Mohammed V from top to bottom.
Photograph by the author.

clear. Our city is not a city of prostitution, not a city of drugs, not a city of
real estate dealers. This is a city of militancy for justice and dignity."[23]

I only had a few days left in the country and was exhausted. In addition
to the topic I had come to research, I had been involved in the events of the
movement—both as a citizen and as an anthropologist. By then, I was also
deeply pessimistic. I felt that there were two main obstacles to real change in
the country—a highly astute regime and a profoundly illiterate population
that could be easily manipulated. The regime had managed, at least for now,
to convince people of the fact that the king had created a new revolution. The
so-called revolution was applauded by the same Arab intellectuals and religious leaders who had denounced Ben Ali, Gaddafi, Mubarak, and Assad.[24]

I left Tangier on December 31, 2011, very uncertain about the future of
the movement. Nearly a year had passed since the beginning of the protests
on February 20, 2011. On the movement's website, from afar, I saw that the
protests were continuing at the same pace. I realized that the movement may
not have been able to implement the radical changes it wanted, at least not
in the short run, but it had definitely made this clear: the regime could no
longer rule alone with impunity—it faced the words and the power of the

Figure 11. Antiglobalization protesters look on as a middle-aged man speaks during a February movement protest in December. Photograph by the author.

street. And while the hogra was still integral to Moroccan politics and culture, its cure was also integral: the nation's youth were totally mobilized against it. As I followed their activities on Facebook and YouTube, it became clear that they had entered a new phase. Calls for escalation and for continuous sit-ins—even for real intifada—were being posted frequently. Slogans explicitly threatened the king, who a year ago was considered sacred; now he was being told he would be next (*'oqba lik ya al-malik*). In the end, what I witnessed and narrate here was just a phase. A second phase started on February 20, 2012, a year after the birth of the movement.

Seven Years Later

The February movement that was the main actor of the revolution that began in 2011 and whose ethnography I wrote in 2012 is still alive and active. It still descends to the streets, celebrates February 20 every year, and makes itself heard about a range of social and political issues. But what happened in 2011 was beyond that movement, the same way that we could say that what happened in Tunisia, Egypt, and Libya was surely beyond the actors themselves. It was a drastic change that was captured by a movement but that sprang from a long modern history of repression, exclusion, and marginality. The figure of the harrag is arguably the most tragic figure of the social, political, and cultural conditions of the region. But they are other tragic figures that are silent, anonymous, yet resilient. From time to time, a story of one of them makes the news and triggers more protests and more claims for social justice. There are those who burned themselves like the vendor in Tunisia, those who threatened to kill themselves in front of the parliament in Rabat, those who went berserk, and those who defied the makhzen by shouting in the streets. There are also the unemployed graduates or the educators who at times were beaten by the police in the streets. Perhaps the most tragic event happened in October 2016 in the Rif, the region of Tangier, in an adjacent city called Al Hoceima.

A fishmonger by the name of Mouhcine Fikri had his cart confiscated by the police because the fish he was selling, swordfish, was not allowed to be caught in that season, and thus it was illegally on the market, according to the official story of the makhzen. Mouhcine's cart was emptied into the back of a garbage truck. Seeing his precious merchandise, his entire capital, thrown away, the young man jumped in behind it, in a desperate effort to salvage it. A police officer still standing next to the truck gave the order to the driver to "Crush the mother-fucker!" (*t-han mmû!*), and the driver did indeed engage the truck's compactor and fatally "ground the fisherman."[25]

Photos of the dead vendor's arm extending from the back of the truck went viral on social media. And immediately, the people of the Rif, including the residents of Tangier, took to the street with a sense of rage. This was another outrageous act of the hogra perpetrated by the makhzen against "the children of people" and also against the Rif itself, which perceived itself as particular victim to the hogra under the entirety of the rule of Hassan II. Protests have been regular since the tragic death of the fish vendor. Several cities have joined the protests in solidarity with the Rif. These include Fes, Meknès, Casablanca, Rabat, Agadir, Taza, Marrakesh, and Tangier.[26]

This is generally not seen as part of the Arab revolutions of 2011. It is rather seen as a *hirâk*, "a move" or movement, and it is now known as Hirâk Rif (the movement of the Rif), despite the fact that the leaders of the Hirâk themselves participated in the February 20 movement. Unlike the movement of February 20, the Hirâk, still an unfolding event in the Rif, has a leadership that speaks on its behalf and that makes specific demands on the makhzen without agreeing to sit with any government officials or even human rights organizations. Their demands are directed to the king. They demand the lifting of the hogra from the Rif, the development of infrastructure, building of hospitals, employment of youth and other inhabitants, the end of the militarization of the region, and the end of corruption. Their demands are undoubtedly regional but still strongly resonate with people in the rest of the country. The leadership of the Hirâk includes its most charismatic figure, a forty-year-old man by the name of Nasser Zefzafi, whose grandfather was the minister of interior affairs in the Republic of the Rif (1923–26) under Abdelkrim al-Khattabi. The existence and identity of the Hirâk's leadership must have worried the makhzen and its supporters. The political scene in Morocco seems now to have a cast of actors and opponents. On one side there are the makhzen, led by King Mohammed VI and his closest advisers, such as Fouad Ali El Himma, and on the other side there is Zefzafi with his comrades—all children of the people with a symbolic connection to the 1920s government of Abdelkrim to boot. "Are you a government or a gang?" is a slogan borrowed from Abdelkrim that Zefzafi has repeated. The opposition, pregnant with symbolism, now seems real to the makhzen, and because it is real, it is serious and threatening, even though the leadership of the Hirâk Rif asks for nothing but basic rights. The makhzen has escalated.

Officials of the makhzen as well as its many ordinary supporters, commonly called 'Ayâsha,[27] accuse the Hirâk of separatism, of being the dirty hand of other states (read Algeria).[28] They also systematically warn other Moroccans of the situation in Syria. They have tried to turn the Hirâk's leader, Zefzafi, into an "outlaw," even a terrorist, by comparing him to Abu Bakr al-Baghdadi, the then-leader of the Islamic State of Iraq and the Levant (ISIL). Racial expressions describing the inhabitants of the Rif as "treacherous," "back stabbers," and "children of Spain" have surfaced over and again, especially on social media.

The makhzen sees this bold sustained movement as being of the type of protests that erupted in 2011. This also means there is continuity, albeit indirect, between the movement of the Rif and the protests of February 2011, especially considering that protesters hold the flag of the February movement as well as the Amazigh flag along with Moroccan flags to underscore the idea that the Hirâk is not a separatist movement. This has alarmed the makhzen, which now know that this period of street stress and anxiety is far from over.[29] In one incident in 2017, seventy people, including two

minors, were arrested in the Rif and were transported to Casablanca. Zefzafi and several of his comrades were also arrested.[30] By the end of 2017,
hundreds of protesters were arrested and transferred to a jail in Casablanca
where they stood on trial for different accusations, including participation
in unauthorized protests, humiliation of agents of security, and threats to
national security. On Tuesday, June 26, 2018, the verdict against the fifty-
three accused came heavy: a twenty-year sentence for Zefzafi and two of his
companions and fifteen-, ten-, five-, and one-year jail sentences for the rest.
The verdict, deemed "cruel and unjust," even by people who traditionally
aligned with the makhzen, prompted many people on social media to express the feeling that the repressive years of Hassan II, known as *les années
de plomb* (the years of lead), were not far away after all. It confirmed once
again that the conditions against which the February 20 movement stands
are indeed intact. For the people of the Rif, it seems injustice, hogra, and
oppression are still their lot. It is doubtful that jail sentences will put an
end to the Hirâk. They may even fuel it.

In any case, the Hirâk has been marked by brutal police repression. Yet
in its unfolding, there is a noticeable link between this repression, or the
state of the hogra, as I call it, and the activity of lahrig. The Rif has been a
region of emigration to Europe since Morocco's independence. Over decades
of marginalization, an estimated 40 percent of the population has migrated
to Europe. As Laurie Brand noticed, "With independence in 1965, migration from the Rif . . . was particularly encouraged, because of its reputation
for both opposition and limited economic stabilities."[31] The repression of the
Hirâk itself has now further "fueled exodus to Europe."[32] Young people from
the region continue to attempt the crossing of the Mediterranean. The link,
then, between hogra, race, and migration is undoubtedly real and tangible,
as the next chapters will explore.

Chapter 2

Migration, Space, and Children

But say, my brothers, what can the child do that even
the lion could not do?

—Nietzsche

The mid-1990s witnessed a new phenomenon linking two shores of the Mediterranean, Moroccan and Spanish: the birth of the child migrant. Migration then was the affair of adults, men and women who would take the risk using both legal and illegal means. Children often accompanied them, but at the will of their parents. The new child migrant has a will of his own. It is his decision to migrate—and he often does so using the most drastic of means, gripping the undersides of commercial trucks being ferried to Tarifa or Algeciras, only thirty-five and forty-five minutes away from the port of Tangier, or finding a way to grip the ferry itself by, say, wedging a wooden board into one of its lower portholes. With the appearance of the child migrant, a new name was also invented, the *harrag*. These children are all boys; girls are never seen hanging out. The port is too dangerous a space for females, whether minors or adults—not only the port but also Moroccan streets. Hence the fact that despite the visible phenomenon of street children, street girls are absent.

The name *harrag* comes from the verb *hrag*, "to burn" in Moroccan parlance. The act of "burning," or *lahrig*, has different meanings, depending on the context: violating the law against passage to Europe, crossing the sea by an act of transgression, or traversing the long road from an inland shantytown to the big and dangerous port city of Tangier. And so a harrag is someone who metaphorically burns himself, that is, who disregards his own self to undertake the risk of death to "make it" to Europe. The term is also used to refer to someone who has overstayed his visa in Europe and thus become a harrag, that is, an "illegal" migrant. In this use of the verb *hrag*, it is as if one has burnt the visa itself. As an activity, lahrig may change and take on new forms.

Despite the variations in meanings and implications, the harrag is in all cases an "unauthorized" migrant—either one who is *sans papiers* (without legal documents) within the borders of a European country or someone who is outside such a country but preparing to cross. It seems, then, that both the intent to migrate and the act of doing so are part of the operation of the harrag, an operation involving the transgression of the law and exposure to danger, including a high risk of death.[1] Acutely aware of all the risks, and when asked about the purpose of his being in the port, a harrag will often say, "We want to burn" (*bâghin nahrgû*) or "We want to risk" (*bâghin nriskîw*). The "we" here indicates that the enterprise of lahrig, though it can be an individual act, is most often a group enterprise. The harrag is almost always part of a group of *harraga*.

In this chapter, I shall examine the conditions of the harraga, the space in which they live and operate, and how, as social actors,[2] they create and change cultural forms and, through acts of transgression (lahrig), display agency.[3] The harrag is a phenomenon associated with the condition of globalization and the accompanying trend of rural-to-urban movement. Most often he is from the countryside or from shantytowns outside the big cities of the country. He is found in coastal cities, and Tangier is considered his capital. In this chapter, I will explore the everyday life of the harrag, or rather, through an ethnographic description, I will construct the social world of the harraga and their material conditions in the city, specifically its port. I will consider their motivations, their strategies for survival, and their tactics[4] for crossing. In all cases, the harrag's motive is clear: he will change his destiny—or rather rectify it—from being a shantytown or rural kid with no prospects to a resident of Europe, which is a status in and of itself.

Children as Migrants

The harraga of Tangier are as young as six, seven, and eight years old; most I met are teenagers, thirteen and fourteen years old. At this very young age, they have already "burnt" a lot. They have burnt bridges with their families.

They have also burnt miles, long and difficult, traversed on foot or by illicit means, to arrive in Tangier, where the greatest burn and transgression awaits them: the crossing of the sea to Europe. They come from all parts of Morocco, often from the poorest areas, the shantytowns of Casablanca, Meknès, Beni Mellal, Salé, and Ksar el-Kabir, but also the remote countryside and its villages. They usually come to the city via an illicit train and sometimes bus ride. Because of their age, they can pass unnoticed or they can mischievously distract the ticketing agent.[5] They usually leave home in small groups of three or more, but sometimes the decision to head to Tangier is an individual one. Once in the city, they instantly make friends among harraga of their age and their condition, even those who are not from their region. Nongovernmental organizations such as UNICEF and also the local francophone discourse heard on public media refer to this population as children, *les enfants*. The name "child" in this context is meant as a legal term, to signify the status of a minor. However, it is worth interrogating the cultural category of the child in order to shed light on the dynamics of his migration to and from the city. What is the meaning of this category, "child," in a society such as Morocco's?

Since the work of Philippe Ariès, social science has come to understand childhood not as a natural stage of life but rather as a cultural one. The concept of the child, according to Ariès, is modern. With the Ancien Régime (that is, the French political order broken by revolution in 1789), it came to be determined by the family and the educational system, both of which not only re-created the concept of the child but even extended the span of childhood.[6] The child also became subject to measures of isolation and even imprisonment similar to those of other marginalized groups—a topic tackled, in the footsteps of Ariès, by Michel Foucault. Foucault also argues that education "accentuates" the separation between childhood and adulthood.[7] In a westernized, once-colonized society, such as Morocco's, the child is determined by race, class, and region. This is to say, because the category "child" is related to age, it is defined relationally and according to context. The child is thus "deictic," "a social shifter."[8] For large masses, especially in shantytowns at the outskirts of cities or even in small villages, children are often perceived as a potential source of social security for their parents, who they are expected to support when they grow up. They will look after their parents financially and affectively—often the first is taken as tantamount to the second. Consider the Moroccan idioms *yathallâ fik* (take care of you, look after you) and *talqâh fâsh takbar* (they will take care of you when you grow

Figure 12. Sleeping at the Corniche. Photograph by the author.

old). These sentiments, preponderant among poor families, make the harrag child feel it is an obligation to find ways to be ready when the family needs him. And the family is already in need—or may be always in need.[9] Often, when I asked, "Why do you want to cross?" I got the answer, "To help my family" (*nâʿwanu mâlin al-dâr*).

Many of the children I met come from broken families: single mothers struggling, rather unsuccessfully, to raise several children; alcoholic fathers who do not provide or care. Their parents either have no jobs or very modest ones, as restaurant workers, taxi drivers, well diggers. At the port one July evening in 2008, I asked an eight-year-old harrag, "What does your father do?"

"Nothing [*wâlû*]," he replied.

"Your mother?"

"Wâlû."

"You have sisters and brothers?"

"Two sisters and one brother."

"What do they do?"

Figure 13. Getting in the port before 2010. Photograph by the author.

"Nothing."

"How do they live?"

"My grandmother."

"What about your grandmother?" I asked.

"She supports us."

"How?"

"She grows crops [ʿandhâ laflâha]."

The parents usually have several children to take care of and no means to look for the missing one. Too young and too poor to be literate, the harraga drop out of elementary school or never went there in the first place.[10] Among the many I met, only a handful made it to the second grade.

"My mother died at the end of my first year in school. I never went back. My father married again and I left," said a fourteen-year-old with terribly sad eyes that leave lasting emotional marks on the listener. He had just been expelled from Algeciras and released by a Moroccan judge the day I met him.

The child of the upper class, and even of the middle class, is socialized in a modern way, as determined by his family, whose last name he bears, and by the educational system, often French and also increasingly American, especially with the opening of American private and semiprivate schools. These children not only have a future that belongs to them—that is, they are not anyone's "social security"—but also often have great material and symbolic capital waiting for them when they grow up. By contrast, most children from poor backgrounds, and even sometimes from middle-class backgrounds, are looked at by the family as its own social security. This explains in part why the harraga are exclusively boys.

Ordinary young girls from lower classes are generally expected to marry and take care of their children or, rather, to be taken care of by a husband, who will be the only breadwinner in the household. Even going out at night by herself tends to create a cloud of suspicion around a woman's reputation and may associate her with the activity of sex work.[11] Rahma Bourquia notes that even for a woman to stand outside the doorway of her own home (of course alone and frequently, she should have nuanced) exposes her reputation to scrutiny. The tendency of Moroccan society, she continues, is to "value the woman who is closely associated with the home."[12] In the entirety of my fieldwork, from 2008 to 2016, I never met a girl harrag. I only heard from a *harrag* boy who said that he met one in the port one day but never saw her again. Moroccan families tend to be more protective of girls than of boys. Protecting girls is protecting family honor (*sharaf*).[13] Hardship for a boy can turn him into a man (*râjal*), so it is often believed. Life in the street for a girl is an immediate and sure danger; it turns her into a *bint zanqa*, a street girl, and ruins her family's honor and concomitantly exposes them to shame.[14] Migration can still be considered a good option for a girl when she grows up, but often through means that are less dangerous and more secure, such as marriage.

The harraga, meanwhile, or most of those I met, have no childhood and are neither enclosed in an educational system nor nurtured in a family background. In his acclaimed autobiographical novel, Mohamed Choukri portrays his early years in the city of Tangier without something that really looks like a family, wandering around, living on theft and occasional "sex work," scavenging in cemeteries and eating from garbage cans.[15] The family—also a modern concept—makes the idea of childhood possible, and that entails intimacy, care, and protection, in the view of Ariès.[16]

Contrary to the ideals of the bourgeoisie in France, who imposed universal education and thus according to Ariès and Foucault extended infancy,[17] in Moroccan society, education has been used, for a long time and especially today, as a means of segregation. Morocco has a high illiteracy rate, which means a great number of persons do not experience that separation between their lives as children and their lives as adults. Foucault considers the divide between the child and adult to be unique to Western societies. Michel Peraldi notes that "the lines and the frontiers between the life of the family and life in the streets" are blurred in a number of African societies with high illiteracy rates and significant child labor.[18]

Schools create, then, that clear modern separation between adulthood and childhood, but they also create separation between the modern (educated) citizen and the unmodern ones. A school is not only a hallmark of the modern but also an institution that produces differences and inequalities. A child's access to school or exclusion from it determines her future as a citizen. This discovery was important for the elite in Moroccan society who, after an initial boycott, ended up "having an acute passion" for French education.[19] They must have discovered its great virtue in promoting social mobility even within colonial society itself. Hence, quickly, education became not only highly sought after by the elite for their children but also an object of competition from which the children of the poor were discouraged. Robert Montagne speaks about how education contributed to the creation of a modern bourgeois youth and how, by the same token and because of economic and political dynamics of exclusion, also created the Moroccan proletariat.[20]

The opening of the school by colonial authorities was not of general benefit to all; in fact, access to it was limited. Yet in its limitation, education was extended, by a certain amount, to individuals in society who were not part of the elite. Colonial authorities sought through education to increase the base of their loyalty, believing that French education would indeed create French subjects—and in a good number of cases, it did. However, this goal clearly clashed with the priorities of the *makhzen*, who saw it as opening the door of competition beyond class parameters by qualifying and inviting children of the masses.

This strategy stood in contrast with that of Western societies, which conceived of schools as a means to separate children from adults and where the means became, in the view of Foucault, a form of imprisonment. In Moroccan society, the children of the masses are "freed" from this sequestration as early as possible, and in many cases, they are never included. They find themselves from an early age in the world of adults, working in the fields, in small shops, in construction work, in the souk selling vegetables or woven bags, and so on. The harraga constitute perhaps the extreme case of a child engaging in an adult practice—migration.

Be that as it may, education in Moroccan society has continued to produce inequality and guarantee exclusion in ways that are more drastic than in France, as indicated by the work of Pierre Bourdieu on France.[21] I mention France not only because, as a former colonial nation, it continues to serve as a reference point for its former colony but also because the Moroccan system itself became, even before independence, an extension of the French educational system for the Moroccan elite.

Since the early 1990s, education, even an extended one, no longer opens doors. Prior to the 1990s, all Moroccan schools were public, and despite economic inequalities, children of the poor also had access to them. The Moroccan government then had interests in investing in education to cover public services such as education, health care; in short, the government had to husband its human resources, derived from the masses, in order to maintain the function of modern institutions (hospitals, schools, post offices, etc.) left by the French. Even by the 1970s, Morocco was still dependent on *coopérants* (French and other mostly European personnel, including from Eastern Europe, with some from the Middle East)[22] to occupy these posts. But from the early 1990s on, public services became more politicized, the theater of an "intense social clash around hegemonic social positions."[23] At play, too, was the push of international finance institutions to open the public sector to private investment, backed by loans and financial aid—part of a global, neoliberal economic trend with profound effects. The sense of defeat and despair among the masses became increasingly palpable. In the decades since and even today, public media, including newspapers, frequently cover the protests of unemployed youth who are calling for what they believe is their right of employment in the public sector. The coverage often shows police forces dispersing the protestors in ways that are humiliating and without regard to gender.

In this context, education, especially public education, has come to be seen as maybe the surest road to failure, that is, to a life of unemployment, whereas in the past, it was the surest way to changing one's social and economic conditions.[24] One of the very few harraga I met who had made it to the second grade, a boy who greatly impressed me with his verbal ability, asked me, "What have those who went to school gained? Have you not seen educated people and doctors unable to find a job? Have you not seen them protesting and asking for employment?"

His questions are clearly rhetorical. That education produces unemployment is common knowledge in Morocco nowadays. That same day of my dialogue with this child, I saw, on the front page of a Moroccan newspaper, a photo of an unemployed woman, a doctor, being beaten by a policeman in front of the Parliament in Rabat.

In the face of despair, migration is seen as a means to success—despite the fact that the harraga are keenly aware that the enterprise of migrating is fraught with danger and a high risk of death. However, unlike education, which generates desperate unemployed people who are often mocked and despised in society, migration generates hope. Successful migrants almost always come back home with many signs of success: cars, money, houses, foreign white wives. In fact, the mere fact of living abroad, in a Western society, is itself an achievement; it provides one with a social status. While discussing the urge of young people to leave, a Moroccan woman told me one day, "We do not make here the difference between someone who is a professor, like you, and someone who works in a restaurant in the U.S. We see both of you as the same, Americans, you both live in that world. You are even the same [bhâl, bhâl]. People say so-and-so married someone from America, not a professor in America. What counts is just where you are, where you live."

In any case, the harrag as a child is determined neither by education nor by his family; this is to say, he is neither confined nor nurtured like the modern child in Europe. One may even go so far as to say that the harrag child has not yet been invented as such, that his childhood is absent, that he is an adult with a few years under his belt. He has nothing of the characteristics of a child, and he has almost all of those of an adult. He has a mission, a political will, and a consciousness that the world in which he lives is worth leaving. He acquires his skill, develops his knowledge, and sharpens his intelligence on the street. In terms of everyday survival, he out-skills children of schools. He thinks about the future before they can do so. He is determined to live according to his dreams. Hence, his determination to change his destiny, to substitute it so he can find what is worth living for and perhaps also what is worth dying for: *Europe as a home.* The harrag could not choose where he was born, but he believes he can choose where he will live.

I met a harrag boy early on in June 2008; he had a scar over his left eye that he barely hid with sunglasses. I was already sitting on a bench at the Corniche with three harraga, speaking about the condition of the country. They were all saying, rather laughingly, "this country is fucked up" (*mqawda*), "it gave us nothing" (*mâ'tâtna walû*), "it is taken by thieves" (*ghir dyâl sha-farâ*) when he chimed in: "I would sign a contract to give up my nationality right now."

"Would you sign to give up Islam?" I asked provocatively.

"No, never, our religion is the best."

"Why give up your citizenship, then?" I asked.

"It has brought us nothing but misery [*quhra*]." He repeated the sentence three times.

"What happened to your eye?" I asked.

"I fell from a truck yesterday morning!"

Quhra is a unique term that does indeed define the condition of these children and, by extension, entire segments of poor people at the margins of society. While one can translate it as "misery," it has a much richer meaning and evokes a constellation of meanings that are culturally rooted. Quhra surely means a situation of total poverty, of owning nothing and hoping to own nothing. It is not only the lack of an ability to live a decent life but also the condition of utter deprivation, of despair that tomorrow will be no better, and the feelings of duress and distress that come with not even having enough to eat. Quhra refers to a material condition of livelihood, but its meaning is also emotional. Quhra is defeating; it wounds one's dignity, often fatally. Quhra in Moroccan parlance is often associated with *zmân* or *al-waqt* (life, time). And so one gets the phrases *qahru zmân* and *qharatni alwaqt*. It is as if quhra is a condition of adulthood, those defeated by the hardship and harshness of life; rarely does one hear quhra associated with the condition of a child. The question of age—"How old are you?"—was a recurrent one in my interviews with both kids and young adults. In a group interview, one fourteen-year-old told me, "Each one of us has the life experience of a forty-year-old man. We have seen so much. We have been in Europe, in jail, in the street, we have seen it all."

Here, the child himself defines himself and his peers not by the number of years but rather by a life experience, that is, by the knowledge accumulated in the street. Defining oneself by how much one has known is also found in other societies.[25] It is true, street life ages children, and it has been noticed that children who spend much time in the streets become conversant like adults.[26] Moroccan culture has several words for "child," each used in a specific context: *darri* (plural *drari*), *barhûch* (plural *brâhich*), and the literary Arabic *tifl*, as well as the francophone press and public *les enfants*. *Darri* can be used to indicate any young person, regardless of a specific age;

Figure 14. Hanging out: the author (second from the right) with harraga on fishermen's nets, August 2011. Photograph taken by a harrag.

barhûch is used in the same sense, with the additional meaning that the young person lacks maturity—to the extent that the adjective *mbarhach* can be applied to anyone, of almost any age, to indicate a juvenile manner. While the state uses a legal concept, the category of "minor" (*qâsir*), society itself has rather ambiguous terms for the child. Not only is it unclear when childhood starts and when it ends, but the concept of the child (*enfant*) is not associated, as in modern Europe, with concepts of rights and citizenship. Hence, a number of types of "child abuse" are not considered as such mainly because the concept of the child is ambiguous, to say the least.

The Space of Lahrig

Lahrig is an act, an activity; it is even a performance, and one that only a few people can undertake and even fewer can undertake successfully. For lahrig is not only an attempt to cross to Europe but also an effort to change one's destiny—social status, country of birth, and so on—and in doing so to change one's own life and self. This activity is performed in specific places, at the edge, at the border between Europe and Africa, between reality and dream, between destiny and will. It occurs across the entirety of the North African shores, from Tangier to Alexandria, but Tangier remains a privileged spot for the enterprise. There is, of course, the enclave of Melilla that migrants, even those temporarily stationed in Tangier, choose as a crossing point. But Melilla is under Spanish rule and thus technically a European territory that migrants may enter only "illegally" as they would any European city. They wait behind the fence.

Tangier is altogether a different story. It is a Moroccan port that anyone, even from other African countries, can enter freely. Whereas the city constitutes the border between Africa and Europe, the port constitutes a liminal space, both Moroccan and European, because of the presence of European commercial trucks and ferries. At the port, one is as close to Europe as one can be—and here the eyes may embrace Europe, meaning the European landscape—with the view of the Spanish town of Tarifa and the city of Algeciras and the British Rock of Gibraltar. Europe is in the field of vision of the harrag. He need not just dream it; he can see it. The port is also the stage for the harrag's performance. The competence of the migrant as a burner is acquired: he learns how to wait, and where and when a ferry leaves; he makes connections with other harraga; he masters the space of the port and learns to divert the attention of the police and their dogs.

"What is the main problem you face when you want to cross?" I once asked a twelve-year-old with old clothes and sneakers that showed his right toe. As if he were smoking a cheap cigarette, or rather half of it, he inhaled, and said:

"Our problem is the police near the ferry. They do not let us pass. They have dogs that can spot us. They used to have this ferocious dog that could smell a harrag from far away. He can spot you in a crowd of people and comes straight to you. Look at me, he bit my leg one day as I was entering the port. Son of a whore, he had an axe to grind with us [*li dârbû dârbà 'linà*]!"

"Is it Saddam?" I asked, having already heard about the infamous dog many times. But I had never seen him, or maybe I was unable to identify him in the midst of the many stray dogs in the port.

The kid laughed and said, "Yes, you've heard of him?"

"Yes, I have, but never seen him. How do you manage him?"

"He is not here anymore. We poisoned him."

"You did what?" I said with surprise and shock.

"He bit many of us around, he messed up our lives, so we put poison in his food one day," he said laughingly.

Knowledge of space and what is within it, boldness to defy obstacles and danger constitute the competence needed for the harrag to cross. He may fail, and he often does. But each failure endows him with more knowledge and more know-how, and this emboldens him even more because he is now, more than ever, convinced that crossing is possible and that it is a matter of timing, or luck (*zhar*). Thus, the space of the port is a space of migratory performance as much as it is also the space of migratory competence. Hence the fact that a harrag child is neither a street child nor a gang member.[27] Rather, he is a migrant child—a peculiar one at that. Streets are familiar to children, who are seduced by their spectacles and their opportunities for fun and play.[28] But the port is not a street, and the street for the harrag is only a means, a way to go to run errands having to do with his survival. The spatial focus of the harrag is the port; all other forms of space, including the street, either take him there or bring him there. Often I would see harraga— and by then I knew almost each one of them—walking in the street far away from the port. For instance, I used to see them standing in front of Bakery Florence downtown, adjacent to Boulevard Mexico, and I always felt they were out of place.

"What are you doing here?" I often asked to start a conversation.

"We are looking for something to eat [*kandabru 'lâ man qassîw*]. We will be back. Tayeb is there, you can hang out with him; we will be back," they would say once they had become well acquainted with me.

However, the space of the port is encompassed; it is part and parcel of a larger space, the city, which is itself part of the larger nation-state that we call Morocco, a postcolonial space where relations of power with Europe can be felt and seen in everyday practices and everyday discourse. The harrag expresses that relation since as a child, and even as an adult, he offers himself to Europe in a sacrificial act that seems to most as the ultimate act of disappearance. We can also say that he is attracted to Europe by its sirens (all signs of the modern) that he can neither ignore nor resist. Even though there is a migratory movement from Europe to Africa, there is no equivalent moving in that direction; there is no European harrag. The Europeans move freely to Morocco. No visa is needed, and a passport is not a privilege for a European but a civic right.[29] The harrag is in the port, in Tangier, and in Morocco. He inhabits multiple spaces at once. All of these spaces are subordinate to Europe—politically, economically, and culturally. And this subordination is the result of colonial history, or better yet, it is its continuity. Migration has shifted from being forced to being volunteered to being obligated.

However, Tangier is not only a liminal space, a main gate to Europe for the harraga—children or not, Moroccan or not—but also a kind of destination in itself, a taste of Europe. The city preserves its European past with café and hotel names like Rembrandt Hotel, Café Paris, Le Petit Berlin, Café Davinci. Several of Tangier's beaches have Italian and English names. Even inside the city, new European and American restaurants, cafés, shops, and pubs open with names such as El Porto, Van Gogh Parisienne, Panorama, London Pub, Irish Pub, and so on. In this city that was once located within the Spanish colonial zone in Morocco, French names are fewer, though not absent. Most European languages are spoken and heard downtown. It is also in Tangier that many, perhaps most, of the migrants from Europe pour into Morocco, especially during the summer. A walk down the Boulevard Mohammed V (or, simply, the Boulevard) in the midst of July revealed to me that the very noise of the city conveys Europe, not to mention the many cars that fill the streets of the city all summer long[30] from almost every corner of Europe. Recently called the Las Vegas of Morocco, the city has reinvented itself under the rule of Mohammed VI to become the second largest economy in the country after Casablanca, to which it was connected, in the summer of 2018, with a TGV, a French high-speed train that bridges the distance between the two cities in only two hours.

Europe—in its physical sense, seductive, clean, and powerful—is on the other side of the sea but still, it seems, within immediate reach—only 14 kilometers away. Tangier is closer to Tarifa (only thirty-five minutes by ferry) than Tarifa to Algeciras (forty-five minutes by bus).[31] Here, despite the strong European presence, the harrag is in Africa or rather in Morocco; he does not conceive of the African continent, only of the place they call *blâdnâ* (our country). In any case, there are ferries that come and go; they bring people to Europe, and bring Europeans and people of Europe (*nâs al-khârij*)[32] to the city, reminding the harraga that there is a movement, a crossing, a link, a connection, a bridge—in short, a real possibility. Two tourist boats alternate in bringing people (the privileged ones, the ones blessed by the right to cross legally) from and to Tangier. One of the boats that comes and goes from one continent to the other is massive enough be seen and heard from a distance. It is called *Biladi* (my country).[33]

Between the port and the beach, there is the terrible long and gray wall. Like all walls, this one was built to separate "us" from "them." "Us" are the Europeans and the fortunate Europeanized Moroccans and Africans who have "made it" and can enter El Dorado freely via Tangier's port. "Them" are the Moroccans and West Africans who want to make it. The wall, 6 meters tall, surrounds the port to the edge of the Mediterranean. Yet the harraga boys have domesticated it in their own way. They use it for different purposes. The wall is their register. They write their names on it and tag it, in a gesture of complaint. The word "*ghurba*" is inscribed on it. *Ghurba* means exile, but it also means "out of place," "stranger," "foreigner." The boys are all of these. It is clear that they feel in exile in a city that is not theirs. They also climb the wall, either using a thin but solid cord, crafted intelligently to give them support, or using the bars of old windows set in the sides of seafood processing plants that are contiguous with the main wall. Once inside the port, they can catch hold of a truck or sneak inside the car or minivan of an absent-minded or sympathetic driver. The top of the same wall is large enough to serve as a safe bed at night for their small bodies. The wall, designed to keep them away, ironically protects them from the police and all the *haggara* (bullies) of Tangier. The boys do not fear the wall; they take refuge in it. By contrast, the police, out of fear, have stayed away from it as much as possible ever since 2005, when one of their number tragically fell to his death while chasing some harraga boys. Maybe, at least in part, because the harraga defeated the might of the wall, local authorities no longer rely on it to keep them away.

In May 2008, early on in my fieldwork, I was just realizing how tightly closed the port was to the harraga, and police presence within it was omnipresent. I joined several harraga in a discussion on the bench of the Corniche: "How do you cross?" I asked.

A six-year-old explained, "We spot the trucks at the red light; we know they are heading to Spain, usually the driver is Spanish. At the red light, the truck stops and we slide beneath it. It gets in the port and then into the ferry. Once in the ferries we get up and wait till we get to Algeciras, then we slide again, and we make it to the city. But with scanners, it became more difficult."

"What do you mean?"

"The trucks pass through scanners; they can detect us. So now before we get to the scanner, we get off, then slide again once the truck passes the scanners. Or, when we can, we get on top of the truck that carries fish. Then it becomes easier. The scanner cannot detect us if we mix with the boxes of fish."

Mohamed, a thirteen-year-old boy from Marrakesh, has burnt six times. "I get caught in Spain. The scanners there are more sophisticated [*mkhayrîn*]."

"What about here?" I asked.

"We get off when we near the scanner and then catch the truck when it passes." That is when one used to risk running into Saddam, the ferocious police dog known to and feared by all the kids. It is impossible to pass the scanners in Algeciras.

"But some do pass?" I reminded him.

"Yes. It is easier to pass in a fish truck or if you are on the truck beneath curtains, not if you are under the truck."

I asked, "How do the truck drivers treat you?"

"Some of them help us by either ignoring us or even showing us where to hide. Others report us to the police. And others do not know we are beneath the truck. They can't see us."

I spoke with a boy who made it by chance and was returned by mistake. He made it all the way to Madrid. He then wanted to go to Barcelona, but inadvertently, he got into the wrong bus, returning to Algeciras. In Algeciras, he was caught and sent back to Tangier.

"Where did you sleep there?" I wondered out aloud.

"The best sleeping places are the garbage cans," he said. "There is an ongoing hunt for the harraga in Algeciras. The Spanish police are merciless. They insult us and call us *morros*. It is a racist term [*kalma racista*]. They also beat us up when they catch us."

Several of these kids have a European connection—a brother in an unknown location in Madrid, a cousin in Brussels, an uncle in Amsterdam.

"Do you know where your brother is in Madrid?" I asked one of them.

"No, but I will find him when I get there."

The children sleep unsafely in the streets, at the entrance of residences, on the sand of the beach, on the benches of the big plaza, on the massive gray wall, or on a construction dumpster next to it. During the day, they hang out, but they are always alert, their eyes wide open in search of a truck, always ready to burn. The port for them is at once a refuge, a temporary dwelling, and a liminal space from where they can change their destiny.

Space Reconfigured: From Marsa to Tanger-Med

Between May 2008, when I first engaged in this project, and December 2010, when I returned for a yearlong stay, much had changed in the city but not in the conditions of the harraga. Many of the dialogues recorded above took place during the summers of 2008 and 2009. I returned in May 2010 for the

entirety of the summer, and again in December 2010 for the entirety of the
year. Each time, I conducted more interviews and hung out with more
harraga—children and young adults alike. By early August 2010, I felt I knew
every single one of them. Upon my return to Tangier on December 24, 2010,
I noticed an important change in the port area. It was open, and the harraga
youth and children were allowed to enter, leave, and stay as they pleased.
The port had ceased to be a commercial port, and all the trucks now left
from a new port built near a town called Ksar es Seghir, 43 kilometers northeast of Tangier. Ultra-modern, with highly sophisticated surveillance tech-
nology, the new port was also designed to reduce the chances of "illegal"
crossings. The old port in downtown Tangier was devoted exclusively to
transporting travelers to the town of Tarifa, Spain.

The old restaurants near the port were all gone by 2013. The government
intended to renovate the city, clean it, and make significant new developments
as part of the grandiose project Mohammed VI had envisioned for the city. By
demolishing those restaurants, nightclubs, and bars, the space of Tangier was
fully open to the horizon of Europe. Making the space of Tangier one with
Spain meant that there was no need for these names. You can see Spain, very
near, from almost every corner of Tangier and most clearly from its Corniche.

The Western signifiers were not all eliminated. The ones downtown, on
the Boulevard, are still there. Café Berlin, Café Central, Café Paris, Café
Davinci, as well as hotels such as Hotel Continental and El Minzah Hotel, are
part and parcel of the core of the city. They remain almost unchanged. Their
presence evokes an important part of the colonial memory of the city. However, since 2008, a number of new places have been built on the other side of
Cape Malabata. In this part of the city, one can now see a series of new Italian cafés and restaurants as well as a McDonald's and a Taco Bell. Architecturally, these restaurants are integrated into Moroccan space, designed to fit
the local urban landscape. In and of themselves, these restaurants are a dem-
onstration of how the local and the global are intertwined to signify the idea
that global modernity is not exclusive, not an import, less so an imposition,
but a willing adaptation, an opening to others while remaining oneself—a
richer self, modern and traditional all at once.

Every Moroccan king of the Alaouite dynasty[34] has made his mark on a
particular city to define his rule. Each of them is known to have a city—the
king's preferred city. Hasan II had a clear preference for Marrakesh, where
he spent his vacations and played golf. His father, King Mohammed V, seemed
to have a privileged relationship with Fes, his birthplace, the home of the

Istiqlal party, the political backbone of his throne. It was as if he wanted to reassure the bourgeoisie of Fes that even though the capital had moved to Rabat, the heart of the king remained in Fes and that the king himself was a Fassi (by birth) residing in Rabat. Hence his Fassi attire—a refined gray or white *djellaba*, white *babouche*, and not a Fes but a Nehru type of cap, slightly bigger though—beneath which one could clearly see the Western shirt and tie. King Mohammed VI, on the other hand, came to power as a figure of change and hope. A young king, thirty-six years old, he chose Tangier to make his mark. With highly aggressive neoliberal policies, he transformed Tangier from a provincial, relatively poor, and even neglected city into a truly global city[35] within the first ten years of his rule, from 1999 to 2009.

If Tangier expressed its modernity through Western names before Mohammed VI's ascension to power, with him, global modernity is signified by an important revolution in space. This revolution seemed daunting during the rule of Hassan II (1961–99), who first considered it. Indeed, when he submitted an application for Morocco to join the EU on July 20, 1987, the revolution was envisioned as the building of a bridge between Algeciras and Tangier, thus physically linking Africa and Europe. The project was soon abandoned by Hassan II himself because of its exorbitant price. With Mohammed VI, the urban revolution was easy and pragmatic. By demolishing the restaurants, discothèques, and bars at the Corniche, he removed a curtain between the city and Europe. That was all that was needed. And it was a highly intelligent urban maneuver. The city reinvented itself as more modern, more attached to Europe, than ever before. Tangier now shares the same space as Europe. Wherever you go, from almost whatever direction, you can see Europe—the port of Tarifa and the city of Algeciras, even Gibraltar itself.

While the port is still under construction, the harraga children can now access it rather freely and even sleep there at night. By December 26, 2010, I had come back to the port again. Those I knew during the summers of 2008 and 2009 were no longer there. I could not get any information about them; I concluded that some of them managed to cross and others left and maybe even returned home. This did not mean they would not come back in a few months or years. Most of those I knew in 2010–11, 2013, and 2016 had come back more than once, up to fourteen times in some cases.

I interviewed, individually and in groups, formally and informally, many harraga during this time. Despite the fact that the port is now open, crossing is difficult but by no means impossible. While Saddam, the vicious dog, is dead (poisoned by the harraga, as I was told over and again whenever I asked), the barrage of police standing between the harraga and the ferry is still there. Building Tanger-Med in Ksar es Seghir only gives the harraga another route to Europe. First, there are many commercial trucks in line for the ferry, and sliding under them is easier than reaching the ferry in the port of the city. Second, going by way of Tanger-Med means that the ferry will land in the port of Algeciras, not Tarifa, from which it is easier to access the nearest city. Yet, the challenge of Tanger-Med is the distance. It is far and most of the kids cannot afford transportation, so they walk.

"How long does it take you to get there?"

"Thirty-five minutes if we manage to get a ride, otherwise a day walking."

"Do you manage to get a ride?"

"No, we walk."

I met this boy, named Hasan, in front of a coffee shop's bakery just an hour or so before the *futûr* (the evening meal of Ramadan). He was begging and joking about it. Each time someone gave him money, he thanked them profusely. He teased and laughed at those who ignored him. As I was sitting on the terrace, he caught me observing him. He smiled and I asked, "What do you do here?"

"Trying to get futûr."

"No, I mean what do you do in Tangier? You don't seem to be from here," I said.

"No, we are not," he said, speaking for himself and his friend standing not far from him. "We are trying to cross to Europe."

"I have never seen you around," I said, confident that I knew everybody there.

"No, we do not try from here, we try from Ksar es Seghir. We only come here to make some money and go back," he said.

"It is deserted there. Where do you stay?" I asked.

"We rent a room in town with friends."

He laughed and said, "You see, people see us here begging and they say, oh, poor things! But they do not know that we are doing this just for fun. We are from good families [*wlâd al-khîr*]. This is just for fun [*tqalqîl*]."

"What does your family do?" I asked.

"We have plenty of land and we grow crops. We do this [lahrig] just for fun."

"For fun?"

"Yes, it is like a game, an adventure, if we go, we go; if we don't go, we try again," he said, laughingly. He then ignored me to ask a man who was just leaving the bakery, "Sir [*shrîf*], give us something for futûr! May Allah bless your parents!"

The man did not pay attention to him. The boy moved closer to the door of the bakery, waiting for the next customer to leave.

For the harrag attempting the journey via Tanger-Med, Tangier is still vital. It is in the city that he can make a living, meaning he can beg and make a bit of money before he goes back to Ksar es Seghir. Tanger-Med is open and deserted. At the gate, there are police officers who constitute the customs service. I told them I wanted to see the area. When I entered, I could see a flat distance that would take fifteen minutes or so to traverse between the port's entrance and the coast where the ferries were stationed. There was nothing to look at, really. You can see highly sophisticated cameras everywhere, watching you and anything that enters or leaves. I had taken several pictures when all of a sudden, the police stopped me and asked to see my camera and my passport. They saw the photos and asked me why I had taken them. I said for research. A policeman asked me, "What kind of research?"

I replied that I worked on the city of Tangier and on people who want to leave it.

"What is it for?" the policeman said.

"For academic research," I answered.

Then the policeman asked me to accompany him. I felt as if I were under arrest and followed him obediently. Meanwhile, my eighteen-year-old cousin, a native of Tangier, who was accompanying me, disappeared all of a sudden. I started to worry more about him than about myself. The area was open and flat and I was wondering where he could be. I followed the policeman, who entered a police station at the gate of the entrance to the port. My cousin suddenly showed up from nowhere, I thought, and said to the policeman, "Sir [shrîf], he is my cousin, he works on the harraga," believing that this would convince the policeman to let me go. On the contrary. Becoming more suspicious, the policeman told me, "You said you work on the city. But you work on the harraga? What is all of this about?"

"Yes, I work on Tangier, and I am interested in the lives of the harraga in Tangier."

The policeman replied or rather asked, "But you did not say harraga?"

I responded, "No, I did not. It is the same. Just wanted to spare you the details."

The policeman requested that I let him see the pictures I had taken. Before he opened the camera, a young policeman showed up and said, "Hamid, let him go, he is one of mine [*râh min 'andnâ*]."

The young policeman shook my cousin's hand and started talking to him, treating the matter as resolved. The other policeman gave me my passport and my camera and asked, "Is the economic crisis still bad in America?"

I said, "Yes, it is indeed."

This little encounter with the police made me wonder what happens to young harraga when they are caught. The entirety of Tanger-Med seemed under camera and police surveillance. It was still a mystery for me that a harrag could cross from there. The only explanation I could find was that they had come under commercial trucks all the way from Tangier. But that did not seem plausible: how can a harrag know that this or that truck is going to Tanger-Med and not to Casablanca, for instance? The mystery was solved when I met Abdallah a week or so after the incident with the police officer. He was begging in front of Nedjma Bakery down the Boulevard. I later found out he was seventeen years old. He looked much younger. He exhibited much kindness and delicateness. He was clearly poor, with an old blue sweater, blue jeans with holes (that did not look like the fashionable kind), and plastic sandals that showed sun-darkened feet. I started asking him my usual questions about his motives to cross and got the same usual answers, "*Makâyan wâlû bnâ*" (there is nothing to do here). I asked him about his family and he said they did not know he was a harrag; they thought he was in Tangier looking for a job. He was the oldest of three kids. His father had died years before. Abdallah had already crossed three times from Ksar es Seghir, had been caught by the Spanish police in Algeciras, and brought back.

"I don't get caught here," he said, "I got caught in Algeciras. There are three customs agents there, the third one is the hardest; they search everything. That is where I got caught. There is a Spanish officer with his daughter and they do the *skying*."

I did not understand what "skying" is, and asked him.

"I will explain to you," he said. "The man and his daughter tie themselves from the waist to a cord that is attached to the ceiling. They then come all the way beneath every car and every truck. They can see everything. That is what skying is and that is how they caught me."

"But how did you get into the ferry from Tanger-Med?" I asked.

"There is a sewage tunnel twenty minutes from the port. We get into it, and we crawl. It takes you next to the ferry; no one sees us. But lately, they found the tunnel and closed it. I cannot find my way," he said.

A few weeks after my conversation with Abdallah, the kids told me that they found another tunnel they used to cross: "It has much dirtier water than the old one, it is more difficult, but we use it."

Tangier's opportunities for livelihood consist mainly of small donations from people, but also from charity houses and even the Saint Andrew's church uptown that provides lunch once every Wednesday. Abdesslam is one of the kids who has his eye on Tanger-Med. He does not even bother to go to the port in Tangier, which he finds more crowded with much tighter security. He is sixteen years old, but he left home when he was twelve. He went to Kenitra, where he worked in a bakery. He left to go to Rabat to work in another bakery. He then went to Agadir, where he worked in a marble factory and decided that burning would provide a better future.

"Why do you want to cross?"

"Find my way [*ndabbar 'lâ râsî*]."

"What do you mean by that?"

"I want to find work and make a living for myself. God said, *sabbab yâ 'abdi wa anâ n'âwnak*," he said, repeating a known Moroccan proverb (Try, my servant, and I will help you).

"Does your family know you are here?"

"No. They don't."

He told me he goes back from time to time whenever he feels burned out. His family does not know he is here to burn.

"What do you tell your family when you go back?"

"I tell them I work."

"Does your mother believe you? What does she say when you say that?"

"My mother does not speak."

"What did you say?"

"My mother is mute; she does not speak."

"Can she hear?"

"No, she is mute and deaf."

"How do you communicate with her?"

"We use hand gestures."

"What does she do when you come back after a long absence?"

"She does not like it."

"And your father?"

"He scolds me."

He tried to leave through Ceuta, but the makhzen guards blocked the entrance. He then went to Tanger-Med. He even managed to cross from Tanger-Med.

"How did you manage?" I asked.

"I entered a dank sewage tunnel. It is long and dirty. You have to crawl on your belly. It takes twenty minutes to get there. Once there, you are close to the ferry; it becomes easy. But I cannot swim to the ferry. I wait till a truck comes, I slide, and it takes me to the ferry. I stayed on the ferry till I saw the light and could feel the ferry was slowing down to stop. Then, I got out, the crew saw me, arrested me. When we got there, they handed me to the police, who put me on the next ferry back to Tangier. They then took me to the police station before they released me."

He asked me, "Uncle, do you work with the government?"

"No, I told you I do research."

"Are you a journalist?"

"No, I am a teacher. Why?"

"Can you help me?"

"Yes, I can. Listen to me, there is a house, an association called Darna. It is a place where children live and learn a craft [san'a]. You can go there, you will be able to eat and sleep, they will take care of you. I can take you there if you want me to."

"No. I do not want to go there. I don't like to stay in the same place. I want to go to Europe. Can you help me cross?"

"No, I cannot. How can I?"

At that moment, a middle-aged man with a girl that looked like his daughter walked by, holding a half-empty bottle of Coca-Cola in his hand; the boy looked at it and, pointing to the bottle, asked him, "Uncle, may I have a drink?"

The man looked at him with disdain and rudely said, "No."

While I was thinking about helping him get food, several West Africans passed by in front of us. They looked clean and I was certain they were professionals. Abdesslam looked at them and turned to me and said, "Look at these 'waza [plural of 'azzi]! Those are the people that ruined it for us. I see them in Melilla, there are hundreds of them, they erupt by a group of eighteen or so into the gate, they are not scared of the police or anything. They just erupt. Because of them, crossing [lahrig] has become difficult for us; they fucked it up for us [qawduha 'lînâ]."

The field of migration, too, is fraught with competition and racial tensions, I thought.

Nevertheless, the children at the port survive their harsh conditions because the hope of youth makes life joyful for them. They live their lives under conditions they did not choose but are determined to change. They laugh, they tell jokes; they get into disputes and argue and shout at each other, only to turn the argument into a joke again. But I rarely saw them fight. The friendship they quickly form with one another seems to be their greatest asset. It protects them, as much as it can, against *hogra*, against hunger, and gives them strength. Yet, despite their age, some of them had undergone significant trauma. Ahmed was a boy I met, only twelve years old. His friends told me he spent five years in a juvenile prison. When I asked him, he confirmed the information.

"Why did you go to jail?"

"I hit someone."

"Just hit him?"

"No, I hit him with a knife."

"What did you do that for?"

"A dispute."

"What kind of dispute?" I asked.

He did not want to tell me. His friends also did not know. It was his secret.

Symbolic Kinship

If the harrag is not determined by school or by the family, what then determines him? Without parents and without school, how does the harrag child live his life? In the eyes of society, he is a street child, a *wald zenqa*, *haddâwî*, even *salgût*. But the harrag is the first one to reject these slurs. He dissociates himself clearly from street children and would even use the slur against another harrag, "You are not a harrag. When was the last time you burned? You just live in the street." The label *shamkâr* is also used. "You are not a harrag, you are just a shamkâr!" I used to hear that when the kids got into arguments that rarely lasted long.

The harrag inhabits a space, the port, for a purpose: to cross. He is endowed with qualities: he is bold (*nzaq*), intelligent (*mtawwar*), cunning (*masmâr*), a risk taker (*maskhût*), fearless (*sga'*). The enterprise of lahrig is carefully planned within a network of harraga friends. The harrag is rarely a loner, whereas a street child is often described as *mjalwaq* (messed up and lost). The harraga hang out in groups, to plan their routes, to protect themselves against gangs (haggara) and sexual predators. They also sleep in small groups either close to the mosque of the port or, when the weather is warm, in the open, on the beach close to the Boulevard, where night's movements almost never stop.

Among them, the place is like a home, or rather it is a home; they maintain it, they nap in it, they come back at night to sleep in it, they furnish it with cardboard and old blankets. They may even adopt pets, usually cats, to make the little place more like home, with the warmth, the protection, and the comfort that a home is supposed to provide. In other words, the child harrag is never alone and is always part and parcel of a small group of younger and older harraga whose dynamics change rather quickly. This refutes the common idea that these children are antisocial with no values[36] except those of violence and aggression. The police at the port warned me several times not to go there because they "will rob you and hurt you." In fact, I witnessed genuine friendship and feelings of protection between them, which also were extended to me, if only because of the time I spent with them.

In any case, the daily lives of the harraga confirm the idea that children in the streets "organize into groups . . . group solidarity extends to the sharing of food and other goods and provision of protection and support in crises."[37] When one of the children somehow finds an opportunity and crosses, his absence is immediately felt among his friends—often with sorrow. The feeling of sadness predominates because, after all, it is in the moment of separation that attachment knows its real depth.[38] It is also at this moment of separation that the harraga ponder the danger that may be out there, the least of which is *ghorba* (exile)—for them, another exile since, according to their narratives and their wall graffiti, they are already in exile in what may be the most exclusive of all Moroccan cities.[39]

"You know Mounir?" I was asked by a small group of children.

"Which one?"

"The one who always hang out with us; he is from Khenifra."

"Yes, I do."

"*Tgharrab*," they said.

I was at first surprised by the use of this verb to convey an act of migration, with connotations of estrangement, exile, and melancholia. I always believed that for children who risk everything to cross, the success of crossing should be celebrated as a victory over hardship. But it is in that moment of crossing, of leaving, of separation, that the children feel the burn of burning. It is not love of country but of one's own that causes the feelings of rupture between a life that is familiar and one that is not.

The children did not cheer his departure but rather were sad. But soon, his story became one of those hundred stories that prove, once again, that leaving is possible. The group overcomes the feeling of sadness and quickly moves on. It is an open group. A newcomer integrates, or a child is burned out and leaves to go back home. The small group of harraga is like a family; the loss of a member does not change the feeling that this is a family unit. The child can switch to another group easily and rather quickly, especially since these small groups constitute cliques that are constantly in touch with one another.

A subset of the group—of, say, two or three members—works as a team. They beg for money and food together; they share with each other. And like siblings, they also occasionally fight with each other, only to reconcile again except when the fight is too severe; then the child may change to another group to which he is already connected. These dynamics of survival are also noticed among street children in other countries, such as Egypt, Kenya, India, and Brazil.[40] But because the harrag is not a street child, his connection with his peers and with older harraga is different. The small group is also closely tied to groups of adults, usually harraga in their twenties and thirties. In many significant ways, while children of a certain age, say, six to fourteen, tend to constitute groups for companionship and support, these groups are inseparable from both groups of other children and groups of adults. Thus, in the absence of parents, the children depend, if only for protection, on the older harraga. They thus display what is usually considered the "specificity of the child," that is, dependency on the adult.[41] But again, this is relative. The dependency of the harrag child manifests itself most in his dependence on his peers. At first sight, the separation between child and adult seems clear. But this clarity was the product of my own perception, having already accepted the modern idea, now totally self-evident, that a childhood exists.

Narratives of Sexual Violence

How can one speak about violence when these children are born in a structure of violence within poor and/or broken families, with no right to education, protection, and "the rights inherent to life," as the United Nations

Convention on the Rights of the Child (UNCRC) indicates—a convention also signed by Morocco? However, I would like to remark here on an extreme form of violence that these children are subject to or, rather, on narratives of violence that circulate among them and that are part of the cultural condition they face daily.

In a city with the terrible reputation of being a city of sexual tourism, the child harrag finds himself at the mouth of the wolf. The city attracts sexual predicators from everywhere.[42] Child abuse is associated with sexual abuse, which is in turn associated with the idea of a child.[43] Harraga are children with a narrative, meaning that they have a clearly articulated reason why they have become what they are. Language is an important medium of the harraga. It is as if these children, by virtue of their social condition, articulate a narrative indicating that they are indeed in the world of adults. Hence the fact that, at the port, the two worlds are one. Before conceptualizing the narratives of both children and adult harraga in the next chapter, I would like to allow them to speak or rather, and to be more precise, I would like to serve as their translator. By this, I do not mean only translating their stories into English but also translating their logic into one that can be understood by a public.[44]

Despite the system of protection that the children create against everyday violence in the city, they are not immune to it; they can only minimize its effects—to a point. Here, I will not be tackling the issue of hogra, which is a cultural violence generated by the state and practiced through its agents and institutions, but will rather examine an extreme form of violence that the children are subject to, namely, the sexual abuse that is part of their everyday life, especially in a city known for its sexual tourism—international and national.

The term *tgharrab*, which a harrag may use when one of his companions burns, conveys, once again, both the feeling of sadness at the separation and, perhaps more, the feeling of exile and estrangement. Even though the children hope to find a better life on the other side, they are all too aware that life there is not a bed of roses—far from it. Stories of exploitation, of abuse, including sexual abuse, circulate among children and adult harraga.

Hadi is sixteen years old. Like many of the kids, he has crossed several times, and he still hopes to cross again. He told me about a young harrag who crossed with him three years back. One time, while walking by himself, he ran into a Serguini, that is, a man from the province El Kelâa des Sraghna. The man offered him food and even cigarettes. But the kid did not smoke, so he declined. The Serguini then asked him to take a walk with him on the beach. They walked until they got to an isolated area and the man tied him and raped him. He came back to his group of harraga friends totally destroyed. They knew something awful had happened to him, but he refused to speak, out of shame. Eventually, the kid told his friends what had happened. They were horrified and immediately called the police. The police arrested the man and took the harrag victim to "the best center," I was told, where he could get excellent care and training. The man was sentenced to sixteen years in jail.

Such stories of sexual abuse are also firsthand knowledge among the harraga. While chatting one night during the month of Ramadan at the port, next to the mosque, not far from several stray cats, Tayeb, thirty-four years old, told me a story of a sixteen-year-old boy by the name of Tarek. The children present seemed to know the story also. Tarek met a doorman one day. The doorman asked him whether he needed anything. Being in need of everything, Tarek went with him to his apartment on the first floor of a building where he worked. There, the doorman gave Tarek food, clothes, and a shower. At night, the doorman told Tarek that he could sleep in the apartment instead of going to the cold and dirty port. At night, however, the doorman came to Tarek in his bed, fondled him, and performed oral sex on him. In the morning, he gave him 20 dirhams. The boy came to the port and bought breakfast for his friends.

Tarek went back to the doorman the following day. The doorman showered him and shaved him and started performing oral sex on Tarek. The group of children asked Tarek where he disappeared every night and why he showed up with money in the morning. Tarek told them. The children were horrified. "What do you do, wretched one, do you know what happens when a male is on a male? Do you know that makes the throne of God shake!? Do you know a male on male stirs God's wrath [dkar 'lâ dkar rabbî yakfar]?" After hearing this, Tarek was terrified. For three days he did not go to the doorman's apartment. Then the doorman came looking for him at the port. The children chased him. Exposed, the doorman never tried again.

Tayeb was one of the oldest harrag in the port and known to all the children, who trusted him. And he genuinely cared about them. Despite his past as a drug dealer in Spain, he acted as the moral conscience of these kids. He represented the world of adults for them and thus provided them with repères solides,[45] that is, a reference in moral conduct. He would advise a kid not to hang out with street children who indulge in sniffing glue. He even acted as a protector against their abuse, including any threat of sexual abuse. In short, he kept his eyes on these children. He told me that one day an old man invited a child to eat in a restaurant. Tayeb was watching and noticed that the old man stood behind the child and started fondling him. Three other kids intervened, moved their friend aside, and stared at the old man with hostility to communicate to him that he must cease and desist. Tayeb was present then, and he watched the situation and how the other kids were dealing with it. Tayeb looked at me and, with his usual gentle smile, said, "You would not believe it, *ustâdh. Wallâh!* This is an old man, with a white beard [a sign of piety in Moroccan society]; we were too embarrassed to even talk to him [*hshamnâ nhadrû mʿâh*]."

The topic of sex and narratives of sexual abuse are very rare among the harraga. This is mainly because of the strong sense of shame associated with the topic, which most often remains a matter of secrecy. Yet, given the culture of sexual tourism in the city, sexual abuse must be more common among the harraga than I was led to believe, precisely because of their vulnerability as children in the street. (Though I would never call them "street children," in Morocco, no distinction is made.) Everywhere, the street kid is perceived by society as "the embodiment of the untamed, feral child."[46]

Stories of abuse are as common as stories of success. But the children tell those stories that do not expose them to shame more freely. I met Hamid, who stood out among the group of five harraga I was speaking to one evening at the port, on the fishermen's nets. He was wearing a nice black shirt and fashionable jeans with Adidas sneakers. He looked more confident and did not display any of the signs of poverty I often noted among the harraga.

"Are you a harrag, too, or you are just hanging out here like me?" I asked.

He smiled, and he said he was one of them.

"Have you just arrived? I have never seen you."

"I have just come back."

"From where?"

"From there, and from Beni Mellal."

"There? Spain?"

"Not only Spain. I have been in five countries: Spain, France, Belgium, and Italy."

He did not mention the fifth one, but I went on asking him, "How did you get there?"

"*Hragt* [burned]."

He was sixteen years old when he crossed. His family paid a smuggler to help him. He was the only harrag I met whose family was aware of and involved in the burning experience. The family hired a smuggler and paid him 10,000 dirhams (about $1,200 at the time). The smuggler helped Hamid cross and delivered him to a man waiting for him on the other side. The man took Hamid to his apartment, treated him nicely, provided him with food and shelter, then called the parents and asked them for money to free him. Hamid was a hostage, he immediately understood. The man asked for 20,000 dirhams ($2,400) as ransom. The parents could afford only 5,000 dirhams. Eventually, knowing that he could not get more, the man accepted the money and let Hamid leave.

"That was a *sequestro*," Tayeb said. "Everybody knows about them. They keep children hostage and call their parents for a ransom, usually 30,000 or 50,000 dirhams [$3,600 or $6,000]."

These narratives of abuse are part of the culture of lahrig. This is to say that the experience of migration is made not only of those who crossed, made it, and came back wealthy and prosperous. It is made also of stories of those who are raped, those who are beaten by the police and the haggara, those who are arrested and deported, those who spends nights sleeping in garbage cans in Spain to hide from the police, and those who get abducted by kidnappers. Stories of death are, surprisingly, the rarest. The children tended to ignore them when I brought up the topic. For death, in their view, pertains to destiny, against which one can do nothing. Lahrig, by contrast, pertains to life, to the chances that one can take to change the direction of destiny, not its final destination.

Conclusion

The new figure of the harrag caused an emotional sensation among the Moroccan public in the 1990s. Children, too, were being infected by "the virus of departing"—in the words of Tayeb Saleh, "*adwat al-rahīl*."[47] Even more surprising was the harrag's willingness—no, his determination—to confront a deadly danger, the waves of the ocean, to cross to Europe. The lives of these harraga children, as I ethnographically describe in this chapter, are complex. In the port (or, before 2010, in its environs), they create a home, build networks of friends, and substitute the old, often broken family with a symbolic family made of their peers with whom they are affectively attached.

Their social world is intricate and includes those harraga adults with whom they share their everyday experiences and who are bound to them. The children are thus provided protection against the haggara and also against sexual predators. They are also initiated into the world of adults, which they enter gradually, most often while they are still at the port. Several of those I interviewed and even hung out with had started early, as early as six years old, and were still at the port by their late twenties. Most of these had managed to cross, often several times, but had been returned immediately or a few months or years later. Upon their return, they further contribute to the culture of burning—and by this, I mean an ensemble of stories that the harraga tell about themselves.[48] Many are real, many are exaggerated, and maybe a few are fictitious. All focus on the activity of lahrig and what it entails: how to cross, where to cross, where to wait, what to do while waiting, what to expect, what to find, what to do when you cross, what to do when you are caught, who crossed, who made it, and so on. These are often told narratively, meaning through stories of so-and-so and so-and-so and so-and-so. In many ways, the harraga have developed a narrative tradition similar to the one developed by European mariners,[49] turned into European myths in some cases and into classical works of fiction in others. Writing their experiences, giving them voice, seems to me important. Not only because writing the history of the marginalized is in itself important because it widens the scope of our view of a society but also, for the case at hand, because examining the lives of children and youth will not only shed light on the dynamics of the makhzen and Moroccan politics but also help us understand global geographies of politics and production.[50]

Many times, at the end of the night, past 4 a.m., I leave the port area amid stray cats and dogs in the dark. I walk from the exit of the port through the Boulevard Mohammed VI. On my right, a series of cheap restaurants specialize in fish; across from them a middle-aged man walks back and forth, engaging in an intense conversation with himself on various topics. His speech is as articulate as it is incomprehensible. He is there every night, unconcerned by the passersby as much as they are unconcerned by him. On my first right, I take the street Salah Al-Dine al Ayoubi, which becomes a hill, and as I continue, it gets steeper. I turn again, left, on Boulevard Anwal. It is even steeper and thus more difficult to walk. By the time I finish off the hill, I am in front of stairs—and I still feel like climbing. The street now is entirely dark. I take the stairs one by one, cautiously. I leave the port far behind me. I keep climbing the stairs and decide not to stop. By the time I reach the top, I have climbed almost a hundred stairs—104, to be exact. Here, the streets are lit, almost bright. And ahead of me, there are even more lights. It is the Boulevard Mohammed V. I stand there, looking ahead, and decide, then, to look down. I do. I stop and turn. I see the entire port area and squint to focus on the area where I had spent the evening. It looks awfully dark and wretched. It is the image of hell. It is dark where the children are sleeping. I feel relieved the place is far from me. I look again, as if for the last time, and walk toward a different life, a bright life, of privilege. To fight my sense of guilt, I say, "I will come back tomorrow!"

Chapter 3

Burning Matters

There were between four and five hundred *harraga* near the port when I first started this research in 2008. This number significantly increased by 2011, when the city of Tangier opened the port to all, including to the harraga, and inaugurated Tanger-Med, a commercial port 30 kilometers east of Tangier.[1] The port of Tangier became even more attractive to the harraga as they could now enter and leave as they pleased, as well as reach the ferry in a matter of minutes. Dispersed across the city during the day, they gathered at the port in the evening. In the late morning, they could still be seen sleeping at the foot of the port's walls and on the fishermen's nets, using flattened cardboard boxes as mattresses, and with no covers. During the rest of the day, they were usually begging in front of bakeries or just hanging out in the city streets. I used to see the small ones, between six and ten years old, playing with the kids in the neighborhood of the medina, only a mile or so from the port.

My research assistant, Chakib, laughed when I asked him whether despair gets into the hearts of these kids who wait here for years in front of a totally sealed Europe. He said, "Listen, when someone has his eyes fixed on the ferry twenty-four hours a day, seven days a week, he will cross no matter what. If not sooner, surely later."

I did not agree with him, but said nothing. Not that I was right and he was wrong. It is more complicated, as social phenomena always are. Yet, I believe that crossing has as much to do with luck as it does with intelligence and perseverance. Some of these young people cross; others get stuck in Tangier for years and eventually give up. The truth is that many of those who persist eventually cross. Dozens of those I met have crossed, gotten arrested, and been sent back; they persisted and crossed again—some up to fourteen times. Often, I came back to the port and I heard that so-and-so had crossed: however, one is never sure if he has started a new life out there, died at sea, or is just sitting there, waiting to be deported in a day or a month or even a year or two.

One hears only success stories; even aborted attempts have some element of success. Regardless of the outcome, these attempts indicate that crossing is possible and doable. This fosters the culture of hope that feeds the resilience and determination of the harrag. If he crosses once and is turned back, he can always cross again. Even when he is returned yet again, the road has been paved for him. Now, he knows it well. Failure is experience and experience is the precondition of success.

The success stories of those who have crossed are often embellished and exaggerated, and some may even be invented. Yet, they circulate among the children and youth. In their spare time, harraga tell these stories to one another. The stories, some of which I will narrate, feature the values of persistence, hope, courage, belief in good luck, and, above all, resilience. It is these values that make the harraga (at least many of them) stay in the port and not leave. They either wait for the chance, or try to find this chance by attempting to cross almost every day—or at least as many times as possible. The more one tries, the more one increases one's chances of success. Their eyes are indeed on the port, as Chakib said, and they know the details of its daily patterns. They know the schedule of the ferries and the ones that are easy to get onto. I was told countless times, "The ferry at 4 a.m. every morning is the good one; there are less police around, and everybody is sleepy or asleep."

The harraga get on the ferry at dawn, either directly, through the main gate, or stealthily, by swimming a hundred meters from its side. The latter strategy is secure but represents greater danger since the *harrag* lodges a board into the ferry's side, at one of its portholes, and then stands on it during the entire trip. If the board breaks or he slips, it is fatal.

In the previous chapter, I recounted mostly the voices of the children I met at the port during the summers of 2008 and 2009. By the time I returned to the port in December 2010, to stay an entire year, I could not find any of the faces I had known. They were replaced by new ones—new children and new youth, most of them teenagers. Some children turn into adults at the port, rather quickly. But whether child, teenager, or young adult, they all hang out together, plan together, live together. They rely on each other, the way a child relies on his older brother. Their social world is the same, with the younger ones learning from the older ones. Sometimes the roles are reversed. A child may have more life experience, especially with *lahrig*, than an older newcomer. Thus, newcomers learn from the children.

As I discussed in Chapter 2, the separation of child and adult is itself cultural.[2] It depends on cultural definition: when does one become an adult and cease to be a child? In Morocco, the distinction is fluid, and a youth can be called the same names as a child (*drâri, awalâd, brâhach*).[3] At the port, many pass from age six to age eighteen or from age sixteen to age twenty-four without having had a break in their life experience that might distinguish "childhood" from "adulthood."

In this chapter, I would like to revisit another question I raised earlier, but this time in conceptual rather than in dialogical terms: Why do young people and children want to migrate? Why are they willing to take the highest risk? How do they challenge the constraints to their mobility set within and beyond the city? Undocumented migration is often approached from the vantage point of the law; here, I would rather ask not how the harrag violates the law, but how the state violates its own laws by creating the social conditions of the harrag's death. And how do the harraga survive in the city, especially within the cultural structure of violence commonly called *hogra*?

The Logic of Burning

The media often make a sensation of the phenomenon of burning. Relatively recently, the phenomenon has drawn the attention of a few anthropologists who see it as representing a new form of migration, at least in the Mediterranean region.[4] So far, the phenomenon of lahrig has been explored from two main perspectives. In an early study, using insights from the work of Nancy Scheper-Hughes on the production of neglect in a Brazilian shantytown, Núria Empez Vidal argues that the phenomenon is a product of the institution of the family, more specifically parents who have neglected their children or recklessly encouraged them to cross and, in so doing, exposed them to danger.[5] Stefania Pandolfo looks at "burning" from the angle that most intrigues and even shocks the observer, namely, that of young adults playing with death, under the assumption that their attempt to change their lives is nothing less than an attempt at killing themselves—a suicide.[6] Instead, the first and basic question I would like to ask is, What has inspired these youth to engage in such actions? Why did the passion for lahrig emerge only in the mid-1990s, to intensify since then? And even if we assume that death is a possibility seriously considered in the mind of the young adult, I would like to ask, What makes one prefer the possibility of death over the certainty of living "safely" (in poverty or not) at home?

The most well-known phrase to describe their actions is lahrig, hence their name, harraga. However, the most common expression I heard is *nriskiw* (from the French verb *risquer*, "to risk"). The term "risk" is clearer than the term "lahrig." Risk means that one crosses and assumes all the risks associated with the act of crossing: the risks of being caught, of drowning, of being beaten if caught, the fear of the unknown and of not making it, and of failing. Whereas the term "burn" is metaphorical, as I explained in the previous chapter, the term "risk" is literal—the enterprise of crossing is a highly risky one for sure. When one crosses, friends describe the outcome as *tgharrab*, an expression that does not have euphoric implications despite the fact that it refers to a successful outcome. For *tgharrab* means "went out of place" or "went into exile," and it connotes the state of becoming a stranger, an outsider—all associated with discomfort and hardship. Yet, by seeking *ghorba* (exile, foreignness), the harraga still believe that it is better than here (*blâdnâ*, "our country").

The dialogues of the previous chapter were conducted in the summer, when the city becomes active and prosperous because of tourism—national and international. However, in the winter, the city becomes something else, especially for the harraga, who depend on the generosity of tourists and good weather to survive. In the winter, they are at risk even when on land. I was able to comprehend the depth of their misery more during the winter than during the warm months.

Upon my return in December 2010, the port was truly dismal, gray, with more signs of poverty and utter misery than I had noticed in the summers of 2008, 2009, and 2010. An ambience of despair was in the air; stray, thin, sickly cats and dogs everywhere; a nauseating smell of rotten fish and food; the soil I was walking on was damp, and it seemed there was dirt of all sorts coming from all corners. Cheap restaurants specializing in fried fish were still open and serving food to a few customers one late afternoon in winter. I crossed an entire line of them to get to the other side, where I could see the sea and the boats, many of them painted white and blue. The sight there was rather beautiful since by turning one's back on the restaurants, one could see only the vast sea. At the horizon, one could also see the Strait of Gibraltar. The port was nothing like it had been the previous summer. In the sum-

mer, the port area has an aura of festivity and is crowded with visitors from
Morocco and from abroad, especially at lunchtime and in the afternoons.

I got there and was finally convinced that the season was winter. Despite the sunshine that day, I felt a chill, though nothing could possibly compare with the blizzards I had left behind on the East Coast of the United
States. The port was almost deserted and that, too, was a sure sign of winter. For, during the summer, the port is one of the most crowded corners of
the city. It comes to life with the numerous fishing boats that come and go.
Fishermen gather around boxes of fish, and fish merchants and residents of
the city pour into the port in search of fresh, less expensive (but not cheap)
fish of all types. But today, the port was deserted. I decided to leave, then
noticed two teenagers staring at me, or rather looking at me with open curiosity. I saw them and walked in their direction, but not directly to them.
As soon as I got closer, one of them approached me hesitantly, and shyly
asked, "Uncle, would you give us something to buy breakfast?"

"Breakfast?" I asked with astonishment, "but it is not morning; it is past
5 p.m."

One of them responded, "By Allah, uncle, we have not had breakfast
yet."

I looked at him again and saw he was sincere and not just trying to get
money by appealing to my sense of compassion, as is often done by beggars
in the streets of the city.

"By Allah, uncle, we have not had breakfast yet," he repeated.

The two of them looked sickly thin, with skin diseases all over them—
their hands and their faces. They were not teenagers, as I initially thought.
Driss, the older one, was thirty years old. But he looked almost ten years
younger. He had very brown skin, rotten teeth, and eyes that told about an
ocean of pain and suffering. His companion, Mohamed, was twenty-three
years old. His skin was also damaged: his hands and his face seemed to have
some skin disease, probably eczema. His teeth were very yellow, with big
pieces of food (from days before, I thought) between them.

"What are you here for?" I asked.

"*Bâghyin nriskîw* [to risk]."

"Why?" I asked directly.

"*Ndabrû 'lâ râsna* [to save ourselves]."

"Why don't you manage here [*a'lâsh mâdabrûch 'lâ raskum hnâ*]?" I asked.

"This country gives us nothing."

"What do you mean?"

"There is no work, no opportunities here. It is fucked up [*maqawda hnâ*]," Driss said, becoming a bit shy as he pronounced the word "*maqawda.*" He still had a sad smile on his face.

"Where are you from?"

"Fes."

Both Mohamed and Driss had crossed before, I learned. Mohamed had crossed just two months before I met him. He and another friend of his swam to a cargo ship, were able to get onto it on time, and were then on the way to realizing their dream. But they were caught just as the ship arrived in Spain. They were so hungry that Mohamed got out of their hiding place to look for food. All he could find was a box of chocolates. He took it and went back to his hiding place. A member of the Spanish crew immediately noticed that the box of chocolates was missing. He alerted his coworkers and started a search that ended by finding Mohamed and his friend. They were sent back on the next ferry.

"Did they beat you?"

"No, they scolded us in Spanish, calling us *morros.* They put us on the ferry that was already waiting to go back to Tangier. When we got to Tangier, they handed us to the police, who took us to the police station in Plaza Toro [downtown]. They questioned us, kept us for a few days, and asked us to go back home and not try again."

This was the same story I heard over and again from those arrested in Spain. Driss crossed much earlier, in 2005, he told me, and again just two days before Ramadan in 2010. The first time, he was eighteen and could slide under a commercial truck. But he was found a few days later when the truck got to the frontiers of France. The second time, he was arrested by the police in Spain and sent back. As always, he spent three days in the police station in Tangier and had to appear in front of a judge, who released him.

"Fucked-up luck [*zhar mqawwad*]," Driss told me. "We get all the way there and we get sent back."

"Are you going to try again?"

"Yes, we have to save ourselves," he said, clearly also speaking for Mohamed.

Both Driss and his friend have "bad luck" at finding a better life. Most of the kids I spent time with at the port share the social condition of poverty. But the idea that it is only poverty that makes these young people want to risk and cross is not accurate. I also met young people whose background was relatively good by Moroccan standards. Some have "decent" jobs and still come at night to gauge the possibility of crossing. Sometimes, they even cross.

One Ramadan night of 2011 (during the month of August), I went to the port unusually late. It was 12 a.m. I did not see any kids except a blond boy who looked more like a *shamkar* (street kid) than a harrag. I continued my walk toward the mosque, where I saw a dark man sleeping: he looked more like a homeless person than a harrag. I turned back, thinking that most of the kids must have gone back home to spend *eid* (the celebration of the end of Ramadan) with their families when all of a sudden, I saw one sitting in the dark. I walked toward him, said hello, and asked him if he had seen the kids. He said, "They all went to Malabata for a music concert."

"And you, why are not you with them? What are you doing here by yourself?" I said, feeling sad for him and thinking that he had problems that prevented him from going with them for entertainment.

"Nothing," he said, "I am just relaxing. They just sent me back from Spain."

"Just now?" I asked, unable to hide my surprise.

"Yes, just today."

"How did you get onto the ferry?" I asked, considering how tight security is at the gate of the port that takes one to customs and then to the ferry.

"I just walked. I was nicely dressed, and could not be noticed."

I looked at him—he was indeed clean, well dressed: nice gray trousers, clean and stylish shoes, a blue denim jacket. He also looked educated. It was relatively rare to meet a harrag who looked like him. He exhibited a bit of social privilege.

"Why do you want to *risk?*" I asked, using the harraga phrase both to connect with him and to be better understood.

"This country is not good for us [*hâd lablâd mâ'tatnâsh*]," he said.

He had last come to the port a week back, but he was familiar with the place: he started frequenting it at the age of eleven. He was now eighteen years old.

"Why did you start this early?" I asked.

He laughed and said, "Listen, by Allah, I will not lie to you. Crossing is an addiction [*lahrig balya*]."

He laughed even louder. I joined in. He then continued, "Burning is an addiction. I have to burn. I cannot help it. My family used to live in Azrou. I used to see people from abroad coming with cars, money, and all of that. I used to hear people talking about how wonderful life is abroad. Those were

people who have never been there, though. It is then that I got the idea
to cross. I came to Tangier at age eleven to stay with my sister. She used to
work at night and while she was at work, I came here and tried to cross. I
was in bed before she came back from work in the morning. But one day the
police arrested me with thirty other kids and took us to Plaza Toro [a police
station in downtown Tangier]. The police split the group of kids into two
groups: those who were native to Tangier and those who were not. Then,
they put those not from Tangier in buses to send them home. I lied to the
police and told them I was from Tangier. They still kept us for an hour and
a half and let us go. By then my family knew. My sister called my mother
and then she called the police to report me missing. The police told her I
was at the station. My family came to fetch me. They wanted to take me
back home, but I told them I would on one condition. They said what? I
asked them to find me a way to get to Europe. I wanted my family to buy
me a contract. They promised they would, but they did not fulfill their prom-
ises. So, I resumed my attempts to cross. Now, I am here. You see, my body
is here but my mind is in Europe. I live a contradiction."

Pointing to his head and then to his body, he said, "I want my body and
my mind to reunite [*yatlaqâw*]." He then laughed again.

"What about your family?" I asked.

"What about them?" he said.

"Do they know you are here?"

"No."

"Do you ever think about reuniting with them?" I asked, purposely
using his expression "reunite" (*yatlaqâw*).

He laughed.

"When was the last time you talked to them?" I asked.

"A few days ago."

"Would you like to talk to them now?" I asked, handing him my cell
phone.

"Yes," he said.

He took my cell phone and dialed a number. His call was quick, as he
was speaking to someone who was clearly worried about him, most likely
his mother. He kept saying, "I am just here, everything is fine. How is Dad?"
and he ended the phone conversation reassuring the person he was fine and
asking her not to worry.

"Was that your mom?" I asked.

"Yes," he said.

He was not in touch with his sister, who lived in Tangier. She worked as a nurse in a clinic. He was here on a mission. His name is Khaled. He told me his name later, after our first conversation, when he felt he knew me well enough. Khaled had tried at least fourteen times to "reunite body and mind." But each time he made it to Tarifa, Spain, he got caught on the ferry and was sent back. He would spend two or three days in the police station and then be sent to the court. The judge would then release him. Khaled, too, asks for money and for food, like all the other kids at the port. He also, like them, strictly observes the fasting obligation of Islam during Ramadan. He spends the day sleeping at the port and wakes up in the late afternoon. He hangs out and then goes to one of the several charity centers in the medina that serve *futûr* to the poor and the needy, many of them harraga.

Before I met Khaled, my understanding of the harrag was of someone who had nothing to lose and everything to win by attempting the dangerous journey to Europe. But I was wrong: Khaled (and later I met several like him) was not running from poverty. All things considered, he was a child of privilege. I cite the rest of his story raw as I wrote it then in my field notes.

August 2, 2011
This morning someone called, woke me up, and I did not pick up. The person called again and again. It seemed urgent. I thought about a tragedy in my family, did not recognize the number, turned off the cell phone, and went back to sleep. I simply convinced myself that someone had dialed the wrong number. This morning at 10 am or so, the same person called and I picked up. It was the voice of a young lady. She told me her brother had called from this number. I said yes, I asked him to call his family. She asked me about him, and I told her. She told me he wanted them to buy him a contract [to go to Europe] for 10 million [10,000 euros] and that they were poor and did not have that much money. I mentioned the uncle and she told me that the uncle promised to just help him cross and then leave him, which the family refused out of concern for his safety and well-being. She told me that he had failed in his baccalaureate [high school diploma] and left school. She did not seem to know he was addicted (as he himself put it) since he was 11 years old. I did not mention this. She sounded terribly worried and talked to me about her sick mother and her sick father. She begged me

to convince him to come back. I promised to do my best and buy him a
ticket back to Kenitra. She wanted to come to Tangier, but she did not
know Tangier and asked me if I could wait for her at the train station.
I said I would and asked her to wait till I called her that night.

I went that night to the port to look for Khaled and was surprised to
see him with his mother and sister. They had arrived from Kenitra, just hours
before the *futûr*. They had not waited for my call and had taken the train
that same day. Both mother and sister were relieved and expressed gratitude.
Khaled seemed to be happy to see his family and did not blame me for telling them. However, they still had another worry. They now had to look for
his friend, Nabil. That was a piece of information Khaled somehow had neglected to tell me. Khaled came from Kenitra with his friend Nabil, who
was also a high school student. Since I knew the haunts of the harraga by
heart, they asked for my help. Khaled's mother then started to confide in
me. Everything Khaled had told me the night before was correct. His uncle,
as his mother confirmed, conducted some business in "contracts." These are
temporary labor contracts for seasonal agricultural workers in Spain that
some people use as an excuse to cross to Europe. She told me how her son
had never been in need of anything. She had given him everything he wanted,
and he was even a member of the national Taekwondo team. She pulled a
number of cards from her purse and showed them to me: "Look, here is his
Taekwondo membership card, this is his running club card, and this is his
soccer club card—he does not need anything."

She did not understand her son's determination to go to Europe. We
walked toward Hotel Continental, across from the port. Harraga usually hang
out at a corner outside the big walls of the hotel. Khaled was silently walking behind us. His mother and I kept talking. At one point, we stopped to
ask a group of harraga gathering at the corner of the hotel about Nabil. The
mother was surprised to see these young people, some of them children, in
the street. She addressed them with great passion: "My children, why are
you doing this? Do you think about your family? You can make whatever
life you want for yourself here. Why do you want to go to other people's countries [*blâd al-nâs*]? Why do you think other people's land is better?"

She then continued speaking with great conviction (speaking indirectly
to her son): "You never know where the *rizq* [lot, source of living] is, my
child. Why venture into other people's countries [*blâd al-nâs*] and risk your
lives? I will tell you a story. A woman borrowed 8,000 euros with *riba* [*riba*

is interest on credit and is strictly forbidden in Islam]. She went to Italy to work and was later found dead."

Yacine, also a harrag in his late twenties, one of the older youth, interrupted her: "That is called fate [al-qadar], mom. When death comes, you cannot stop it."

Ignoring Yacine's comment, Khaled's mother continued as passionately as before: "The woman has children. Now they need to pay the money back. You see, you can make money and live here yourself. There is this young man I know. By Allah, he was raised in an orphanage [khiriya], he studied and became a gendarme [a police officer in the countryside], a captain. His hands are full of money now; gold comes out of his hands [dhhab kayakhraj min yaddih]. You don't know where good comes from, my children. Why jeopardize your life like this?"

They listened to her without responding. I looked at them as she was speaking: they seemed unconvinced, untouched by what she was saying. They just listened with no nodding and no facial expressions. I knew they had heard this discourse many times, but they did not understand. Neither could she understand their reasons for wanting to cross and go to blâd al-nâs. Like her son and his friends, it is not about the money. It is about destiny and the will to change it. As we went back to the port, Nabil was waiting for us. Some harraga had told him that we were looking for him. He knew we would be back in the part of the port where most of the harraga meet. Nabil, too, looked like Khaled. He even looked more dapper.

Lahrig, then, is not a specialty of poor people, even though it seems that poor people have a monopoly over it. I met many poor young people who do not attempt to cross, who have never thought about it, and who are as poor as the harraga of the city. And of course, there are those who are determined to cross despite the fact that they are not poor, and may even have a good job. That is the case of Mounim, who was in his early twenties. He dressed in the fashion of Moroccan youth: newish sneakers, nice blue jeans and a T-shirt. When I met him in the port area, not far from the mosque, where he was sitting on fishermen's nets, he was staring not at the water but at the horizon where one can see the lights of the Spanish city of Algeciras. I just said salaam and sat next to him, which is customary among harraga. There are no formalities; everyone pretends to know everyone else. By this time, I had been accepted into the group, and the initial sense of suspicion was replaced by a sense of trust and friendship.

"One day, I will reach that land again," he said.

"Again, you said?"

"Yes, I got there, but they sent me back [*kayradûni*], damn luck [*zhar din al-mû*]!"

He explained to me that he had crossed five times, and each time he was caught in Algeciras and sent back to Tangier. Conversation with him, as with many harraga, was spontaneous and smooth. He quickly told me about his family background, when I asked him. His father was a state employee and worked for the OCP Group, the national phosphate company, one of the most important in the world. His mother was a school teacher. His brother had just won a contest to become a police officer. His sister had just completed sixth grade. He was a chauffeur in his hometown, Salé. He came to Tangier as an employee of the Benjelloun Fish Company. Then, he had the idea to cross—just like that (*ghir hukkâk*), he said. He considered his job as temporary.

"I am tired of temporary jobs. I want to risk and find my opportunity in life," he said, when I asked him why he wanted to cross.

"What makes you think that life there is better?" I asked.

He sensed that my question was critical, implying that life there may not be better than life here. He responded, "It is better if you have things to do. I have a high school diploma, I have another professional diploma, and I have a driver's license. The kids you see here have nothing. They cannot even manage here. If you cannot manage here, you will not be able to manage there. I manage here. I make 80 dirhams ($10) a day fabricating fish boxes for export. But the kids you see here cannot manage. They spend days begging. I never beg. I spend two hours a day in a cybercafé looking at the classifieds [cybercafés are not free; it costs $1 an hour to use a computer]. And I can always go home, any time I want."

Mounim's family knows he is in Tangier working in the fish company, but they do not know he is a harrag.

"If they knew, they would not like it and they would want me to come back home," he said, when I asked him.

He stood up and asked me if I wanted to walk with him. I stood up in turn, without saying a word, but expressing by that very gesture that I was up to it. He lit up a cigarette and I noticed he had a packet of Marlboros ($4 equals a daily salary for many people). We continued walking.

"Where do you sleep?" I asked.

"At the hotel or with my friend Rachid."

"How much do you pay for a hotel room?"

"Thirty dirhams [$3], but right now I do not rent a room. I am staying with Rachid. He is my friend; he let me stays with him for free."

Hogra: Structural Violence or Symbolic Violence?

Hogra, as explained in the previous chapters, is the cultural system of violence in Morocco and, to a lesser extent, in the entirety of the region of the Maghreb, where it plays out differently in each nation depending on local dynamics and historical specificities. It is most severe in Morocco, where the old social and economic structures were not disturbed as they were in Algeria. Amid a relatively inclusive system of citizenship, in Tunisia, too, hogra is less pronounced.

Hogra is a structural violence that "has been used to designate violence (and violation) owing to extreme poverty. That violence includes the highest rates of disease and death, unemployment, homelessness, lack of education, powerlessness a shared fate of misery, and the day-by-day violence of hunger, thirst, and bodily pain."[7] Most (though not all) harraga come from extreme poverty and are thus victims of structural violence. Surely, there is a dialectical relationship between poverty and hogra to the point that one may well ask whether poverty itself is a product of hogra. Hogra is also an exclusionary violence—wrongful exclusion from symbolic and material resources. But hogra also exists not only in the absence of poverty but even in the presence of wealth, power, and status. For hogra always plays out between at least two social actors and entails at least a *haggar* (perpetrator) and at least a *mahgûr* (a victim of the hogra). But, of course, often the individual hogra is nothing but a reflection of collective actors; this means it is neither accidental nor random. It is structural, but its structure does not spare any of the social actors save for the king.

Pierre Bourdieu identifies a type of violence that is nonphysical yet forceful, harmful, and exclusionary. He calls it symbolic violence. "Symbolic" here does not imply that it is fictitious, unreal, but rather a form of violence (ensconced in symbolic domination) that uses representations operating at the level of the subconscious to make the agent not only adhere to his own position of submission, of subjugation, but also become complicit in it. For Bourdieu, symbolic violence (unlike many forms of physical violence) cannot exist without the cooperation of the "victim" himself. It operates through categories, schemes of thought, that are interiorized.[8] Male domination, for him, inflicts a symbolic violence on women. It relegates women to an inferior status and excludes them from domains of power and influence—while at the same time making this process appear natural and self-evident. Hence, in Bourdieu's view and in a specific context, twentieth-century France, one sees a relative absence of women in fields accepted as "manly," such as politics and business, and their overrepresentation in fields considered "womanly," as extensions of the family, such as education and nursing. Hogra, on the other hand, is always recognized and the mahgûr may (or may not) be complicit.

Again, hogra is a form of violence both symbolic and physical; its symbolism and its physicality are culture specifics. (Hence the fact that hogra is often misrecognized by outsiders as something else: simple, random, and individual instances of injustice or unfriendliness.) But hogra is also recognized as such by both the perpetrator and the victim and is distinguished from other forms of violence such as *ta'addu* (aggression), *zulm* (injustice), and *dsâra* (bullying).

Hogra is inseparable from the political structure in place in Morocco, which is the system of the *makhzen*—a system of alliances (and thus exclusions) that distributes power and influence (called *jâh*) across segments of society, and across individuals within these segments, according to rules and norms. These pertain to political, physical, and symbolic closeness to the center of the makhzen (the Palace).[9] This closeness is itself the product of history, and as such, it is the object of memory of social actors in relation to this center—hence the importance of families (and family names) in Moroccan societies.

At the center of the makhzen is the royal family,[10] commonly called, in Morocco, *le Palais* or *laqsar*—the heart and the lung of the makhzen. At the center of the Palace (or the makhzen) is the king. The king is the only one exempt from hogra. But his relation to others, or rather to the rest, is one of hogra, meaning he is capable of delivering gratuitous acts of violence (symbolic and physical) not only against dissidents, as has frequently happened since independence, but even against his own entourage, including family members and ministers.[11] The king is above everybody else. He can hire, dismiss, imprison, and so forth. He is not bound by the law; he is the law. His immunity is absolute.[12]

Proximity to the center of royal power is of paramount importance in Moroccan politics.[13] However, two other important concepts need to be taken into account in an analysis of power, its distribution, its effectiveness, and its dynamics in Moroccan society—jâh, culturally specific symbolic capital, and hogra—not as two antithetical concepts that exclude each other (for instance, a holder of jâh is immune from hogra) but rather as two concepts that can coexist. How does jâh reduce or increase hogra and how can hogra itself be greater even with the presence of jâh? Yet, proximity to the center is undoubtedly important, and without it neither jâh nor hogra can be understood as an important concept in Moroccan politics. The closer one is to this center, the more jâh one gains, and the more jâh one gains, the more power one accumulates. This proximity, whether by lineage, alliance, or in any other physical and symbolic form, endows a person with greater power to possibly exert hogra against others (who hold a smaller degree of jâh and are further from the center). Yet, this same position of power also puts that person at risk of enduring greater hogra from those even closer to the center. Hence, the strategy of social actors, both close to the center and far from it, is to circumvent hogra via tactics that consist of internalizing the rules of jâh between the potential mahgûr and the possible haggar: avoiding, ignoring, exhibiting expressions and gestures of submission and obedience, and other tactics to neutralize or minimize the effects of hogra.

One's proximity to the center of the makhzen, or one's position vis-à-vis the Palace or within it, can also greatly alter ordinary politics of gender and race because of the jâh associated with this closeness. For instance, the black Moroccans called Touarga, by virtue of their physical and symbolic closeness to the Palace, are endowed with jâh that is recognized and feared. They are immune to the hogra from below though exposed to it from above. Similarly, women of the Palace, while subjected to androcentric rules within the family (in terms of inheritance, for instance), possess infinitely greater power than men with closer connections to the makhzen but with weaker (or absent) relations to the Palace.

It has been noticed that the social order in the country itself is "founded on belongings more than on citizenship."[14] The degree of the hogra or jâh one experiences in daily life depends on one's class, region, ethnicity/race, gender—and also one's relation (or lack thereof) to the makhzen. Yet, one can argue that anybody is a possible victim of hogra: anyone, even close to the center of the makhzen and endowed with significant power (jâh), can, at any time, face the adversity of someone with a higher political and social status (closer to the center) and greater power. Thus, hogra traverses Moroccan society from the center out, from top to bottom. Since hogra is located within the system of the makhzen, the system of the makhzen itself is a system of hogra. Within it, the king is able to exert power over his own entourage, who are ritually and publicly forced to demonstrate their total subjugation by kissing his hand and by bowing in front of him in ways many find ridiculous or at least outdated. Others believe that the hand kissing, the bowing, and the dress of the entourage itself, consisting of a white robe with a hood, are meant to humiliate.[15]

Moroccan families often exhibit astonishing similarities to the model of the family of the makhzen, including the rituals of submission to the father, especially during ceremonies of 'eid (Islamic festivals) when, interestingly enough, he may also dress ritualistically, wearing the jellaba (Moroccan traditional robe), preferably white. Hogra is present within families; it is exerted, with varying degrees, depending on one's position within the unit, one's gender, income, age, and so on. The origins of Moroccan authoritarianism, then, are not to be found in the relation between master and disciple[16] but maybe within the Moroccan family itself.[17]

There are degrees of hogra, just as there are degrees of violent acts as measured by their effects, their acuteness, their permanence and durability. Consequently, the harrag, by virtue of his social condition, is one of the primary victims of the hogra. He is as far from the center as the sky from earth.[18] As a citizen, he is not only unprotected by the state but also harassed by it daily. His vulnerability is extreme, almost absolute. He can be and often is the object of abuse, mistreatment, and violence at the hands of others, including the police force itself—that is, the modern institution that enforces the will of the makhzen. The harrag represents the zero degree of citizenship. His presence in the city is a consequence of hogra, not its cause. Lahrig, the activity in which he is engaged and with which he has become identified (he is a harrag), is an experience of violence from beginning to end. In other words, lahrig is nothing but an attempt to escape hogra.

All in all, the system of hogra itself, which is nothing but the very system of the makhzen, is a system of cultural violence, symbolic and physical. To understand the dynamics of the makhzen, it is important to understand the positions of those at the very margins, like the harraga, those who experience the hogra fully, constantly, and endure its most intense degree with its most nefarious effects. If understanding the law entails understanding its transgression, according to Michel Foucault, then understanding the makhzen as a system of hogra entails understanding the conditions of the victim of hogra—that is, conditions produced by the system of hogra. To put it bluntly, to understand the dynamics of the makhzen, one needs to understand the games not only of its political and social actors (parties, elites, etc.) but also the dynamics, the politics, and conditions of its most vulnerable victims.[19] It is to the relation of the harrag to the state that I shall now turn.

"Illegality" of the State

The Moroccan government is often silent about the youth who risk their lives to cross to Europe. It is generally silent about the horrific conditions of poverty in Morocco's shantytowns and rural areas. The media, especially social and international media, often report on these youth, including the dozens and sometimes hundreds of deaths in the Mediterranean Sea.[20] Some media, such as Al Jazeera, report the existence of at least one entire cemetery in the town of Tarifa devoted specifically to Moroccan harraga and West African migrants.[21] Such news, though, has become routine and lost the power of sensation it once had in the 1990s. These news reports do not seem to incite a reaction from Moroccan civil society, and no organization is dedicated to the cause of the harraga.[22]

The harraga are familiar with the state, which they often encounter in the form of the police force. They are the objects of verbal and physical police violence, especially when Spanish authorities hand them over to deport them to Morocco. Harraga are also subject to random violence when the police come to inspect places suspected of harboring drugs and sex. While I was in the midst of a group interview with dozens of young adults and children on a Ramadan night, a police van suddenly stopped, and the chief of police and his aides got out abruptly, screaming, "Sons of whores [wlâd laqhâb], faggots [zwâmal], what are you doing here? Fucking each other?"

Everybody ran away while I remained, sitting on some stairs, rather calmly. Seeing my attitude, two kids decided not to run away, but they walked a few steps ahead, ready to run at the first sign of danger. The chief of police walked toward me, still shouting: "Faggots, sons of whores!"

My tape recorder was still on, and I purposely did not bother to turn it off. One of the kids said, "We are just talking to the ustâdh [professor]!"

I thought that with my sportswear and my plastic sandals, I did not look like an ustâdh; as it turned out, and age aside, I looked as suspicious as the kids themselves. It was dark; the area had no lighting. I could have looked like any harrag. Plus, the meaning of "ustâdh" had changed drastically since the late 1990s; now it also meant "gentleman" or "sir." It is used right and left to address anyone regardless of status. I stayed calm, not knowing how to react. Surprisingly, the police chief addressed me with deference: "Forgive me, ustâdh, this is not a convenient place for meeting or hanging out. We come here often and we find faggots fucking each other. No disrespect intended [hashak], this is a faggot place. Could you please leave! And please forgive us [smahnâ]!"

The police, it became clear to me, were not concerned about the safety of these children and youth in the street. They also seemed less concerned about their intention—lahrig—which is known to everybody. Rather, as state agents, they were practicing "bio-power"[23] and were concerned only about sexual deviations. In this modern city, too, sexuality is one of the activities most scrutinized and controlled by the state—just as it has been in Western societies.[24]

In any case, most of the harraga I encountered were energetic, adventurous, and highly intelligent. Many had crossed to Europe. They had matured early and sounded older than their age. In a country with one of the highest rates of youth unemployment,[25] the harraga, children and young adults alike, constitute an excess of human labor power.[26] One out of four youth aged fifteen to twenty-four is unemployed and has never been schooled. This constituted 1,685,000 youth between 2016 and 2017.[27]

In the industrial society of the United States, the reservoir for labor, so necessary for the functioning of a capitalist society, is essentially Mexican labor (reserved as illegal).[28] In the nonindustrial yet highly capitalist society of Morocco, the reservoir of labor is the youth from the marginalized segments of society whose parents do not even qualify as working class (since most survive in jobs that put them outside the working-class system). They constitute the underclass, to use the term coined by sociologist William Julius Wilson.[29] The children of this Moroccan underclass, especially those who have made of lahrig a profession, are left to do and die by the state. They are nothing but a surplus of labor that exceeds society's needs. George Bataille remarks that "if the system cannot produce or if the surplus [of production] cannot entirely be absorbed in its production, then it is necessary to waste it, spend it, willingly or not, gloriously or catastrophically."[30]

By this, Bataille must have meant all types of production, including the biological one, from which human labor is extracted. Seeing that labor in human society has also been turned, with capitalism, into a commodity that one can buy and sell, it too can be wasted when it becomes a surplus. That human labor, embodied in human life, whether gloriously or catastrophically, can be destroyed as a commodity is horrifying at first sight. But despite its horror, human labor when it becomes a surplus is no different from any surplus product, even when it consists of children. Disposable human surplus, in all its excessive forms, must be spent and wasted, that is, sent somewhere or destroyed here. One ordinary and most common way is unemployment; an extraordinary one, among others, is lahrig, whereby the surplus of labor is lost in the sea or is transported to Europe by the laborer who offers himself.

In *Das Kapital*, Karl Marx examines the conditions of children in the formation of capitalism in Great Britain.[31] The working class he analyzes contained a significant number of children as young as six years old. Not only does he show how children constituted a major and cheap force in capitalist production, but he also draws attention to the effects of child labor on mothers. According to government reports that Marx cited, British women were forced sometimes to let their children die to spare them a life of utter misery where, as a consequence of inhumane labor conditions, they lived sickly lives, suffered, and died young anyway—in their early twenties.[32] This is different from Nancy Scheper-Hughes's study of the Brazilian shantytown of Reno, where mothers let their unhealthy children die so that they could utilize scarce resources to take care of those with a higher chance of living. This choice was justified by a Catholic belief, according to Scheper-Hughes, that sickly children are angels meant to pass through this life and not stay in it.[33]

While in almost all of the cases I have seen in Morocco, the family is unaware of the actions (and often even the whereabouts) of their children, the state, via its highly effective police machinery and network of spies, knows.[34] It even polices their sexuality in the port area. Yet, the state does nothing to prevent them from exposing themselves to death. By this I reference not only the fact that many of these children come from remote villages with no infrastructure or from deprived shantytowns neglected by the state but also, and especially, that the state does not police their highly dangerous actions. As raw human labor, they are disposable.

In his study of Mexican migrants in Chicago, Nicholas de Genova argues that in U.S. society, migration labor is needed and state laws are designed in such a way as to create "illegality."[35] In other words, the state creates "illegals" who are needed for capitalist production, and their very illegality constitutes the guarantee for a reservoir of cheap and malleable labor. In Moroccan society, by contrast, there is an excess of human labor. The state strategy is to neglect it, even expose it to death. Those who do not die, those who overcome the incredible difficulties and "make it," qualify for labor migration to the EU—both legal and illegal.[36]

If mothers can let their children die to spare them a miserable life full of suffering or so that other children, with a greater chance for life, can live—what of states? Modern states are not mothers but cold monsters, as often described by social scientists. They have been involved in killing not only others but also, first and foremost, their own citizens from the moment of their foundation.[37] As a matter of fact, one of the conditions of allegiance to a state is precisely the willingness of a citizen to die and kill for it.[38] When it fails its responsibility toward its citizens, especially children, the state also kills by neglect, that is, by creating the conditions for death. From January to November 2014, the death toll in the Mediterranean Sea, considered the deadliest route of migrants, was estimated to be 3,500.[39] That year, 219,000 migrants crossed to Europe, ten times more than in 2012.[40] From then to November 2016, the number increased to 10,000 dead, according to the United Nations.[41]

From the previous vignettes, it is clear that the harraga have no expectations from the country; most of them even distance themselves from it by saying "this country" (*hâd lablâd*) and not "our country" (*blâdnâ*). But when I ask a question about the government, the language is even more poignant.

I asked Mohamed and Driss, "If the government gets you jobs, good jobs, would you not cross?"

Both smiled and Driss said, "Those that are here, the sons of whores, thieves, they give you nothing."

Mohamed added, "They will see you dying of thirst and will not offer you a drop of water. Tell me about them [*twarrinî fîhum*]."

"Is the king to blame?" I asked.

"No, he does not know. It is those around him. He cannot know everything."

"Don't you think he is responsible?" I asked, pushing the issue a bit further.

"No, it is all those sons of whores around him."

Hogra as Racism

What the harraga experience is not only daily racism, shown often in gratuitous acts of persecution and acts of brute violence by gangs and bullies, but also structural racism (hogra), a form of marginalization from which most of them are virtually incapable of escape except by an act of lahrig—in itself a courageous and transgressive act. This means that in order to be free from the ubiquitous violence of hogra, the harrag must leave his space. Beyond the country, there is life without hogra. So he believes. He knows this via the many narratives of life in Europe that circulate among his friends as well as in Moroccan society at large. Many such narratives are fabricated by Moroccan migrants who, upon their return, want to prove that their endeavor was a success. They often back these narratives by displays of material wealth: cars, flashy clothes, watches, and, the most certain sign of all, a European wife—a sign of total success, since sexual success implies all others.

The figure of the harrag represents one of the most tragic victims of hogra. Hogra manifests itself as a form of local racism, an exclusion from basic rights, and a neglect that can result in death, in exile, and surely in a waste of one's childhood and youth looking for a chance that may or may not come. In a postcolonial, westernized society, such as Morocco, racism is found in postcolonial relation with forms that were precolonial in France. By this, I mean that though racism is found in the new class formation, it is as old as the colonial experience itself (1912–56). Foucault stated the obvious when he wrote that "racism has developed primo with colonization."[42] However, he is more insightful when he explains how those dynamics have played out, and how racism entails death or a variety of death experiences: "What is racism? It is first the means to introduce a cut in this domain of life that power has taken in charge: the cut between what must live and what must die. . . . Of course, by putting to death, I do not mean simply direct murder, but I also mean anything that can be indirect death: the fact of exposing to death, to multiply for some the risks of death, or simply political death, expulsion, rejection, etc."[43]

Racism not only is categorizing populations according to the notion of race (which has drastically changed over time) but also is fundamentally an effective, mostly invincible mechanism of excluding populations deemed different according to notions of birth, religious affiliation, regional belonging, class, and so forth. This exclusion can take the form of marginalization (which is a form of symbolic death) and even physical elimination, including imprisonment and even murder. Yet, the racism that developed alongside colonization found its origin in class; as Benedict Anderson notes, "The dreams of racism actually have their origin in ideologies of class, rather than those of nation."[44]

In Moroccan society especially, the formation of a modern class out of the old, traditional, feudal-like system gave birth to a colonial dynamic still at work today.[45] When returning in 1990s to Algeria, whose colonial dynamics he knew firsthand, Bourdieu was surprised to see similarities between the colonial and postcolonial societies in the country.[46] It is what Étienne Balibar calls "racism without race."[47] The case of Morocco may be even more severe, as is evident from the events of the so-called Arab Spring and the Hirâk of the Rif narrated in Chapter 1.[48]

One Ramadan night, I was playing cards with the kids and listening to them talk about their lives in the city: "We cannot even get into a restaurant to eat. They will not serve us. The other day a gendarme [a police officer of the countryside] took us to a restaurant to buy us food. He asked us to sit so we could be served food. The owner was staring at us with great hostility. We felt he was going to kill us with his stare."

As has often been noticed, one of the characteristics of racism is its inability to see diversity and its power to reduce the heterogeneous to an essence. In Tangier, the harraga, in the eyes of the residents, are also shamkara—"human dirt," homeless with no purpose in life, glue sniffers. They make no difference, or worse, they pollute the city with their presence.[49] Racism is practiced against them mostly via the state's indifference, which amounts to what Foucault calls an "indirect death": "exposing them to death and even multiplying for them the risks of death."[50] This death is possible at the port any time; it is also possible in the streets and under the trucks, but its possibility is exponentially increased once they take the ferry.

As we saw in Chapter 2, these kids are defined by their ambition to cross, to migrate to Europe. Hence, they are not shamkara, that is, street children wandering without purpose in life. The harraga want to escape social death but subconsciously confront real death. Their goal is not to die; it is not suicide but rather life—they want to live (bghînâ nʿîshu) a new life with dignity, that is, with a job and an income. Paradoxically, the road to this life makes them wait in the very domain of hogra, not only in the street but also at the port that is almost a free zone for discrimination and violence.

Stories of daily hogra are prevalent among the harraga. They share them the same way they share stories of success or tragedy. They are not good at keeping secrets. Often, they volunteered information to me that could have incriminated the person involved. Many were born in extraordinary conditions that are fraught with violence: in shantytowns, in abject poverty, with divorced parents, or parents who died while the kids themselves were small.

I met Abdelhalim in the same area of the port, next to the mosque, where many of them sleep on flattened cardboard boxes. He was only sixteen years old and had been staying in the port since he was thirteen. He had crossed many times (too many for him to remember exactly), and each time he had been caught and sent back. He told me that police abuse and violence are daily routines. His parents divorced and his father married again. He himself does not know where his mother went after the divorce, but he lived with his stepmother for a while until one day her jewelry went missing. He said that his brother stole it, but his stepmother accused him and called the police. He was sentenced to three months in jail in Larache. He is bitter about the injustice inflicted upon him.

"I was tortured in jail," he said, "my stepmother bribed the police to torture me."

"Why?" I asked—so shocked by the revelation, I did not know how to respond.

"To discipline me [*trabbîni*]," he said.

"What kind of torture?" I asked.

"*Trûbiya*," he said.

"What is that?"

"They tied my hands and my feet, they held my feet in the air, and they beat me with a stick and sometimes a belt."

"Oh, *tahmîla*?"[51] I asked after I recognized it.

"Yes."

"How do you know it was your stepmother who made the police torture you?"

"I know," he said.

"How do you?"

"I just know."

He then continued, "I intend to cross tonight at 4 a.m. on the first ferry to leave. If it does not work, I will buy acid and throw it on her face."

Tayeb warned him, "Damn you, bastard! You will get twenty years in jail if you do that."

Abdelhalim is very thin (most likely because of malnutrition), is very dirty, and wears old clothes, but he has a vivid mind and a sharp tongue. He can shut up anyone in the group, including Khaled, who is much older and more educated. When he argues, he raises his voice, looks straight at his interlocutors, and stares at them, saying, "*mrag, mrag*" or "*skut, makatmargush*" or "*wahad dbnadam makymargouch!*" (shame on you! shame on you! or shut up! you have no shame! what do you know?) and then he makes his point as forcefully as possible, while waving his hand in front of the faces of his interlocutors, often leaving them agape with no response.

"What happened to you?" I asked, noticing a bruise over one of his eyes.

"Someone hit me while I was asleep."

"With what?"

"A stone."

"Did you see them?"

"No."

Not interested in elaborating, he stood up and left. I could hear him singing as he walked toward the gate of the port.

Burning as Freedom

Mobility is about freedom—both freedom for and freedom from.[52] For the harraga, movement, often from a shantytown or small village, and then to Europe, is a true exercise in freedom. Their transgressive act is in itself a display of agency.[53] Refusing to accept their condition, they are determined to change it, and in changing it, they will change the condition of their families (n'âwnu mâlin dâr or n'âwnu alwalidîn). Often times, what they mean by the family is not the nuclear family but just their mother. First, they leave their shantytown or village and head toward the city of Tangier. Thus, they are free from the everyday life of their home.

"Why stay in Shishawa? There is nothing there, just watermelons [makayan wâlo ghîr dallâh]!" Abdelilah told me, laughing, while his friends and his younger brother Abdallah, all from the same village south of Marrakesh, joined in the laughter.

They had been here for five months; they shared everything, including meals, and slept at the port.

"Listen, ustâdh," Abdelilah continued, "look at us here. We are in Tangier, on the beach. We have everything, food, cigarettes, soda, and all. It is like we are on a vacation, a long vacation! Praise be to God!"

His companions continued laughing.

Being in Tangier is in itself an accomplishment for the harraga—a big one at that. They are able to leave their isolated place of birth for the city. They share the space of the city with everyone. But the city is not their final destination, nor is the port their permanent dwelling. The harraga have their eyes and their hearts set on Europe. Their freedom of movement has not ended in Tangier, nor is it hindered by the walls, the police, and the sea. In a different historical context, though applicable to the harraga, Hannah Arendt noted that "being able to depart for where we will is the prototypical gesture of being free, as limitation of freedom of movement has from time immemorial been the precondition for enslavement. Freedom of movement is also the indispensable precondition for action, and it is in action that men primarily experience freedom in the world."[54]

Departing for the harraga is also "a gesture of being free." However, in their case, departing is itself an action. What is the precondition of this action (of departure)? It is the harraga's willingness, their determination to be free, as well as their knowing they are free. This is what made them leave, and it is also this that prevents them from feeling trapped in Tangier when they cannot cross. The harraga know the way to Tangier; they undertake it often by bus or by train—and almost always "illicitly," meaning they ride without a ticket. Once in Tangier, they quickly learn the culture of lahrig in the street and at the port—the way to cross, how to cross, when to cross, and what to do once they are on the other side. It may take a harrag a day or two to leave Tangier or it may take him a year or more. Often, those in the port have tried several times and waited. Waiting is not being stuck; it is rather the precondition for movement. It is true, however, that departure can be the precondition for another action: departing again. The harrag waits for the moment of the grand departure when he crosses continents, a departure (and thus an action) that will be followed by other departures—departure from Tarifa to Algeciras and from Algeciras to whichever direction in Europe. In a number of cases, it is a destination where he has a relative on whom he can count. Often the connection is already made, and a brother or a cousin is on the other side, waiting for the arrival of the harrag.

These departures can be aborted at any time. The harrag may get caught and return to his point of departure in the city. Even when he is sent back, he waits to depart again. This exercise in, of, and for freedom is lived in a variety of ways by every harrag I encountered. His life is illegal in the view of the state. Freedom is exercised by a transgression of the law constraining the harrag's movement. Freedom is the ability to overcome this constraint—to be free of it so one can be free to move. Hence, an interesting dynamic between the harrag and the state arises: between his ability to be free, to move, and to freely follow his dreams and the state's repressive power that constrains the citizen—especially the citizen deprived of his rights. The

Universal Declaration of Human Rights (1948) makes freedom of movement a human right, while the state (both in Morocco and in the EU) constrains this movement with an array of laws and with an entire "infrastructure of arrestability."[55] Hence the tension between freedom (located in human will) and unfreedom (located in state law). The harrag, as a new figure of globalization, epitomizes this human will. If power, race, and citizenship allow others to have the freedom of mobility, to turn the world into a flat terrain easy to cross in all directions, the harrag finds that freedom in his own will. He practices guerrilla mobility. Hence the huge challenge the harrag presents to the state, including to the EU.

This challenge consists mainly of the idea that despite drastic measures and huge spending on the part of the EU to stop this movement, the harrag not only crosses, but the number of migrants who die at sea put the humanitarian morality of the EU into question. Europe has seen over 33,000 young people die at its gate. A discourse deployed against the harraga and migrants in general is that they are potential dangers to security. The connection between migration and terrorism has thus been created. However, migration from a country of origin not linked to terrorism is unlikely to be associated with terrorist attacks.[56] The harraga and the West African migrants have not been linked to any terrorist attacks in Europe.

Even at the peak of the war in Syria in 2014–16, as Tangier provided more combatants than any other city in Morocco to jihadi groups fighting Bashar al-Assad, I never heard about any harrag being recruited. As in Europe, from where combatants joined jihadi groups, the Moroccan jihadists who went to Syria were recruited in mosques and prisons, not at the port and not even in poor neighborhoods where harraga often come from. The argument that poor people are easy prey for jihadi recruiters adds to the large number of negative stereotypes about lower classes—if you are poor, you are likely to become a terrorist—while, by now, it should be known that terrorists, of all brands, come from different classes, with leadership often coming from upper classes and the educated.[57] The harrag remains a would-be migrant in search of a better life, not a would-be terrorist seeking to destroy lives.

Again, the very existence of the harrag constitutes a problem for the state, one that the Moroccan state tackles by ignoring or through minimal oversight, most of it violent. But the harraga and what they do are one. They burn and they are burners. Their very presence constitutes a transgression against the norms of society, including against their families. Even when they

are not crossing, they are delinquents; living in the street is being a delinquent. By virtue of the 2003 Moroccan law that regulates migration, attempting to cross without proper documentation is a petty crime.

Khaled, the high school student whose story I reported earlier, is both
a delinquent and a petty criminal. But he does not know it. Comparatively
speaking, Khaled is a child of privilege. He is from a middle-class family, he
went to school, he was a member of a martial arts club, and he even participated in national martial arts tournaments. He has a family that looks
after him. Yet, when he is in the street, he becomes a delinquent, a candi-
date for petty crime. Each time he is burned out, he goes back home to recharge his batteries, so to speak. He has the luxury to do so. He then returns
within a few months to resume lahrig. He is not trapped or stuck. He is
always engaged in an action expected to lead him to his dream—to cross to
Europe.

Those who are caught crossing are often arrested, then deposited in a
police station or the old city train station to appear sometime in front of a
judge. I did not meet any youth who had spent significant time in a European jail; at the most they had spent three days at the Moroccan police or
train station and had been passed on to a tribunal only to be released with a
warning from the judge.

Tayeb's was a different kind of case. He was one of the few harraga suspicious of me, yet always affable. He always declined to answer my questions
or he responded ambiguously, telling me he just wanted to cross "to see that
world." I explained to him several times that I was doing research to write
an academic book. He opened up to me gradually and within eight months
he seemed to trust me. This is what I wrote about him while I was in the
field.

> [Tayeb] is 34 years. He has been in the port for eight months or so,
> waiting for his "chance" to cross. He is gentle, polite, and with a sense of
> humor. He wears the same clothes every day—a blue sportswear and
> khaki trousers. He is always clean shaven. The children seem to trust
> him well. They rely on him the way they would rely on their older
> brother. Communication between them is smooth; age or life experience
> does not seem to be an obstacle or a problem. He also seems to genuinely
> care about them. I knew him for several months before he told me his
> story. He crossed legally "by a contract" (when crossing was still easy),
> made it to Spain, got a job in a pig farm, and even got married to a

Spanish woman and had a child with her. He then started selling small doses of powder [cocaine]. "I buy 100 grams, consume some of it, and sell some." Gradually, he bought more and sold more. He then quit his job and became a full-time drug dealer. Everyone knew him in Girona. Business boomed, he said, and he continued to sell drugs against his wife's advice. But the police started watching him. He was under surveillance for six months. By then, the police knew all about him, and decided to arrest him. "One day," he said, "my wife woke me up, and told me that the police had encircled the entire neighborhood. I saw policemen wearing hoods from the window. I quickly ran away, from one villa's roof to another. I ran and ran and ran. Finally, while jumping between roofs I injured my foot on a piece of glass, and started screaming. The police then arrested me. . . . They brought me to the apartment and searched everywhere for powder and could not find anything. 'Son of a bitch, where did you put it?' a policeman asked me. It was just there, not far from them. I had hidden it in the oven and I could see the police dogs getting close to it, but all they could smell was food, spaghetti, and chicken near the unwatched oven. The police went berserk, could not believe it, as they did not want to go back empty-handed to their chief. So, one of them put a gun on my wife's head, calling her puta *[whore]. He tried to scare her so she would tell them where I had hidden the drugs. But she was a good wife, she did not say anything. Finally, they handcuffed me and took me to the police station. They took my wife in a different car. At the police station, they asked me whether I wanted to make a declaration, to speak to a lawyer, or to a family member. I chose a lawyer. He came and I told him what happened. I wanted to sue the police for threatening my wife with a gun. But the attorney advised me not to sue the police because they may retaliate. I asked him how? He said next time they may come with powder in their pocket and claim it is yours. But my wife did sue them for putting a gun to her head."*

"So, when were you arrested then?"

"Two years later. The second time they came to search the house, wherever they put their hands, they found powder [ghobra]," [Tayeb] said laughingly.

He spent six years in jail for selling cocaine. His Spanish wife divorced him, remarried, and remade her life. When he ended his jail time on January 18, 2011, he was deported to Ceuta, and from there he was sent to Tetouan. In Tetouan, he was arrested by the Moroccan police. The judge released him after he learned that he had spent time in prison for what he did.

For eight months or so, Tayeb had been in the port, wanting to cross to Spain. But his motives were different from the harraga I knew. He confided to me that he had "merchandise" hidden somewhere and that he wanted to go back to get it. "It is worth a lot of money," he said, "I need to recuperate it. I have to." I finally understood his suspicion of me; he was protecting himself.

Tayeb was not the only man I met with stories of selling drugs and spending time in jail. I met several others who had similar experiences. These were usually older, like Tayeb himself. Jailed and deported, they too come to the port to find opportunities to cross again. Often, they bury their past and keep it secret. They too are harraga waiting for their chance to cross—their chance to be free. Or rather, they want to get back to a different life they once had and lost. Their dream is not about "what it is not yet and will be" but rather about "what it once was and will be." It is a different type of hope—hope for repetition.[58] A repetition of freedom.

Hope and Resilience

Despite the tremendous challenge of life in the streets, despite the tight security around the port and at the ferry gate, and despite the "failed" attempts at crossing or even crossing only to be sent back within days, months, or years, one thing is certain: the harraga are known not to give up—or at least not easily. The harsh conditions I have described are meant not only to communicate how exceptionally hard life is for these youth but also to demonstrate how strong and unshaken their will is, how steely their resilience.

Resilience is a physiological concept. It presupposes trauma and requires an ability to regain control, reinvent oneself, and pursue another option for development. It has been reintroduced as an operational concept to anthropology by the work of Boris Cyrulnik, who understands it as "a biological, psycho-affect, social, and cultural mechanism that allows a new development after a psychic traumatism."[59] This process, Marie Anaut notices, is based on a number of factors categorized into three orders: those that concern the "interior of the subject," such as cognitive abilities, defensive modalities, types of personalities, and so on; those that pertain to the family, such as family support; and those that concern the socioenvironmental context, such as friendships, community, religious supports, and so forth.[60] However, resilience has ultimately to do with the ability of the individual to manage under adversity, and as such, the question of resilience is one of agency.[61]

It would be difficult to specify the trauma in the lives of many of the kids here at the port. People who have experienced trauma usually experience a life of normalcy, an ordinary life where the extraordinary has not yet happened. And usually the trauma, even in extreme cases, is overcome with the help of others—relatives, therapists, and so on. But young people here have lived in a traumatic condition all their lives. Many of them were born into it. Even Sigmund Freud speaks of trauma as a moment and uses the phrase "traumatic moment," which in his understanding "paralyzes the function of the pleasure principle and gives the situation of danger its significance."[62] This means again that the traumatic moment is an extraordinary moment. It is an occurrence in one's life that is rare, but with lasting effects. Hence the concept of resilience as the ability to overcome the "traumatic moment" and start again.

However, like hope, that ability seems to be inherent in human beings. Vincent Crapanzano notes "the extraordinary resilience humans have to the unsupportable, to hopelessness, and despair."[63] This is what he calls "hope-in-hopeless."[64] Hope is associated with faith,[65] "two essential characteristics of human existence."[66] What is important, in my view, is how certain conditions of utter despair are surmounted and how cultural and personal factors are determined in this resilience. For indeed, even suicide, which may seem the total giving up on life, is in crucial ways an attempt to get out of unlivable despair. It is true that in the case at hand, other poor and ambitious youth do not choose lahrig as a way out but look at other options, including theft, sex work, petty jobs, and so on. They are no less hopeful and no less resilient than the kids who take what seems to be a drastic measure, lahrig. In the face of such a high death toll, most of us, or at least I, look at this endeavor from the viewpoint of risk, and this viewpoint must also be culturally embedded. For the youth I met, death is a question of destiny, not a choice and less so a risk. As Yacine told Khaled's mother, "That is fate, you cannot stop it."

For Mary Douglas, the question about risk is "How safe is safe for this particular culture?"[67] However, safety itself needs to be defined in order to ask what is "safe" in a particular culture. For the case at hand, the particular culture is not only a Moroccan culture but also the culture of particular Moroccan youth mostly from a specific segment of society. It is not safe for many of these youth to not take the risk to radically alter their own destiny. Death is not part of the equation for cultural reasons and for reasons having to do with age. Death again for these young people is a pure abstract, and even as an abstract is not thought of philosophically as that nothingness that causes humans great anxiety.[68] Death is an abstract, yet it is also something bound to happen for everyone, and when it is meant to happen, it will inevitably happen in bed, in the street, in the sea, to young, old, or in between. Therefore, for these youth (and children), death is excluded from the probability thinking that is associated with risk. The risk is only that one will be caught, mistreated, beaten up, and returned to the country. Many of those I met have crossed and got caught, insulted, smacked, sent back, insulted again, smacked again; they spent a few days in the police station and then were released, only to start again. However, since the harrag is not safe on the streets of Morocco and especially since he sees his own life as not a life—as a death, in the words of one of the children I interviewed—it is not that the harrag does not adhere to "the cult of safety,"[69] as Douglas calls it; rather, he does so, and firmly. It is this cult of safety that requires him to seek safety where he believes it is safe—Europe—about which he has heard and seen a great number of positive things. He believes that to be safe, he needs to take a risk. There is greater risk in not trying. Passivity in the face of tremendous hardship is not safe. After all, by taking "risks," the harraga are also trying to overcome the trauma of the *quhra* (misery) that most have found themselves in since birth.

The trauma of the harraga is not just a moment, or even moments. Many of the harraga, like Driss and Mohamed, know nothing but traumatic experience. Yet, their resilience may be precisely the survival instinct that pushes them to escape the lives they live—fraught with danger, with constant pain and suffering, structured by the hogra. Their hope is to escape it. Their action is guided by this hope. Their resilience in fundamental ways stems from their hope that another life is possible, another destiny is possible, another land with a decent life is within reach; it is as near as the other side of the Spanish coasts that they can see and often gaze at while resting on the port's fishing nets.

"It takes youthfulness to hope," Søren Kierkegaard wrote.[70] But hope in and of itself can be a factor of inaction. Hope with action and, in the case of the harrag, with repeated action is what makes the harrag a harrag. Not only does he hope to cross, but he does cross; and when he is arrested, brutalized, and sent back for further mistreatment at the hands of the Moroccan police, he waits and tries again. Kierkegaard wrote once, "It takes courage to will repetition."[71] The truth is that it takes courage for the harrag to make the first attempt, to engage in action, and then it takes resilience, not just courage, to repeat his attempts at overcoming the extraordinary burdens of life and to reinvent his own life by a series of repetitions of which he *hopes* one will be successful—meaning he will accomplish his goal of crossing to a better world. One may indeed think of this "better world" as a utopia. But "hope sees what is not yet and what will be," as poet Charles Péguy put it. "Hope loves what is not yet and what will be."[72]

I met a group of harraga one day at the entrance of the port. They were sitting on the stairs of a dirty abandoned building, watching passersby. From time to time, one of them said something, and the rest of them laughed. Then they were silent again, just looking at the people walking by. As I walked closer, I made eye contact with a few of them.

I asked if I could join them and they said, "Why not, uncle? Sit down."

"What are you doing here?" I asked.

"Just resting [*ghîr mrayhîn*]."

"I meant, what are you doing here at the port?"

"We are here to burn [*nhargu*]."

"How is that going?" I asked.

"God has not yet allowed it [*mazâl masahhalsh Allâh*]."

I noticed one of them, a teenager, who was not responding. He listened to his friends' answers with a smile, then looked at me when I asked a question, and continued smiling. His black plastic sandals were too big for his feet, his jeans had holes in them (a sign of poverty, not fashion), and he was wearing two sweaters, one on top of the other. There was something particularly kind and gentle about him.

I turned to him and asked, "How about you? Are you here to cross as well?"

"Yes."

"Why?"

"To make a life for ourselves [*ndabrû 'la râsna*]."

"Why don't you make a life for yourself here?"

"I can if I want to."

"You can? How?" I asked, surprised at the answer.

"I master a craft."

"What craft?"

"I make buttons for caftans. I used to work in a shop in Marrakesh before I came here."

"How much did you make?"

"100 dirhams [$10–$12] a day."

"That is good money. How old are you?"

"Eighteen years old."

"Why did not you keep that job?"

"I could not stay there. I had to leave."

"Why?"

"My parents."

"What about them? What does your father do?"

"My father passed away."

"Sorry to hear that. When?"

"Few years ago, seven years?"

"Sorry again. And your mom? What does she do?"

"She is dead too."

"I am really sorry. How did she die?"

"Just like that [ghir hâkkâk]."

"Was she sick?"

"Yes."

"How old was she?"

"Thirty-six years old."

"How did your father die?"

"Just like that."

"Was he sick?"

"Yes, he was."

"How old was he?"

"Thirty-two years old."

"Do you have any family left?"

"Yes, an uncle in Casablanca, but I am not in touch with him. I have an older brother in Spain. But I do not know exactly where."

"You are here just by yourself in this world."

"Yes. But I will look for my brother when I go there."

"When will you go there?"

"When God allows it [fâsh ysahhal Allâh]!"

The harraga, young adults and minors alike, do not use the word "hope," whether in Arabic (amal) or French (espoir). Yet their experience of the present is embedded in a tomorrow that will be better the day they cross to

Europe. Even if they do not say the word, they use several Moroccan expressions that mean it. All of these expressions are rooted in Islam. For hope is often embedded in a "system of force" called religion.[73]

Fâsh ysahhal Allah ("when God allows it") or *Inshâ* Allah ("God willing")—such expressions denote a conception of hope embedded in Islamic eschatology. It is thought that nothing happens without God's will and that the world itself is God's will. (This is despite the existence of theological and philosophical questions about will and freedom—and conflicting attempts at an answer—in Muslim theology and philosophy.)

The harraga also use secular notions such as *zhar* (luck). And even this notion is often associated with Islam in such expressions as "God blessed him with luck" or, simply, "He has luck." They also use expressions such as "when I will cross" or narratives situated in the future (about "being there," "working," "bringing a car").

The idea here is that the endeavor of crossing is based on the concept of a tomorrow that will change the present for the better—and that tomorrow is not one that the harrag brings or creates; it is God who does so. The harrag can only persist, and his persistence is fed by his unshakeable belief that the crossing will happen no matter what and no matter the length of time it takes. There are those who have stayed in the port for years. Often, they had that chance, that luck to cross, but it was aborted in Spain and for some even farther out, in France or in the Netherlands. That half-chance is in itself an indication that there is hope, that there is a possibility of crossing, and thus the possibility of drastically changing one's life and making it to a new world. Again, aborted attempts are not failed attempts; they are proof that crossing and a new life are possible—that they happen.

Of course, there are those who give up. Several times, I asked about someone and was told he went back home because he got tired of it. But there is always the possibility he will come back. Indeed, I have met several harraga, like Khaled, who go back and forth—they are burned out, they go home, only to face the harsh or boring static life they had run from in the first place, and then they come back to try their luck again.

Nevertheless, the activity of lahrig itself is fraught with danger where luck is an extraordinary occurrence. And luck is not always good, meaning it does not always result in a happy ending. Crossing can be the beginning of a new episode of violence and suffering, if it is completed. And the process itself can involve extreme forms of violence—drowning in the sea, being crushed under a truck, or suffocating in a hiding place. As someone reported to me one time, by the time he got to the British border by hiding on top of a truck he caught in Tangier, he was about to die of cold and starvation. "When the truck stopped, I got out of my hiding place, quivering with extreme cold. The British were nice to me, they covered me, and made sure I was fine. I would have died if they found me a half hour later." Yet, he was at the port, ready to cross again. I witnessed harraga crossing many times. I saw them sliding under a truck, swimming toward the ferry. They know the schedule of the ferry well. At night, usually around 2 a.m., young men came prepared, psychologically and physically.

On the night of August 10, 2011, in the middle of the month of Ramadan, while I was sitting on the fishing nets playing cards with the harraga, a group of four guys in their late twenties arrived. I had never seen them before. They started undressing behind a horse cart in a nearby corner. They called Tayeb and started talking to him. I could not hear the conversation. Then, I saw one of them blowing into a plastic bag, the kind that are given out in the market for groceries. Once the bag was filled with air, he started to check that no air was coming out of it. Then he opened it and put his clothes in it. The other three started doing the same. I did not understand what they were doing. Then Tayeb came and I asked him about it. "They are preparing to burn in a few minutes," he said. I got closer to the group. By then, they were all undressed save for their underwear. They held the plastic bags in their hands and started climbing down to the water one by one. They also had planks of wood with them, I did not know what for. They stood for a minute or two in the water, their hands holding onto a small boat for balance. I approached a fifth guy who was with them. He looked clean and well dressed, in his mid-thirties, reserved, and was gazing with intensity at his friends. They wished him goodbye. Then, they started swimming in the dark toward a ferry that was at least fifteen minutes away.

"Why did you not cross with them?" I asked.

"I don't know how to swim. I do, but I don't know how to tread water," he said while looking at his friends, who by then had disappeared in the dark.

He then continued, "I want to buy a life jacket, but it costs 350 dirhams. The owner asked me for 250 dirhams, but I could not afford it. I offered 150 dirhams. I am going to make my own."

Tayeb later explained to me that once they reach the boat, they tread water for a while until it is about to leave. It is at this moment that they use their planks of wood. Each one lodges his in the side of the boat, near a porthole, and then stands on it for the entire trip. That way, they are crossing without the risk of being caught inside the boat. Once they are about a mile or even two from Tarifa, they jump in the water and cross all the way to the right side of the port where the customs and the guards are. They swim sidewise until they reach the shore, their plastic bags attached to them. Once on the shore, they dress and head toward Algeciras through the forest. They avoid the road in order not to be seen.

"What about the piece of wood?" I said. It did not seem too solid and thus too safe to me.

"That is the risk," Tayeb said. "If it breaks, you drown in the sea. No one will hear about it."

Indeed, in the many reports by human rights organizations and the United Nations, the deaths that are reported are of those who drown in a sinking boat. The harraga who fall from the side of the ferry while standing on a plank of wood may not be reported. For the harraga left back in the port, if those who have crossed are not heard from, it means they made it. They too become a success story—a narrative that sustains hope and strengthens resilience.

Conclusion

I have attempted to demonstrate that crossing—or lahrig (burning), as Moroccans metaphorically call it—obeys a logic, that is, a set of moral and cultural rules. It is neither an irrational act nor a suicidal one. It is rather a calculated effort to change one's life and condition. It is an act requiring hope, skill, courage, and an incredible amount of resilience matched only by despair that conditions at home will never improve—a condition itself described as "death" or "not a life."

The Moroccan harraga are new and tragic figures of globalization in Morocco. They emerged as a phenomenon in the 1990s, especially at the time when Mohammed VI came to power and immediately followed an aggressive neoliberal policy with a clear focus on Tangier. Most often from shantytowns and remote areas of the countryside neglected by the makhzen, these children come to Tangier in hopes of crossing to Europe. While neoliberal policies must have undoubtedly worsened the depth of Morocco's poverty, lahrig involves motives beyond escape. Not all poor people undertake the project, with its risk of perishing at sea, even though they, too, may want to cross. The harraga are children, and youth, determined to refuse a destiny they did not name.

The many harraga I spent time with want a different life, of course, but they also want to see the world (*nshûfu dâk al-danya*). The "illegality" of their desire to move is a transgression of both EU and Moroccan law. But listening to them, it becomes easy to see movement through their eyes: as a legitimate activity that would guarantee them freedom—freedom from hogra, freedom from exclusion and marginalization, freedom to satisfy their human curiosity about another land and another people that captivate their imagination.

The enterprise of lahrig is undoubtedly one fraught with danger and high risk, including that of death. Hence their other name for the project: "risking" (*riskiw*). But is this risk, in fact, greater than the ones already imposed on them? The harraga children are victims of the state's illegality, deprived of their right to safety, dignity, and protection as enshrined in international law that Morocco has itself signed. At home, they are burdens for the state. In a society with a high rate of unemployment even among the skilled and educated, the harraga are unwanted human labor that the state needs to waste in order to limit its own spending (on education, health care, etc.). As an excess of human labor, they are disposable. The state violates its laws by creating for them the conditions of extreme exclusion, even death. The state is indifferent to them; it practices a "let go and let die" policy. Hence, it ignores their activity and limits its policing to occasional taunts.

True, the harraga face an array of laws, police, and centers of arrestability on the other side of the sea—in Europe, especially in Spain. But the sea is their first and most immediate challenge—and an immense one at that, considering the high rate of migrants' death at sea. The totality of the challenge is more than daunting, and many Moroccans think of the harrag's enterprise as pure madness and an attempt at suicide. But for the harraga, crossing offers a way—and maybe the only way—to access a different life. Hence their motto "*rabha walla dabha*" (make it or die).

The harraga do not think about *dhabha* (death) first; they believe in *rabha* (gain) with all the energy of their youth. Hope is their main asset, and so is their incredible endurance and perseverance. Their hope has no parallel but in the despair they face at home. Hence the phrases I heard so many times: "death is here" or "do you call this a life?" Their hope is fed by stories (some heard and some witnessed) of harraga who really made it—stories of harraga who crossed the first day they arrived, of those who crossed a few months later, those who crossed and were sent back and crossed and were sent back again, and those who crossed after several years of attempts. Their night-time gatherings at the port are reminiscent of sailors on a ship, telling stories of adventures, many of them exaggerated. The symbols of fortune are the currency of their talk: cars, clothes, money, women. It is hope for a change in fortune that keeps them in the port for months and years; it is also that hope that makes some of them cross. In short, it is hope that makes them resilient.

Chapter 4

Transit "Illegality"

Danger lies in transitional states.

—Mary Douglas

One morning in March 2005, the Grand Socco in Tangier witnessed a demographic transformation: over five hundred young West Africans had gathered in its small plaza overnight. Neighborhood merchants, café owners, and residents were disturbed by the presence of this large number of West Africans. It was not good for business, they said. At first, they complained to one another and to the migrants themselves, before scolding them and urging them to disperse. They threatened to call the police to make the youth leave by force if necessary. With nowhere safe to go, the migrants refused to disperse and remained in the plaza.

The Grand Socco is a tourist district in old Tangier, famously described by William Burroughs as "the meeting place, the nerve center, the switchboard of Tangier."[1] It combines the flair of the traditional medina with a European accent that it has deservedly earned since colonial times. Now, in this age of globalization, one notices waves of European and American tourists, often seen sitting in cafés or just passing by, idly looking at the historic place. But the sudden presence of West Africans disrupted that, making it look more like a corner of black Africa.[2] I asked Mohamed, a local businessman, "Why should they disperse if they are just hanging out, harming no one?"

With his usual gentle smile, he replied, "They just gather here, many of them. It is not that we do not want them or do not like them, it is just that there are too many of them crowding the place. So, we want them to just disperse and not gather in one place. This is a small business area—when it's crowded, you cannot pass."

There was the unspoken that I did not need to formulate in a question: the issue of race. The place is crowded by Europeans coming in tourist buses—a normal scene in the Grand Socco, one that gives Tangier its color and flair. But the West African youth were not here to visit, to shop, or even to pass through. They were here because it was safe, or so they thought.

Mohamed continued, with the same smile, "One day, I was on the balcony. I could only see black heads at this terrasse right here—I could see nothing but black heads, so many of them, one next to the other. That is all I could see from the balcony: just heads, black heads, black heads, all black, next to each other in large numbers. What a scene to see from the balcony! I even thought about making a painting of that. Just a painting of black heads and nothing else. That would have been a very interesting painting!"

And he burst into laughter.

"What are they doing here?" I asked him.

"They are all waiting to go to Europe. It is odd to see those people here— their bodies are here, but their minds are in Europe. They live in a dream!"

The presence of West Africans in this city is relatively new. I did not notice them when I visited in June 2001. They arrived around 2005, when Mohamed first saw them from his balcony. By 2008, when I undertook this research, the presence of West Africans in Tangier had become a defining feature of the city. Through the lens of both Moroccan and European media, Tangier has since become a transit city for so-called illegal migrants preparing to cross to Europe.[3]

In this chapter, I seek to understand how the relatively recent presence of a large West African population has changed the cultural dynamics of a Moroccan society that had defined itself, since its independence in 1956, as Arab and, for the past two decades, as both Arab and Amazigh (Berber). More specifically, I seek to examine the status of these West Africans in a city that has in modern times associated itself with Europe, particularly Spain—its language, its culture, and, especially, its European whiteness. The chapter contributes to the study of the Mediterranean border, which has drawn in recent years noticeable attention in the press as well as in the field of anthropology.[4] West African migrants move, sometimes with astonishing speed, but in conditions drastically different from those of the Europeans who move to Tangier. Once they reach Tangier, they often find themselves "stuck" in the city—and by this I do not imply the absence of mobility. No, they are stuck as they wait, as they hope, for the possibility of further movement. Additionally, I seek to understand what I call transit "illegality," a legal condition that defines the migratory conditions of West Africans hoping to reach Europe. This chapter sheds light on the road to illegality undertaken by West African migrants, the dynamics of their mobility, and the discourse that justifies and even inspires many to consider a highly dangerous and risky enterprise. Moreover, the chapter also examines the conditions of the migrants in terms of their place within the city, how Moroccans relate to them, how they relate to Moroccans, and forms of violence that they endure even in the midst of sustained acts of compassion that make their stay in Morocco possible. By discussing these topics, I hope to ultimately show that in the twenty-first century, we find a new type of Europe's "illegals" at the very border between Europe and Africa.

Zone of Illegality

From the moment of his departure from "home," the West African migrant steps into a zone of illegality, made up of territories and frontiers of several nation-states. Obtaining a visa in a West African country[5] for travel to Europe "is as easy as getting one to the moon,"[6] as Congolese novelist Emmanuel Dongala once put it.[7] All of the migrants I encountered had not even bothered to apply for a visa and had opted instead to migrate without it. Their migration frequently includes activities in spaces that nation-states cannot or do not entirely control (and are instead controlled by actors such as smugglers, other migrants, and so forth). The zone of illegality is on the margins of the state, yet it still is within the domain of the state, where laws are rarely or loosely enforced. Scholars have examined the question of illegality most often in terms of status and conditions and rarely in terms of space. "Illegality" is often understood to be the transgression of state law, such as that governing borders,[8] shantytowns,[9] or areas at the intersection of several states.[10]

For a Nigerian such as Osman, who I met early on in my fieldwork, this space was entered when he left the borders of Nigeria in 2007. I met Osman with his friend Ibrahim at the cemetery of Marshan one Friday morning. Osman was thirty-eight years old, and Ibrahim was thirty-four. Both were the oldest migrants I had encountered during the entirety of my fieldwork. They told me they were university friends. Both held engineering degrees but were not interested in working in Nigeria because work there would not guarantee them decent lives. They made the plan to go to Europe—to Italy. They departed from Lagos by jeep with the help of Nigerian guides and made their way through Nigerian territory to Mali. They hired other guides called "Arabs" or "Bosos," who were Touaregs well acquainted with the desert roads that lead all the way to Algeria. They adopted the same logic of "illegal" crossing observed in other areas, such as on the U.S.-Mexico border, which consists of taking remote roads where state surveillance is least likely.[11] The Touareg guides helped them cross the Sahel, through the Algerian desert, all the way to Marghnia, a small city on the northwest side of Algeria on the border with Morocco. Once in Marghnia, they encountered the "government," a quasi-checkpoint of organized migrants stationed to help passing migrants in return for a small fee. Osman and Ibrahim each paid 120 euros before they were given "permission" to cross to Morocco and the information they needed to do so. The zone of "illegality," for Osman and Ibrahim, thus encompasses a huge swath of territory of various nation-states. Morocco is the last and easiest part of the zone. From Oujda, on Morocco's northeast border, they took the train to Rabat, where they met with the "consulate" for further assistance. Members of the "consulate" are appointed by the "government" in Maghniya. The "consulate" comprises a few Nigerian migrants who provide information about various aspects of migrant life— from information about housing to names and contacts of Moroccan guides, fees, and other services. Members of the "government" are not permanent but change every five years, taking as a model the presidency of the African Union. This leaves them free to move on to pursue their main goal, which is crossing to Europe.

This is the trajectory taken by all the Nigerians I met. Other migrants from western Africa follow slightly different trajectories through the unavoidable desert routes of Mali and Algeria.[12] This is a large zone that migrants navigate for months, usually between three and six months, and is one fraught with many dangers, from hunger and thirst to theft and even murder. In this zone, the migrant embodies "bare life," in the words of Giorgio Agamben.[13] In this zone, too, the migrant "can be killed, but not sacrificed"[14] since, by virtue of his trespassing and (in the view of the state) transgressing the border, he is killable because he does not belong as a citizen or even a lawful resident who can claim state protection. If "illegality can only be understood in relation to citizenship and belonging,"[15] the zone of illegality is one of "unwanted, un-belonging population." Often at these borders, as I was told, the police, especially the Algerian police, shoot at people. While the Moroccan and international media focus on the sensational deaths at sea, the deaths in the desert through thirst or at the hands of police or gangs are just as common, according to Osman and Ibrahim. They are rarely reported simply because they are not known.[16]

"Illegality," for the many migrants I encountered from 2008 to 2016, starts outside their nation-state, not inside it. All of them depart with a passport and with enough money to make the transition to Tangier with the intention of crossing into Spain. The decision to migrate is never spontaneous. It starts with an idea and develops into a project fed by media images of Europe and stories of success from relatives, friends, and acquaintances. In every city and now even in small villages, the successful migrant, the one who made it and then returns, is a model of success to be envied and imitated. As Henrik Vigh put it, for the case of Guinea-Bissau, "migration makes it possible to rapidly become someone."[17] Those who return make sure that their visit is as triumphant as possible. The material signs of success are displayed: nice clothes, watches, gifts, a car, and the most prized symbol of all—a "white girl" from "there" or a "white man" in the case of a woman migrant—in addition to exaggerated stories of success.[18] One can say that there is an entire migrant narrative fed by abundant literature and a repertoire of images of Europe.[19] Migrants have specific images and expectations about what awaits them in Europe. The symbolic signs of success, intertwined with the material signs, are not insignificant. Being in Europe offers status in and of itself; being in Europe with a job and home is a tremendous achievement. The ensemble of stories, of images and living models of people who have been Europeanized, offers incentive to take the risk and try one's fortune. It is not that people are necessarily running from something bad (as the media by and large depict) but rather that they are running *toward* something—a new life different from and, of course, imagined to be infinitely better than the one left behind, usually one of economic hardship and/or political instability.[20] To put the matter differently, the migrants I encountered were not refugees, they were not forced to leave, and life with its hardships and political instability was livable. Rather, acutely aware of the possibility of another life in Europe (imagined to be better), the decisive motive of young migrants is to explore the possibilities of living.

The idea of leaving Africa is rarely an individual one for West Africans. It is usually a family project.[21] Family members actively participate in its concretization by making serious sacrifices that include borrowing money and selling valuable belongings to make the trip possible. For the trip requires not only a will but also, in relative terms, the means to make it possible. From the point of view of those who depart and their families, leaving home is not an illegal activity, even though surely the trip is an arduous, difficult, and even dangerous one. Its outcome will undoubtedly change the condition of the migrant and that of all family members left behind. The belief that the departure will transform, for the better, the person departing and his or her family is so entrenched in the mind that it makes the trip worth every sacrifice and every danger—including death. For many, it is not only worth the risk but also an ethical obligation. One should do whatever is necessary for the good of oneself and one's kin.

"We are going to die anyway! Death is a destiny, you don't know where and when you die," Osman told me, as Ibrahim nodded approvingly.

All those I met left their home with a passport. That is to say, they departed legally. But the passport was not a means to conform to rules of migration. It was a document, an identity card, that the migrants knew they would need once they got to Europe. With a passport, they would be able to "regularize" their situation, meaning they would be able to have work papers, move freely, and come back home when needed. However, the migrants did not think about the laws of migration and often did not know them. They did not think that they were engaging in an illegal activity. They did not think of crossing as something "illegal." Crossing, from their point of view, was an activity that allows them to pursue a dream, to search for opportunities: in short, to grow and succeed in life. Crossing is an exercise of freedom.

Mohamed, a twenty-seven-year-old Senegalese man, arrived in Morocco when he was twenty-two years old, managed to get residency when he was twenty-six, and works in a street bookstore. Affable, he is well liked in the neighborhood surrounding the Boulevard of Mexico, which is arguably the busiest in Tangier. He still wants to go to Europe. I asked him, "You know crossing without a visa is illegal?"

He laughed and said, "When crossing, we do not think about the law, about visas, stamps, and all of that. We just want to cross."

"What will you do if you cross?" I asked.

"Once I am there," he said, "I will know how to impose myself."

"How?" I asked.

"I cannot say how, but when I am there, I will know," he told me, with unshakable confidence.

We became friends; he called me often just to say hello or to ask why I had not stopped by. One day he told me an Italian filmmaker was making a film about his life. He told me that some of it was already on YouTube. I was able to watch part of it.

The next time I saw him, I said, "You know that you are exposing yourself?"

"How?"

"They are exposing you as an illegal migrant. That is an illegal activity!" I warned him.

He did not like my words and said with a bit of irritation, "This will open doors for me, I have no intention of staying in Morocco."

Clearly, he does not recognize the legitimacy of the notion of the legality of illegality. Among all those West African (and Moroccan) migrants I encountered and those I interviewed, illegality is not a concept to be believed.

In July 2016, I met Abderahman, a migrant from Mali. He was hanging out with four companions from Cameroon. Even though he looked poor—his clothes were tattered, he had old plastic sandals that revealed damaged toes, and wore an old heavy hat even though we were in the middle of summer—he was articulate and spoke excellent French, sometimes uttering a poetic phrase indicating a high level of education. He stared at me intensely when he spoke, betraying a constant suspicion of me. At one point, it was not just suspicion but some kind of anger against me. I felt it had to do with the fact I was Moroccan. His next question confirmed that for me: "Tell me, why is Morocco not playing its role as an African country?"

"What do you mean?" I asked him.

"You know, Libya plays its role, today and in the time of Gaddafi," he said. "Africans could cross into Libya and out of Libya with no problems. They were no barriers like the ones Morocco has."

His friends nodded approvingly. One of them was big and tall, well built, and looked rough, but he smiled all the time, kindly, and said, "right, right" to express his total agreement with his companion. Abderahman continued speaking, clearly encouraged by the signs of approval from his companion: "You see? Libya opens the road, people can cross, and they cross all the time. The number of people who cross to Europe in one day exceeds the number who cross in one year from Morocco. But Morocco, which is an African country too, is not helping; it is closing the road. Why don't they open it?"

I felt obliged to say that Morocco is also under constraints and that there are international laws that Morocco is obliged to abide by. Maybe that is why

Morocco cannot open the border. The EU would not allow them, I said, purposely using "them" to distance myself from the decision makers and hopefully to reduce what seemed like hostility coming from my interlocutor.

Abderahman stared at me again and said, "You know what? One needs
to revolt, one needs to break the rules. That is what Libya does. Morocco
should open the border and allow people to cross. They cannot cage us here.
We need to depart."

"Well, that is considered illegal, I heard. Do you know that it is illegal?"
I said.

He batted my question away with an elegant turn of his hand and said,
still looking at me intensely, "Listen, this question of 'legal' and 'illegal' is
false. There is nothing illegal. Illegal is only what they decide is illegal, whatever deviates from their truth. They create the legal and the illegal. They
arrest you at sea and they say this is illegal and they want you to believe it."

"But you want to cross against the law, don't you think?" I asked.

"It is their law; they want you to believe in their law," he answered
promptly. "Searching for my chance in life cannot be decided by their law.
It is their law. And this is my life."

"You sound like a philosopher," I said. "What did you do in Mali? Did
you study philosophy?" I could not but ask.

He paused, and I thought he seemed flattered but also angry. He replied, "I do not go to the past. I locked up the past and threw away its keys
a long time ago."

"Who are the *they* you talk about?" I asked, going back to our conversation on "illegality."

"You know. I don't need to tell you." His friends laughed in unison.

For the many West African migrants I encountered during my fieldwork,
crossing is not a crime, not a transgression of a law, and therefore not something wrong or illegal. They see the police, at sea or at the border of Europe
or in Spain, as a force that curtails their freedom of mobility, not as enforcers
of the law. In many African countries, as in many places around the world,
police are synonymous with state repression and violence. For many of the
West African migrants, a police officer is the same anywhere, whether it be
Nigeria, Morocco, or Sweden. The police are just one of the many obstacles
to be encountered—and overcome—on the journey to Tangier and their goal.
The police are like the gangs or the bandits of the deserts—all of them constitute threats to their freedom of mobility, which is also a mobility for
freedom.[22]

The mobility of people should be seen as part of a larger set of activities, including the flows of goods in sub-Saharan Africa discussed in recent ethnographies.[23] These activities, Roitman argues, are "more than just an instrumentalist calculation, or a strategy to maximize economic gains or personal interests, they [Roitman's interviewees in Cameroon and Chad] explain this exercise in maintaining illegality in terms of licit behavior, or what they see as practices that, while not lawful (hence illegal) are nonetheless not forbidden. Illegal activities are rendered licit practice. Licit practice is in this sense understood to be what is allowed or what has become normal practice."[24] The many West African migrants I spoke to in Tangier and other cities in Morocco are not aware of EU migration law or even the 2003 Moroccan law that regulates migration and creates illegality. What they generally know is that borders are guarded by police, but once they overcome the police, they believe their destiny will change—they will find work, get papers, and have a life worth living—for themselves and for their families. In short, they will live dreams for which they are willing to sacrifice everything.

The Legitimacy of Illegality

Action, especially social action which involves a social relationship, may be guided by the belief in the existence of a legitimate order.

—Max Weber

It seems almost paradoxical to speak of legitimacy in relation to actions that are clearly illegal. The activity of crossing borders without official permission is not only unlawful but also harmful to the transgressor. Moreover, it may also be against the interests of the transgressor because of the hardship involved, the small chance of success, and the greater chance of death—in the desert, in the streets of a Moroccan city, at sea.[25] Legitimacy, as argued by Max Weber, is either subjective or defined by what he calls "interest situations."[26] Illegality itself is not possible without the state, since it is the law that creates the concept of illegality.[27] And since the state itself is the product of a process of "legitimizing the illegitimate,[28] what a state legalizes cannot always be seen as legal by other actors, in the same way that what a state legitimizes cannot always be seen as legitimate by other actors.

The death penalty or prohibitions of marijuana in the United States, for instance, are well understood: the death penalty is legal and marijuana is illegal in most states. To many, however, endowing the state with the right to kill and outlaw the use of marijuana is not legitimate. The "cardinal activity" of legitimizing the "illegitimate" does not always work—or at least not entirely and not all the time. Hence the advocacy of a part of civil society in the United States to abolish one and to lift the prohibition on the other. Such advocacy can reverse the prohibition, such as in Massachusetts for the death penalty and in Colorado for marijuana, which is further proof that the law is not set in stone but is changeable, abolishable, and so on.

Likewise, in the views of all the migrants I encountered, prohibitions against crossing are not legitimate—and not because they are at odds with the United Nation's Universal Declaration of Human Rights that asserts the right of the individual to leave his or her own country (1948)[29]—but rather because they are seen as an impediment to the freedom to pursue one's dreams. They all knew that crossing, despite the danger and the challenges, may (or rather will) change their lives for better. And it is these interests that make it legitimate.

But what about the chances of success and the chances of death, the dangers of the road and the sea that the migrant must cross? One may well think that the migrant's decision is not in any way rational and thus illegitimate. Leaving "home" for work always carries risk for any ordinary person, including the risk of getting hit by a car. But none of us gives this a thought. Instead, we think about going to work. The migrants do not think about risks; they think about reaching a destination.

"We are going to die anyway," Mousa, a twenty-four-year-old Nigerian man, told me. "It is a destiny; if I am destined to die at sea, I will die at sea. But I know that movement makes history. I need to move to pursue my dream."

The migrants know well that crossing is a difficult and even a dangerous endeavor—not just like leaving home for work. Yet the migrants I spoke with did not ponder the problems not yet posed by life. The question of whether they will make it once on the other side is not a question of immediate concern. As a rational human being, the migrant deals with problems that are either posited already—such as the need to attempt to cross—or those that are immediate, such as everyday living conditions. The migrants do not borrow problems, so to speak. The dynamics of being on the other side, from this viewpoint, are totally different—the migrants will deal with them when they get to them.

It is true, however, that their dreams are on the other side—and the other side is nothing but a world of illegality waiting for them. The West African migrants' ultimate goal is to cross to Europe. Among the hundreds I met and the many I interviewed, I did not meet one who expressed a desire to stay in Morocco. The destination is Europe. Once in Europe, they will study the situation again and will behave accordingly. The goal is to settle, obtain papers, and live life in a specific European country. Once in Europe, migrants deploy different strategies to "regularize" their situations.[30] Often a relative, a friend, or a parent will assist them. But the migrants' intellectual and physical energy, their high endurance, their resilience are all harnessed to accomplish one goal and one goal first: to cross.

Max Weber argued that "action, especially social action which involves a social relationship, may be guided by the belief in the existence of a legitimate order."[31] Weber also maintained that violations of the law can be justified "with varying degrees of good faith" as legitimate.[32] He further argues that that it is not impossible for the two orders—a legitimate order and an illegitimate one—to coexist.[33] There is a legitimate order, or rather a regime of mobility that precisely concretizes this fundamental human right to leave one's country or birthplace. The decision of migrants to leave is nothing but a willingness to exert the mobility of freedom—or the universal human aspiration for freedom *tout court*. Freedom consists mostly of mobility.[34] Bartholomew Dean notes that "rights of mobility provide individuals with a legal framework to realize their hopes."[35]

However, one might well ask, What happens when such rights of mobility are denied? They are still claimed as rights, and these denied rights that are claimed provide the individual with a moral framework, what I call the legitimacy of illegality. Migrants denied the right of mobility by the state (i.e., the EU and its proxy state Morocco) claim the right for themselves. Their very "illegality" is a full exercise in freedom—both freedom *from* (the EU and its laws) and freedom *of* (mobility). They surely see the enterprise as difficult but not illegal in the sense that the state or its legal scholars understand the concept. They also surely do not see themselves as "illegals." Each sees himself or herself as a complex person, part and parcel of a family and a social group. They do not think of themselves as illegal any more than I think of myself as legal.

Since 2003, Morocco has adopted a category designed specifically to name and thus curb the mobility of West Africans. Prior to this date, illegality (*hijra ghayr shar'iyya*) did not figure in the law, even though provisions about the stay of "foreigners" in the country existed.[36] Even today, "illegality" does not involve or suggest labor migration, as it does in the EU and the United States.[37] Instead, "illegality" in a country such as Morocco refers to transit "illegality," a liminal stage for the migrant. Here the last preparations to cross are made—and crossing may still take years, or never happen.[38]

The category of "illegality" is new in Moroccan law. Since colonial times (1912–56), Morocco has been a country of emigration, not a country of immigration. Emigration increased after independence, especially in the 1960s and 1970s, because of the dire need that western European countries had for human labor. The immigration law that created the "illegal" is relatively new, issued in 2003, and has been seen by scholars and human rights activists in Morocco as an imposition and an import of the EU, which is dictating law and attitude toward the sub-Saharan migrants and making a sovereign country play the gendarme of the EU and do its "dirty job."[39]

Race and Embodiment

My body is constantly perceived.

—Merleau-Ponty

In the meantime, the West African carries his body as a burden. His is the most visible body in the city of Tangier. Here, anonymity is a luxury he cannot attain. (Yet, in Europe, he is ironically called clandestine.[40]) The scene at the Grand Socco is revealing. Blackness makes the sub-Saharan body not only foreign but also unwanted in the city and in the country. By contrast, Europeans or rather Europeans' whiteness is perceived as part of the landscape of the city. It is valued, welcomed, and respected. The Grand Socco is often crowded with European tourists who arrive on buses. They gather, look around, and move on. They do not stay for hours. Their presence does not bother the owners of the shops or the residents, even when they do not buy anything—and often they do not.

Whether alone or in groups, the black body, in a city that looks akin to Europe, is seen as out of place, as polluting the city, to use the words of Mary Douglas. In a country that generally considers itself part of the Arab world and not Africa as such, the black bodies of the migrants constitute the outside of the outside of society, one that signals "Africanness" (which in Moroccan imagination is synonymous with blackness—hence the "neutral" name of *afāriqa*, Africans, to designate them).[41]

Didier Fassin argues that "the body is the primary site on which the imprint of power is stamped."[42] One can also argue, paraphrasing Fassin, that the body is the primary site on which the imprint of powerlessness is stamped. Within Moroccan society and not only in Tangier, the black body of the West African represents the ultimate racial other—one that is so impure that it endangers the body of the city and the national body as a whole. For it combines both what Morocco (and Moroccans) does not want to be in terms of race and in terms of class. And as such, the West African is relegated to the position of utter otherness that becomes, ironically, part of the definition of Moroccanness—Morocco is in Africa, but it is not black.

In everyday life, the West African body, commonly associated with the activity of begging, is not only at the city's margin but also outside of it. The Moroccan beggar, usually aged or handicapped, is still at home. The West Africans live on the outskirts of the city, many in a forest near Malabata, others in the forest near Rmila. "Moroccans do not want to rent to us," I was often told. "Native" residents of Tangier relate to Europeans, specifically Spaniards, linguistically and culturally.

Tangier distances itself from the inside of Morocco, considered *l'rubiya* ("the countryside"), and defines itself, more specifically, in relation to Europe. The architecture of its downtown, as well as the strong presence of the Spanish language among its population and even in its daily dialects, not to mention the strong identification with Spanish soccer teams (especially FC Barcelona and Real Madrid), creates a strong connection with Spain, as well as to a colonial past often remembered as a glorious time for the city.

"Why did they have to ask for independence?" a resident of the city told me. "With all the Western infrastructure that the city had, with its banks, schools, and hospitals, they could have kept it as an international city, and Tangier would have become another Hong Kong."

Now still part of Morocco, to which it often turns its back, the city faces the presence of "blackness" in the city. That the West African migrants represent dirt and pollution in the city (as well as in the Moroccan imagination) is evident in the stereotypes of them: they are considered dirty, smelly, infected with HIV or Ebola. Unlike a "black Moroccan" who has been Arabized,[43] the West African is not only an outsider but also transient, adding to both his marginality and his ability to pollute. Commenting on Mary Douglas,[44] Victor Turner states that "transitional beings are particularly polluting, since they are neither one nor another; or maybe both; or neither here nor there; or maybe both; or neither here nor there; or maybe even nowhere (in terms of any recognized cultural topography), and at the very least 'betwixt and between' all the recognized fixed points in space time of structural classification."[45]

If the black body of the West African migrant announces its polluting outsideness, the European white body adds to the modernity of the city, its cosmopolitanism, so to speak.[46]

"This is the Socco, it is famous; in the summer you come here and it is all Europeans, you can even see famous writers and actors sitting in cafés," Mostapha, a native of the city, told me with a sense of pride.

Yet, the visibility of the European body, or whiteness, is also invisible.[47] Europeans, unlike the West African, have the right to anonymity. They can pass unnoticed, or when they are noticed, as is often the case, it is never with hostility or defiance; it is a look of positive curiosity. For the body of the white European is in itself a narrative where both colonial and postcolonial histories are inscribed. Anonymity itself becomes a sort of privilege in this space. I myself walked unnoticed, especially the first few months, feeling a rare sense of freedom to be what I wanted to be. No one knew me; I did not fear to run into someone I knew who would see me through a specific lens. I was free to sit in whatever café, enter whatever hotel, go to whatever beach, and still be free from an inquisitor's gaze, never mind being asked to leave or to provide reasons for my presence in these places.

The West Africans have right to no such privilege, and have right to no rights except the right to bare life—to breathe—and not always, some would argue. In this country, they enjoy no rights of citizenship. They are perceived as a group, all the same. They have no individuality of their own: the individual is indistinguishable from the group, as it is often the case in racist stereotyping.[48] The West Africans are clearly out of place in this national space.[49]

Wearing a long white robe, Ahmed is a tall and dignified Senegalese man in his thirties. He sells African artwork, watches, and sunglasses. He goes to the mosque in the medina and is acquainted with people in the neighborhood. Even though he is in the city to look for opportunities to cross, he is also perceived as a merchant, making a living in an acceptable way. He saluted me in Arabic, "*Salâm 'alaykum!*" and so obliged me to respond, "*Wa 'alikum al-salâm*," thus establishing a certain relation that defies national belonging—mine and his—"we are Muslims" and thus "brothers." He does not express negatives views about Moroccans; neither does he complain about racism.

"Moroccans and Senegalese are Muslims, we have a long history, there are many Moroccans in Senegal who are married to Senegalese women, and there are Senegalese men married to Moroccan women. Morocco for us is like a second Mecca; many Senegalese come to visit [the tomb of Ahmad] Sidi Tijani [the founder of the Tijaniyyah Sufi order], buried in Fes. We Senegalese are not strangers in Morocco."

I looked at Ahmed: he indeed looked too rooted to be considered a migrant. I asked, "Are you here for business or do you want to cross to Europe?"

"My friends and I came here to look for a chance to go to Europe. But we do not do it like the other ones. We do not beg, never. We drive from Senegal to Morocco with merchandise. We do this all year long."

Not all Senegalese have the same experience as Ahmed. Because he had been coming to Morocco for five years, he seemed to have mastered a certain cultural code in Morocco that allowed him to connect and command respect. However, there are also those, even Muslim, who suffer from the same prejudices as other non-Muslim West Africans. Even professionals and students, I was told, are also often mistaken for "illegal" migrants and treated accordingly.[50]

Beyond the *Hogra*

When a West African arrives in Morocco, he has not only progressed on the road of illegality but also entered the land of the *makhzen*—a political and social order like any other: old, based on family alliances at the center of which is the royal family, claiming a Sharifian origin, an order rooted in a specific history,[51] and marked by a unique order of violence called *hogra*.

Hogra is the social, physical, and class violence that crosses classes but chooses its most significant victims among the lower strata of society, men and women, but more women than men, more children than women. The cultural violence that Moroccans identify as hogra was signaled by European travelers before the advent of colonialism.[52] As a system of violence that ensures the political order, it was modernized by colonial authorities and later by national governments. This is to say, when the West African migrant enters Morocco, he enters a domain of unspeakable violence—a domain devoid of rights, fraught with arbitrary rules. And he sees it as soon as he enters. Hogra shows itself in the clothes and faces of its victims. The last thing the West African desires is to be part of this societal fabric; the first thing the societal fabric desires is the body of a poor, black man or woman as a privileged space of its own violence.

Since hogra is structural, exerted from the top downward and from the center to the margins, the West African finds himself at the bottom and at the margin at the same time, and thus suffers its most hurtful effects from those who themselves have suffered at the hands of those above them—class-wise, gender-wise, or age-wise. This is not to say that all those who constitute the lowest classes have a particular taste for indulging in name calling, or gestures, or sheer physical violence. Rather, it is to say that the West African's contacts in everyday life are almost exclusively within those strata of Moroccan society where racism is predominant, where lack of respect for poverty is almost a rule. Hence, his daily contact is marked by everyday violence— mostly symbolic.

"Eighty percent of Moroccans are utterly racist," said Ismael, a well-built thirty-eight-year-old Nigerian with intelligent eyes and a determined will to cross. He exuded confidence and resoluteness. "Very few are not, very few times we meet people like you," he said with a tone of honesty.

I met Alex in front of Rif Hotel. He was nineteen years old, from Gambia, and had just arrived from Mellila, an autonomous holding of Spain northeast of Tangier. His friend died there; he fell from a fence. Alex returned to Tangier to recover himself; he was deeply saddened by the death of his friend. He was dressed well, in the fashion of youth. I asked him, "How are the Moroccans with you?"

"Racists. I can tell you that honestly. You are not the kind of guy I would like to lie to."

"In what way are they racist?"

"They despise us, they treat us like nothing, they call us 'azzi."

Alex told me he had left Gambia with his friend three years back; he was then sixteen. They stayed two and a half years in Libya, until the fall of the Gaddafi regime. They then came together to Morocco, spent a few months in Tangier, and left for Mellila, to cross the Mediterranean to Europe. He went on to explain his position in Morocco: "We are all Blacks [here]; we do not discriminate against each other despite differences in tongues and in religions. But in Morocco, they call us ʿazzi. The Moroccans who mistreat us most are the ones who never left and have never been outside of Morocco. Those who have are nice to us. So are the Muslim ones. They treat us nicely. We are all one because we worship the same God. Good Muslims know this. But 60 percent of Moroccans are not Muslims, they just say they are. But 80 percent of Moroccans are racists."

"How about the police? Are they racists also?" I asked.

"Sometimes I tell myself the police are doing their duty and sometimes I feel they hate us."

Racism was the most common complaint I heard from West African migrants. Osman, my Nigerian interlocutor, explained, "Yet, they know and often admit that not all Moroccans are racist—but are clearly overwhelmed by the general feeling of hate and discrimination."

West Africans tend to regroup together and share their lives irrespective of faith or national origin. As James Clifford put it, "A negative experience of racial and economic marginalization can also lead to new coalitions."[53] This has also been noticed by Abdelmalek Sayad in the case of Maghrebis in France.[54] Whenever I met West Africans in small groups of four or more, it was rare that they were from the same country. Often, they were friends from Nigeria, Mali, Gambia, Ghana, and other West African nations. Even religion or language did not seem to get in the way of the coalitions they made. These coalitions provide them safety and comfort.

In Tangier, the most intolerant to the presence of the West Africans are those on the bottom and at the margins—the gangs, the poorest of the poor, children, and occasionally women. The migrants first suffer from insults, launched in the forms of jokes and accompanied with giggles and laughter: ʿazzi, kaḥlūsh, ʿantiz, but also, recently, Ebola, dirty black (sale noir), slave (ʿabd), or Mamadou. "We call them azizos," Chakib told me, laughing—his laughter aimed at inviting mine. Azizos is clearly a Europeanized, westernized form of ʿazzi, which is synonymous with nigger. In this very westernized name, there are the two contrasts: the Western (white) and the African (black). All the names invented to designate West Africans, specifically in terms of color, are meant to be humorous and provoke laughter. In itself, this racial and racist naming is an expression of power, as naming often is.[55]

But their humor expresses not only the power to name but also the power to humiliate. *Azizos* involves what Bergson calls an "inversion"[56] made in the name itself, transforming it into a Western name while still keeping its semantics to contrast with the inversion—and in so doing pretending that black is white.[57]

Because hogra is social and historical, what is exerted against the West Africans is not local violence as such but rather a new form beyond it. It is exerted from within the body of society against a foreign body—black to boot. Moroccan society also has its "others." It has categorized them and used a plethora of names to define them. To cite a few examples, one finds the name of Jebli (especially in Tangier, these are the Arabized Berbers of the Rif mountains). There is also the Lakḥal (usually black Moroccans who are recognized as part of the fabric of society after a "process of assimilation" that counters their "sub-Saharien affiliation"[58]) and the Yhoudi (a Jew).[59] There are negative views and attitudes associated with all these groups.

But the West African migrants are newcomers, and because they are newcomers, they are not part of the dynamics of the hogra. The dynamics of the hogra are between Moroccans. The West African, in the eyes of his *haggara* (bullies), does not qualify. His rights are nonexistent; hence, "crimes" against him are not punishable. It is another form of "bare life," except here it is not the state as such that makes violence execrable but everyday contact with people who are themselves victims of the hogra. For the link between the hogra and its "beyond" consists of the fact that hogra is exerted from the more powerful to the less powerful. And so those with minimal power in society exert it against those who are on the threshold of society or rather those, like the West Africans, who are literally outside of it—without being desired or invited to be part of it. "Damn you, you overpopulated the country [*Allah yan'alkum 'ammartou 'lina la blad*]!" I heard one visibly poor Moroccan shout as he passed a few West Africans, who of course could not understand him or even hear him on a busy street.

The West African's body is the most visible in the city; it is also the most vulnerable, unprotected by the 2003 law that aims at excluding it, and this makes the violence against the black body legitimate. He is one, everywhere, with no individuality of his own. As Sarah Ahmed noticed about race, "Bodies come to be seen as alike."[60] He has no stories worth hearing, dehumanized and stripped of dignity or the ability to have one. Yet, behind or rather inside every black body, there are stories of suffering, of endurance, of hope, of resilience, and of grand dreams whose chances of success are relatively small—because of the wall of laws Europe built once it realized that even the dangers of the ocean, the desert, and the high risk of death do not deter someone who has already decided that the life he lives is not worth living. The sole value of this life is to be used to cross. A real gamble: if it is lost, so be it. If the migrant wins, he will win big—a new life in a land of rights and opportunities. So he thinks.

Space and Racial Violence

It has been argued that urban protest is often about space.[61] This protest, which is in itself a form of struggle, can be undertaken to liberate space from domination or to defend it from contamination, as with the case at hand. Protests can also aim at claiming the right to occupy a space. David Harvey and others argue that "the demand to liberate space from this or that form of domination and reconstitute it in a new image, or to protect privileged spaces from external threat or internal dissolution, lies at the center of many urban protest movements and community struggles."[62] Since 1990s, Tangier has become a space of protest by Moroccans against West Saharan Africans. My research assistant, Chakib, told me that when the West Africans began to arrive en masse in 2005, they were subject to intense harassment, even violence. Children followed them, laughing at them, calling them names, and throwing stones at them. Men, usually gang members, thieves, and "bad boys," stole their cell phones and jewelry. "You know blacks like to wear gold and silver jewelry," Chakib told me, "so the Moroccans used to bully them and take their valuable belongings, the poor ʿazzis were afraid, they could do nothing." In many ways, at first, these acts of theft and harassment were in themselves a protest against the presence of West Africans. They were meant to dissuade them from coming to the city and sharing its space. As stated above, the West African migrants, because of their race, their transient status, and their illegality (confirmed or assumed), were perceived by and large as polluting a city whose inhabitants (tanjawa) generally see themselves as not part of Africa.

Yet the newly arrived West Africans were not living in the city. Most lived in the forest of Malabata. The city was important to their survival, however, as it is to the countryside. In it, they could make a living, mainly by begging, and inquire about ways to cross the Mediterranean, making contact with Moroccan guides who are usually fishermen in the port. The intensity of violence made the city a dangerous space for West Africans. As a strategy for survival, they started to move in groups.

Chakib told me, "One day a group of ʿazzis were attacked next to the Corniche by a group of Moroccans at daytime. The ʿazzis fought back, they were strong. The Moroccans retreated and started throwing stones at them. The ʿazzis threw stones back. I saw with my own eyes a big ʿazzi throwing a stone with his full force, and hit a Moroccan in his head, his head was fractured. From that time onwards, the Moroccans started not to mess with them, and ʿazzis imposed themselves. Now, no one talks to them."

Chakib meant no one attacks them. Generally, that is the case; physical violence against them has diminished. Moroccans know that the West Africans fight back and that they are tough. However, attacks of a different type began, in the form of social protests.

On December 8, 2013, in the neighborhood of Al Irfane 2, hundreds of Moroccans, holding the portrait of the king, took to the streets protesting against the blacks who now live in their neighborhood.[63] The protesters preemptively denied any accusation of racism: some held a banner that said, "*Nous ne sommes pas des racistes*" ("We are not racist").

Considering that several media outlets as well as human rights organizations regularly denounce racism against West Africans, the Moroccan protesters claimed that the problem was not the presence of West Africans in their neighborhood but rather their practices that make the neighborhood unsafe. They claimed that the West Africans traffic in drugs, engage in prostitution, own arms, and do not respect the inhabitants of the neighborhood. They urinate on roadside walls even as women and children pass by— which, if it is true, is not only a practice of West Africans.

The space of the neighborhood has thus become the object of struggle between the West Africans who inhabit it and the Moroccans who hope to exclude them from it. As Allen Feldman says in a different context, "Space become(s) power and an animated entity."[64] The neighborhood is the focus of a power struggle between Moroccans and West Africans. Its Moroccan residents fight to keep it "purely" Moroccan, something for "us," from which "the other" should be excluded. In fact, the protest is also about resisting demographic change and not letting the neighborhood become black. The West Africans, who once lived exclusively in the forests outside the city, have started to make a place for themselves within the city and share its space as residents. In other words, they too claim the space of the neighborhood.

On June 24, 2015, Moroccan newspapers reported news of several violent attacks against West Africans in a Boukhalef quarter.[65] It was reported that the major problem in this neighborhood is what is called squatting—mainly the fact that migrants move to occupy apartments of Moroccans living abroad. The newspapers often show sympathy to the plight of West Africans. They reported that in this neighborhood on the outskirts of the city, sub-Saharan Africans (as they are called by local press) occupy empty apartments that belong to Moroccans. In the news report, the West African seems to have added to his illegality by an illegal act of invading and occupying Moroccan houses and apartments. In other words, not only does he invade the public space of the city (believed to be owned by the tanjawis and only them), but he also invades private homes.

It seems from this and other print and social media reports of similar events that there is a cultural misunderstanding at play. On one hand, the migrant homeless cannot understand the logic of property, especially when he is sleeping outside, not far from unoccupied apartments whose landlords live abroad. On the other hand, the landlord, his family, or simply the neighbors cannot understand the logic of the homeless migrant who occupies an apartment not his. The migrant appears to them to exhaust all the possibilities of "illegality"—he is illegal in a country, in a city, and in an apartment. The irony is that the African migrant occupies the apartment of another migrant who is absent because he is in exile in Europe.

High tension and even physically violent conflicts have erupted, often when the migrant comes back to find his apartment occupied or when members of his family in Morocco come to know about the situation. Moroccans in small groups, it was reported, went to the neighborhood and attacked West Africans. The police refused to force the West Africans to evacuate, and when violent clashes erupted, they refused to intervene. Several West Africans and Moroccans were injured and taken to the hospital. One day, the clash ended with the killing of a young Senegalese man and the injury of two Ivoirians who subsequently died in the hospital.[66] It was only then that the authorities summoned the police force to evacuate the squatters.

By the time I made it back to Tangier in June 2016, the affair of squatting was over. I visited the neighborhood several times. There seemed to be far fewer West Africans than described in the newspapers I read—no more than two dozen compared with the 800 reported. Most likely, they relocated amid the danger they felt in the neighborhood.

Several young West Africans had gathered next to the last building on the development's fringe. They were from Cameroon, and only one of them was from Mali. One of them was selling cigarettes; another had a shoe-shining table set up. Their version of what happened was entirely different.

"I heard that West Africans squatted," I said.

The tall, robust guy from Cameroon who seemed to be in charge of their small business operation said, "Yes, we were in the forests and Moroccans came to us and told us there are empty apartments here, why don't you just live in them? We did. It was the Moroccans who told us to move on. We would not just move in if the Moroccans did not tell us."

"Where do you live now?"

"We live in the forest, in Rmila."

While I was interviewing them, a Moroccan resident came to buy cigarettes. He told me he had lived in several African countries and they treated him well. I told him, "Please take care of them!" and he replied, "Of course. They are good people." He bought the cigarettes and kissed the salesman on each cheek, in the Moroccan manner that conveys feelings of love and brotherhood.

My friend, Samir, who owns an apartment in the same neighborhood, confirmed this version of the story. While opening his apartment, he told me, "Listen, the poor ʿazzi [using the racist term, which he combined with 'poor,' meskine, to express his sympathy for the West African migrants] would not dare to enter an apartment which is not his. They are foreigners here; they are scared. Moroccans are nasty [waʿrin], you know! What happened to them, poor things, is that brokers made money out of them, forced the doors of the apartments of Moroccans living abroad, and started renting to them cheap."

Conflicts between West Africans and Moroccans do not first erupt over ways of life but rather about the space they share. In that space, ways of life then become a problem to justify the conflict. Meanwhile, civil society and human rights organizations organize protests in favor of West Africans.[67] This means that the conflict between West African migrants and Moroccans translates into a divide between Moroccans who reject the presence of West Africans and Moroccans who are not hostile to their presence and may even welcome it. It is also a divide between Moroccans with racist views and those who have a more accepting attitude and more empathy toward the West African migrants. Two campaigns have been launched to educate Moroccans and sensitize them to the issue of race and especially the presence of West Africans. The first began on March 21, 2014, and was called "*Je ne m'appelle pas Azzi*" ("My name is not Azzi"). The second, launched in May 2017, is called "Zero Racism, We Are All People." However, these efforts, sporadic and few, have very limited effects. The lives of West African migrants remain marked by daily racism and violence.[68]

Muslim Compassion and the Strategy for Survival

> You shall give due alms to the relatives, the needy, the poor, and the traveling alien.
>
> —Quran

I was at the cemetery one Friday morning on June 2009, interviewing a group of four West Africans, when a Moroccan lady came and started handing them bills of 20 dirhams each ($2.50, which is generous by Moroccan standards). She skipped me and gave a bill of 20 dirhams to the person on my right. I was wearing a shirt, sportswear, and sandals. My attire did not distinguish me from my interviewees. The only thing that did was my skin color.

"Hey, Madam," I said, "why did you skip me? You won't give me something?"

She looked at me, getting my joke, and said, smiling, "*Ma baynaash fikk* [your need is not evident]!"

After she left, I continued interviewing the group, and most of my questions were answered by Osman. Given the happy event of the woman's gifts of money, we started speaking about how they make a living in Morocco. Osman told me, "We come here to beg. When you are away from home, you do whatever to survive. Here I beg. I have a degree in engineering, but I cannot work here, so I beg. I am incognito here, so I do what I do to survive." He exuded dignity as he spoke. "In Nigeria, I would rather kill myself than extend my hands to someone for money."

The cemetery is a good spot where one can see Moroccans displaying compassion to the poor, with a clear preference for foreigners (i.e., West Africans). It was in the cemetery that another young lady was giving money to a group of them when a Moroccan teenager came and said, "What about me?" She looked at him and said, "Those are the ones who first deserve it. You are here in your country, you have a home to go back to, they are here as foreigners, poor things, far from home." Most West African migrants I interviewed said that they lived on begging and that they made between 30 and 70 dirhams a day; in the summer, with the arrival of tourists and Moroccans living abroad, they can make up to 200 dirhams a day.

At the Cervantes Institute, where I was taking Spanish classes, the students suggested a party to celebrate the end of the semester. The teacher decided to organize it and asked for contributions. Each contributed 50 dirhams, and it was only at the end that the teacher realized that we had much more than we needed. Instead of giving us the money back, she suggested to give it as *sadaqa* to the "Africans."

I asked, "Why the Africans and not just poor people, whether African or not?"

The teacher responded, "Africans are poor people. They come here to cross and they get stuck. It is better we give them the money than give it to others who may not need it. Africans [*msakin*, poor things] need it most!"

Then she repeated the same discourse about Moroccan beggars "being rich but in disguise" that I had heard many times, including once on national television and from time to time in a news article about the phenomenon of the "the rich poor":[69] "The beggars we see are not poor; they fake it. Begging is a business for them. The government did research and found out that some of them own three storehouses, and another one was so rich that they found cans of old money buried in his hut."

Compared with West Africans in New York City, as described by Paul Stoller,[70] West Africans in Tangier live an utterly miserable life depending almost exclusively on mendacity to survive. The difference between the first and the second can only be explained by the difference between New York, a global metropolis of the utmost importance in the world economy, and Tangier, which, after all and despite recent progress, qualifies as a Third World economy. Even compared with Western Africans in an African city, such as Brazzaville, described by Bruce Whitehouse,[71] the West African population of Tangier lives in conditions not enviable by any standards. They live on no trade, with very few exceptions, and are single men, with only a handful of women in the city. But the main difference consists of the fact that the West Africans in New York are settled, while those in Tangier are decidedly transient. Tangier for them is only a liminal place where they have to make the preparations to cross. While they are doing so, they live on mendacity in a country with a high rate of unemployment.

Aware of the Islamic notion of sadaqa, the migrants often pretend to be Muslim.[72] They invent Muslim names for themselves (such as Ibrahim, Mousa, Boubker) and learn basic Moroccan phrases that they use to appeal to the compassion of passersby: "*Sadaqa*, please, may Allah bless your parents [*i'tini sadaqa allah yarham biha al walidin*]!"

In early Islam, sadaqa was meant to be given to the poor and the destitute regardless of whether they were Muslim or not. The idea that sadaqa should go only to Muslims emerged later. And so a beggar, in medieval Cairo, for instance, might pretend to be Muslim to benefit from alms.[73]

The cemetery is only one location where West Africans "make a living." The rest of the week, one sees them on every corner of the streets, in the boulevard, in front of bakeries, or in coffee shops, asking for sadaqa in Moroccan Arabic, appealing to the compassion of believers.

This does not mean that those who give are always devout Muslims. Someone who is not devout might still believe that giving is a work of good (*khir* or *hasana*) that will not go unrewarded. Stories of those who do good and encounter good are common in Moroccan culture: A man was a drunkard, a story has it. One day, a beggar knocked at his door, asking for sadaqa. The drunk man had nothing to give. He looked around and all he saw were empty wine pitchers [*kidh*]. He picked one up and opened the door and gave it to the waiting beggar. The following day, a friend of the drunkard knocked at his door bringing with him ten pitchers of good wine as a gift.

The drunkard was a Muslim, and drinking wine is a sin for most Muslims. Yet, he was still compassionate to the plea of the needy and the poor. On the one hand, he sins and thus transgresses one of God's important commandments, "thou shalt not drink," yet he also observes one of God's equally important commandments, "thou shalt give due alms." But since he was drunk, he did not give in hope of receiving a reward but rather in compassion for the poor and the needy. The story is also meant to demonstrate the veracity of the Hadith according to which "God rewards an act of charity with ten better ones." Clearly, ten filled pitchers of wine are better than empty ones!

In Islam, there is the belief that those who have are obligated to help those who do not have. Sadaqa thus is voluntarily giving alms consisting of "small acts of kindness performed without fanfare."[74] The West Africans regularly receive sadaqa in the form of money, food, and even clothes. These donations may be significant. I have met several West Africans who sleep in a Moroccan garage for free. Others rent in a popular and highly populated neighborhood called Masnana. Yet, as noted, many continue to live in forests. Whether in a garage, in a small room in a poor neighborhood, or in the forest, their living condition underscores their transitionality.

Conclusion

The topic of West African migration at the border of Morocco and Spain is a new one. Despite the fact that this crossing has become a phenomenon and has spilt so much ink on the pages of international media, the field of border studies of the Mediterranean area is in its infancy. Migration studies have focused on migration within European countries and rarely on the borders and even more rarely within sending countries. In this chapter, I hope to have contributed not only to the study of a border but also to the study of migration within a country of emigration, Morocco. Because of the task at hand, I sought not to focus on migration policy but rather on migration as a dynamic that changes the city. By focusing on what I call "transit illegality," I looked at how West African migrants manage their condition within what I call "the zone of illegality," including in the city of Tangier. Transit illegality, as I sought to demonstrate, is not a permanent illegality typically associated with labor;[75] it is an "illegality" that has been constructed as such, not via the nation-state but rather via the EU policies that set "the cause of fighting illegal immigration" as one of the defining features of diplomacy with the countries of the southern Mediterranean. In the so-called age of globalization, "illegal immigrants" are not only those who live within the territory of the nation-state in question but also those who live in transit, outside it, in neighboring nation-states of the so-called global South. To put the matter differently, Morocco, once a migrant-sending country, has now turned, because of neoliberal dynamics, into a receiving country but one that hosts the EU's "illegal" migrants.

Chapter 5

Europeans in the City

We "good Europeans," we also have hours when we allow
ourselves a warm-hearted patriotism, a plunge and
relapse into old loves and narrow views.

—Nietzsche

In 1956, barely two months after the declaration of Tangier's independence in April, Paul Bowles, then a renowned resident of the city, not to mention an internationally known literary figure—albeit a less known (but maybe more original) musical composer—published a piece in the *Nation* called "View from Tangier," later reprinted under the title of "The Death of a Cosmopolitan City: Tangier."[1] From the outset, he depicts a scene in the Soco Chico with a sense of pessimism: "Walk down into the Soco Chico any night. In the little square lined with cafes you can see that in fact, if not officially, the integration of Tangier with the rest of Morocco has already taken place. Instead of the customary assortment of European tourists and residents elderly Muslims in *djellabas* [traditional robes] and native Jews from the nearby streets of the Medina, you are likely to see sitting at the tables no one but young Moslems in European dress—mostly jeans."[2]

Bowles then wonders, "And the Europeans who used to be here every night, where are they?"[3] "They know better," he continues, "than to wander down into part of the town where they are not wanted."[4]

The term "cosmopolitan" in Bowles's piece is not defined, but it seems to refer to the presence of Westerners in the city and to connote that this presence is positive. He mourns not only the absence of this population, but rather the presence of the local population, irrespective of their jeans (a modern dress) or their youth (the modernly preferable age). It is their *nativism* that is the marking point. "Not being wanted" is the negation of cosmopolitanism and "contrary to natural right"; this inhospitality is a defining feature of the people of Immanuel Kant's[5] "Barbary Coast": "The inhospitable behavior of coastal dwellers (as with the Arab Bedouins), who regard their proximity to nomadic tribes as a justification for plundering them, is contrary to natural right."[6]

Yet between 1956 and 1996, Tangier's cosmopolitanism, as understood by Bowles, remained alive and well.[7] Bowles himself remained in the city long enough to see that the European and American population did not decrease as a result of decolonization but rather stayed on. And before he died in 2001, he witnessed its notable increase, which included not only the usual "elite" but also people from the middle and working classes. In short, the European population has diversified (in terms of class and gender) since the early 1990s. The experience of residing abroad—an easily accessible situation during the earlier colonial period—has become possible again and is even easier—much easier, as I will show—in the so-called age of globalization.

The concept of cosmopolitanism, now associated with globalization, is one of the most problematic ideas one finds in the discourse of social science. The first to acknowledge its ambiguities and its highly problematic use(s) are its own users. Jacques Derrida notes that "the concept is today as problematic as it was in the time of Kant."[8] Despite its ambiguity, *cosmopolitanism* has a few semantic elements that seem if not invariant then at least common in its usage. Over the past two decades, it is chiefly associated with elitism—a status enjoyed by businessmen especially but also writers, artists, diplomats, tourists—in short, all those who can afford to leave "home." Second, it connotes detachment. Not only are the "cosmopolitan" elite able to leave home, but they also have a detachment that enables them to embrace the entire world as their home, and not only the second place in which they choose to reside. Thus, as Martha Nussbaum puts it, their "allegiance is to the world wide community of human beings."[9] Similarly, Amanda Anderson argues that cosmopolitanism "denote[s] cultivated detachment from respective forms of identity."[10] Living somewhere, with a commitment to their place of residence as part of the entire globe in which they live, makes them (so we are told) transcend the narrow frame of the nation-state, the dominant polity in the twentieth century whose death has been announced too early, too loud, too often, and without weeping since at least the 1990s.[11]

Many of those who theorize cosmopolitanism focus on the wealthy, the privileged, a certain class to whom the world belongs,[12] or interrogate their own lives to demonstrate its existence.[13] The idea of cosmopolitanism itself is an elitist concept; it connotes a certain way of life that only money can buy. To be cosmopolitan is to be not only modern but modern plus. And that plus consists precisely of a privileged worldly experience.

While the aim of this chapter is to examine European migration to the city of Tangier, I also test the idea of cosmopolitanism in my discussion. My goal is not to draw a general conclusion about the validity of the concept (or lack thereof) but rather to use it as a guiding principle in my discussion of "white" European mobility. Cosmopolitanism is conceived both as a way of life and as a concept that supposedly accounts for a phenomenon of our time, not the crossing of cultures as such (which is as old as humanity) but rather the transcending of one's nation to embrace the entire world as one's home. I aim to show these contradictions as I discuss the motives, motivations, and conditions of Europeans who settle in the city as migrants.

Encountering Race, Again

Doing ethnography with West Africans and Moroccan *harraga* did not pose any exceptional or unpredictable challenge, and I can even say that it was relatively easy. The contacts were, at the beginning, initiated by them. Walking along the Boulevard Mohammed V (or, simply, the Boulevard) was sufficient to encounter several West African migrants asking for money and willing to talk if I asked them questions—though sometimes they would put a price on their conversation as soon as they discovered my interests and project. Harraga, by contrast, spoke more freely (at least to a Moroccan) and did not ask for money to talk. The Corniche—especially the port area—was a mine of information. The relative challenges pertained more to the difficult conditions of the harraga's lives, which one needs to share with them, if only temporarily, to grasp. For instance, one needs to withstand the discomfort of hanging out in the port area, especially where they gather and rest—that is, on the fishermen's nets hopping with all kinds of bugs, most of which you can feel on your body but not see.

Encountering a European is a totally different matter, especially for a native. European residents tend to be suspicious of Moroccans, especially the ones they do not regularly encounter. Talking to them about their lives, their motives, their reasons to move and settle, their everyday contact with Moroccans is asking to "see them," as Jean-Paul Sartre would put it, and Europeans do not like to be seen. As Sartre said a long time ago, "For three thousand years, the white man enjoyed the privilege to see and not to be seen; he was a pure gaze."[14]

Indeed, anthropological research, historically carried out by "white" men, focused on the native, which, by definition, is not white. The West African migrants are accustomed to interrogation by anyone, including ordinary Moroccans. *Why are you here? Why do you want to cross to Europe? What do you expect to find in Europe?* These are questions the West Africans have answered hundreds (if not thousands) of times since they left home. They have been the object of repeated documentaries and media reports since they emerged as a phenomenon in the early 1990s. Not the Europeans. Their move to and within the city, especially a city such as Tangier, is considered the most natural action. Their presence may be celebrated, but their movement goes unremarked upon and unquestioned.[15] Tangier is the creation of Europeans—both its physical reality, the materiality of the city itself, its boulevards, its cafés, its streets, its names, and even the contours of the city, as well as its myths, that is, the ensemble of images, narratives, and feelings surrounding the city. To be interrogated by a native is fantastical, a cause of real suspicion.

My early efforts to meet, interview, and hang out with Europeans were totally unsuccessful. The American way, which consists of introducing yourself, by saying your name and putting out your hand toward a stranger you meet, increased their suspicion and appeared to strike them as bizarre. One needs to be introduced; that is the custom. My Spanish landlady in the city was not of much help when I asked her. She was engrossed with preparations to return to her native Barcelona. An acquaintance I had known years back in Paris, Mohamed (now a real estate agent in the Casbah itself), seemed to know all the European residents of that attractive neighborhood.

"Twenty-five thousand euros," he said, when I asked him to introduce me to European people he knew—and he seemed to know them all by virtue of both his profession and his residency in the Casbah.

"Twenty-five thousand euros for what?" I asked, puzzled, not sure I understood what he meant, uncertain whether or not he was serious.

"Twenty-five thousand euros to help you with your research and introduce you to all the Europeans I know."

"Twenty-five thousand euros is a lot of money," I said. "Where am I going to get you this huge amount?"

"You are writing a book, are not you?"

"Yes," I said, confirming what I had already told him.

"Well, you will be writing a book. It is fair that I get some of the profit from your book if I help you," he said, convinced that academics make a hefty amount of money out of the books they write.

Convincing him that this is not the case was more challenging than convincing a harrag that life is not a paradise in Europe.

I had a breakthrough in meeting one very helpful person, a middle-aged French woman by the name of Chantal. We met in Café Rif, a place where Europeans and Moroccan *assimilés* ("French mimics"[16]) hang out. The place had been reinvented by a French Moroccan artist, Yto Barrado, and had become a meeting spot, especially for francophone, rather elite, youth and French residents of all ages. In her early forties, Chantal settled in Tangier with her two children after a divorce. She did not work, but she supported herself and her children thanks to alimony and child support from her former husband, as well as additional financial support from the French state. With her French income, she led a comfortable life in a city that, despite locals' complaints about the cost of living, is still affordable to a European with an income, however modest. She was, then, a full-time mother, but she had hobbies that consisted mainly of activities in the city, including writing a blog that updated Europeans (and others) about local cultural activities of all sorts. There, she regularly introducing her readers to French residents she interviewed.

At first, Chantal did not seem suspicious of me and volunteered information freely. I spoke to her about my research, as well as my difficulties in meeting people, and asked for her help, a request she promised to grant.

From the outset, Chantal was very critical of Europeans. "They are racists," she said.

"How so?" I asked.

"They are here in Tangier," she said, "they come to Morocco, and they want things to be done their way."

I asked her to explain this to me.

"Do you want concrete examples?" she asked.

"Yes, I do."

"Well, French employers criticize Moroccans in front of Moroccan employees. They [couldn't] care less about what they think or feel. A Moroccan maid who is paid 50 dirhams [$5] a day, if she leaves five minutes early, they take 5 dirhams [50 cents] out of her pay. Another Moroccan maid was harshly scolded because they found her praying in the house."

Chantal went on, "We, the French, are racists. They taught us from [an] early age to fear the Arab and Islam. This is why it is difficult for you to meet Europeans," she said, addressing my concern that I had found it difficult to do so.

Chantal used categories that are common currency among the French in the city and in France itself. "Arab" is a typical postcolonial French category used to refer to any Maghrebi (another postcolonial category).[17] In Morocco itself, the categories used by people to refer to themselves are, first, the national category: Moroccan. Other labels are also used, depending on the context: outside the city, regional categories such as Fassi, Casawi, Tanjawi, and so on are used. Inside a city, the denomination is different: one is known by one's last name, tribal name, craft, father's name, and so forth. This is a person's *nisba*, which, as Clifford Geertz point outs, is context dependent.[18] Other identifiers such as Chalh, Sousi, Jebli, Rifi, and so on, referring to a particular ethnic/racial group,[19] can also function as a nisba.

As it is context dependent, today the nisba reflects changes in the global world that are also reproduced locally. Within a city—say, Tangier—a man is the son of so-and-so, he is marked with a family name, yet since he shares that with his brothers, he may bear other denominations, such as "the American one," "the French one," or "the Saudi one" (if he resides in the United States, in France, or in Saudi Arabia), differentiating him from his brothers who reside in Tangier or Casablanca. The nisba can also relate to a world event or a global movement. So-and-so, the son of so-and-so, do you know him? Which one? The Sunni one? The Salafi one or the Daeshi one (if the son is known to be a Sunni or a Salafi or if he has joined ISIL in Syria, for instance)?[20] Needless to say, these denominations did not exist in the 1960s when Geertz conducted his research in Sefrou, Morocco. Yet the nisba still operates today, and with the changing world, Moroccans find new ways to identify—and be identified—that is, to be different and to be differentiated from those who are near and those who are far (both spatially and socially).

It should be noted, however, that Geertz, even as he raises these issues, paradoxically overlooks racial denominations—despite the fact that he himself repeatedly used categories with strong racial connotations such as Arab, Berber, and Jew rather freely and without problematizing them. These categories are modern and do indeed have a colonial history—they were constituted, from the beginning, as racial denominators, first in the context of Algeria, as well as later (which means now, since they have survived in this region, and of course in France itself).[21] For example, Arab in relation to

Berber perpetuates a dichotomy, as does black in relation to white (for both Europeans and Moroccans who think of themselves as white).[22]

In France, the term "Arab" refers to anyone from the region called the Maghreb (irrespective of whether that person believes he or she is Amazigh or not). The term "Arab" refers to a Maghrebi[23] and may not include people from Lebanon or Iraq, who are rather referred to as Lebanese or Iraqis. Despite the absence of the concept of race from Morocco's official political discourse (unlike in the United States), the term has been claimed by these same "French Arabs" lately to draw attention to the rampant racism against them. They often contextualize the racial discrimination they face in terms of the civil rights movements in the United States and in South Africa, looking to them as models for liberation. They translate and revive icons of that era such as Malcolm X and Steve Biko. They have even gained the support of more contemporary figures such as Angela Davis and Cornel West.[24]

From a postcolonial French perspective, the population in the city are all Arabs, as they are all Muslims. Since the Salman Rushdie affair in February 1989 and the veil controversy in France in October 1989, the "Arab" population in France has been assigned another name, a colonial one at that: les musulmans de France (Muslims of France).[25] Islam is racialized in France; it is a religion of Arabs, and being Arab is, then, a racial identity in France, and it is anything but positive, to say the least. Its many connotations are all rooted in a long, unchallenged colonial representation that is alive and well—both then and now.

Chantal's implicit evocation of "race" was paradigmatic of my experience with Europeans in Tangier. As Nicholas de Genova puts it, "Europeanness itself [is] a racial problem—a problem of postcolonial whiteness."[26] Small wonder, then, that the racial dynamics that exist in France between "Arabs" and "the French" was imported to Tangier.[27] Racial lenses and racial categorizations are predominant among the Europeans in Tangier, as they are in Europe. I found hanging out with the Europeans in the city to be similar to hanging out with the French in France. The experience was generally marked by suspicion, aloofness, and, at times, arrogance.

Be that as it may, in a book about migration and race, it is important to mention that the Europeans are not thought of as "immigrants," even though that is what they are. They think of themselves in national terms—as French or Spanish—and then in extra-national terms—as Europeans. Media coverage displays an array of beautiful names to designate them, such as "aesthetes" and "legendary expats."[28] The Moroccans, who have a plethora of names for West Africans, refer to all the Europeans (recognized by skin color) as (1) *Nsara* (from the name Nazareth, Jesus's birth place, meaning Christian), (2) *gawri* (from the Turkish name *Gavir*, itself from the Arabic *kafir*, which means infidel, or also possibly from the word "*Gaules*"), or (3) and, sometimes sarcastically, as *shurfa* (nobility).[29] These populations are seen in a highly positive light overall, and their presence is believed to contribute to development, bringing "projects of life and new experiences."[30]

In any case, race and racial tensions are real in Tangier, constituting colonial-like dynamics between Moroccans, West Africans, and Europeans. These tensions exist between Moroccans and West Africans (i.e., blacks), and they likewise arise between Europeans (whites) and Moroccans (who, by and large, have white consciousness). Consider the protest I mentioned in Chapter 4 against West Africans in the brand-new neighborhood Al Irfane 2, on the way to Rabat, close to the Tangier Ibn Battouta Airport. That event became an important point of exchange between several Moroccans and a number of local French residents. I heard several French women denouncing Moroccan racism against "blacks." The Moroccans, on the other hand, felt that such accusations are themselves racist, intended precisely to cover up French racism against themselves. According to one Moroccan, the proof of this was the fact that France was then bombing black men in Mali, but none of the French who denounced racism had yet said a word about it. A French woman intervened and told this Moroccan, "Your language is aggressive," attempting thus to displace the conversation from the pertinent topic to effectively accuse the local of not conducting himself with "civility." This exchange reminded me of something my acquaintance who wanted to charge me 25,000 euros had said: "Listen, all this is acted. It is done on purpose. An incident happened in which a black person tragically died. But this was turned into a payback affair. It is to harm the Moroccan image. It was also done to damage the relation[s] between blacks and Moroccans."

As we saw in Chapter 4, relations between Moroccans and West Africans are fraught with racial tensions, despite the existence of feelings of compassion. Yet, between the Moroccans and the Europeans, any event pertaining to the treatment of West Africans becomes itself a domain of racial tensions between the Europeans and the Moroccans. This often happens on social media, where European residents (and nonresidents) comment on these incidents and denounce racism against West Africans. Yet in these denunciations, there is an implicit claim of European innocence that is itself an affirmation of a moral superiority (i.e., Arabs are racists against blacks, "we good Europeans" are not).

Race and Space

When I returned to Tangier in May 2010, the medina had just put to rest an issue that the people of the neighborhood struggled with for several months. A local French resident had erected a wall on the roof of his house in a way that deprived his neighbors of their view of the sea. A view of the sea is extremely important in a city such as Tangier, as it may significantly increase or decrease the value of a house or an apartment. Often when you announce to someone you bought a house or an apartment in the city, their first question is, "*Wash katchouf labhar?*" (Does it look out over the sea?). Outraged, the neighbor spoke to the French resident and explained to him that his wall was depriving him of a view, decreasing the value of his house in the bargain. The Frenchman responded that it was his house and that it was within his right to build a wall if he so chose. The neighbor then took the issue to the city hall and argued in terms of value and *le bon voisinage* (good conduct toward one's neighbor; it is an obligation for every resident to take into account the peace and rights of their neighbors as to construction, making noise, etc.). The neighbor seemed to have a case, and the officials at the city hall called on the French resident and informed him that it was not within his right to build a wall and block the views of his neighbor. At this point, the French resident gave up the position of absolute property rights and unexpectedly used another argument that he possibly thought would fly in a Muslim country. He argued that he was married and that his wife liked to sunbathe on the roof, and thus, he did not want men to look at his wife naked, necessitating the wall's construction. The authorities responded that if he did not want people to see his wife naked, she should not undress on the roof, which is similar to a public place.

This story in fact involves a French media celebrity, Bernard-Henri Lévy. Several years before this open conflict in Tangier and immediately after the ban on the veil on March 15, 2004, Lévy was interviewed by National Public Radio (in the United States) about the veil. Joan Scott summed up his interview in the following manner: "After listing a number of objections to the 'veil' and explaining the need for a law banning it in public schools, he ended up by talking about how sad it was to cover the beautiful faces of young girls."[31]

I cite this incident not only because of its ironies and because it involves a media celebrity but also because it is a story of the struggle over space between a Frenchman and his Moroccan neighbors (or, more aptly, Moroccans and their immigrant French neighbor). Compare this to the sporadic protests that erupt in the city between West African and Moroccan neighbors. These protests, led by Moroccans, always involve claims of wrongdoing (allegations of crime or bad conduct) meant to exclude the West Africans from sharing space because of the racist belief that they pollute it, make it unsafe. Even within Moroccan society, admitting racism is shameful; therefore, expressions of racism often take the forms of "legitimate concerns." Ironically, with Europeans, there are no such protests. The case of Bernard-Henri Lévy seems to be one of those exceptions that confirm the rule. He infringed on his neighbors' right to view the sea. But, generally, the expectation is reversed. I interviewed Fatema, a Moroccan architect with a long interest in the Casbah and its renovation. She told me, "There was often conflict between Europeans and Moroccan residents of the Casbah, especially young people. Europeans try to make them [the Moroccans] behave in a certain way so as to impose a code of conduct. That did not go well."

"Conduct such as what?" I asked.

"Young people staying out late at night, smoking, listening to music, and chatting. That bothered some residents who are used to going to bed early, and they complained about the 'noise' in the neighborhood."

When I lived in the Casbah during the summer of 2010, I did not see any friction between the two communities. However, there was no interaction between the two. The two communities coexist while ignoring each other. Moroccan families, several of them really poor, live their lives as always, without paying attention to the presence of Europeans. Europeans do the same. As Anton Escher and Sandra Petermann observe regarding the European residents of Marrakesh, "Europeans are still attracted by a world which seems strange and mystical to them, and which may evoke sentiments of being a colonialist amidst the omnipresent poverty of the Moroccans."[32]

However, Moroccans, whose memories of colonialism are rather vivid, tend to legitimize the sentiments of the Europeans by recognizing European language and culture as superior to their own. In fact, it is the general Moroccan attitude that confirms the European privileged racial position. Relations of domination, as Pierre Bourdieu noticed, need to be recognized by the dominated in order to be effective, and it is this recognition that makes the victim complicit in the act of domination. To cite the words of Bourdieu: "When the dominated apply to what dominates them schemes that are the product of domination, or, to put it another way, when their thoughts and perceptions are structured in accord with the very structures of the relation of domination that is imposed on them, their acts of cognition are, inevitably, acts of recognition, submission."[33]

Self and Space

Chantal not only criticized the predominant European racism toward Moroccans (regardless of the motive for this revelation); she also denounced their tendency to "lie" about their identity. Chantal went on to tell me how most Europeans who live in Tangier lie about who they are.

"Someone just took a class on psychology in a school in France, here they claim they are a psychologist; some sold a single house one day, now they claim they are real estate agents."

As I later interviewed many other Europeans, I became aware that Chantal's comment was not just a critique but rather an observation of a real phenomenon in Tangier. Furthermore, I heard the same statement over and over again about specific individuals. I realized many European residents gossiped about one another and made jokes about how others lied about who they really are. "I cannot figure out Eric, I do not know who he is," a French resident by the name of Juliette told me. "He says he is a psychologist, but he does not sound like a psychologist." Juliette told me, just a few months after Eric's arrival, that he claimed he was a psychologist with a degree from the University of Paris.

Reinventing oneself is not specific to Europeans who move to Tangier. New places always reinvent us, sometimes in good ways, sometimes not, whether we want them to or not. As we saw in the previous chapter, West African men and women reinvent themselves and are reinvented at the same time. They most often reinvent themselves by hiding their past (or at least by not talking about it). They are reinvented by the place in the sense that they become Mamadou, 'azzi, HIV, Ebola, and so on. The European residents, by contrast, reinvent themselves by often claiming middle-class occupations— such as real estate agent, therapist, photographer, antique dealer, and so forth. However, they are also reinvented by the place in that they become the

European, a white man or woman in a postcolonial (brown) space, conferring status and prestige reminiscent of colonial times. One can see that the
racial dynamics of the colony continue to deploy themselves in the postcolonial city—as they do in France itself.[34]

A space does not mean only the body in space. As with the West Africans who see their entire persons changed because their black bodies, "constantly perceived," signify in this new space, Tangier, what is "ugly" and what is
"bad" (to use Frantz Fanon's expression),[35] the European white bodies, because
of the same postcolonial space, see their status changed significantly. They become white men and women; their whiteness becomes an important symbol
that secures advantages such as being treated with respect wherever they go,
including (among other things) receiving comparatively faster service within
the Moroccan bureaucracy. The signs of this symbolic capital are also recognized by the locals via the language, the white body, the attitude. In the
racial discourse of modernity, black people have been relegated to one of the
lowest rungs of the racial hierarchy.[36] Hence Fanon's prophecy that "the negro will always remain a negro wherever he goes"[37]—a statement that goes
beyond even that of W. E. B. Du Bois: "the problem of the twentieth century
is the problem of the color line."[38] For it continues nowadays to be so, and
the prospect of a society without race (a raceless society, about which Sartre[39]
spoke) does not seem to be on the horizon—and definitively not on the
horizon of Tangier. The color line continues to be a problem, a symbolic bar-
rier, well into the twenty-first century. Reinventing oneself is one of the
reasons Europeans (and everybody else) relocate.[40] Places are extraordinarily
important in the making of one's identity and even in the reimagining of
one's past. It does not necessarily mean that one "lies" or even simply "wants
to impress"; rather, it means that places require reinventing the past, the present, and even the future—if for no other reason than to resituate them, to
make them meaningful in the new context the different place entails. As
Gaston Bachelard put it, "Space is everything because time does not like
memory."[41] Moreover, relocating means also that one's own body is, in a sense,
reconfigured in another space. Or as Maurice Merleau-Ponty put it, space is
"the means by which objects (*les choses*) become possible."[42] Therefore, there
is no space without body. However, the relation between the body, or the
subject, and space can be reflexive or not. When it is not, Merleau-Ponty
speaks of "spacialized space" (*espace spatialié*). In this case, the subject just
"lives in space" without thinking about the relations of body and objects.[43]
When it is reflexive, Merleau-Ponty defines it as "*espace spatialisant*" (spatial-

izing space): the subject of the body does not just live space but thinks it, describes it, and carries it. There is then a white space in Tangier, a space lived and imagined individually and collectively by the European community.[44] In this space, one relocates his or her body in relation to other Europeans (whites) and in relation to Moroccans (not white). It is as if one needs to insert his or her own body in this ensemble of relations in a postcolonial city. To do so will undoubtedly require coming up with new narratives about oneself. It is an adaptation, a repositioning, a self-reinvention required by a postcolonial space.

Nevertheless, I soon realized that because Tangier is a city of people from different parts of the Euro-American world, many of the residents were not of privileged classes. Actually, a number of them moved to Tangier (at least in part) for economic reasons (though different from the ones of the West African migrants). Hence, I compare migrants to migrants, not migrants to "flexible citizens," such as former secretary-general of the United Nations Kofi Anan or fashion designer Yves Saint Laurent (d. 2008) and his partner Pierre Bergé (d. 2017).

The person I thought represented an eloquent version of this trend was Piero, who introduced himself as a successful artist. He was Italian, fluent in English and French. He dressed as a dandy and lived in a house he bought for $75,000—it used to belong to an American celebrity. Upon our first meeting, I myself was convinced by the image he created of himself and was eager to see his artwork. He promised to show it to me several times. And, several times, I went to his house only to find he was not there. One time, as I was leaving, he arrived out of breath, having just climbed the long hill that takes you to the Casbah, the second-shortest hill providing access from there to his house. Breathless from his climb up the steep hill, he politely told me he was too tired to host me and asked me to call him to arrange a visit. I called and finally got an appointment to meet him in his house. As I was preparing to go the following day, he called me and asked me if we could meet at Madame Porte, a French café built in 1954.

At Madame Porte, I was surprised to see Robert, a gay Spanish priest I had met several times before, who told me he, too, was waiting for Piero. Piero soon arrived, elegantly dressed, and apologized for, yet again, not being able to meet me in his house.

"My house is very messy," he said.

As we sat down and started talking about his life in Tangier, I expressed to him once again my desire to see his studio.

"I did not know you were interested in art," he replied.

"Yes, I am. Actually, I would be interested in buying something from you," I said, not mentioning the fact that I had spoken to him about his artwork several times previously.

Robert then told me in a way that I found condescending, "Well, you cannot afford it. Professors in the USA are not well paid. I know that."

I avoided engaging Robert on this topic and addressed Piero instead. I said, "Seriously, I would like to see your artwork and may be able to buy a painting or two from you."

Piero then explained to me that he was unable to sell his artwork because he had a contract with the Marlborough Gallery in New York City, and violating that contract would cause him legal troubles. I believed him and respected his decision, and went on interviewing both of them about their experiences in Tangier. I was aware of the artistic significance of the Marlborough Gallery, even though I had never visited it. I knew one of Tangier's well-known artists, Claudio Bravo, had a contract with that gallery as did Dali, Picasso, and other luminaries in the painting world. The fact that Piero, too, had a contract with them impressed me greatly and made me even more eager to see his work. I went online and could find nothing except one or two interviews with him.

The following week, I returned to the United States. I stayed in New York City for several days. Curious about Piero's work, I went to the Marlborough Gallery to see it. The gallery had an exhibit of the work of Claudio Bravo. I asked a young woman about the work of Piero, but she was not familiar with it. Confused, she called the director to help me. A gentleman in his early forties, polite and down to earth, the director looked puzzled as he, too, had never heard of Piero. He then handed me the list of all the artists with Marlborough Gallery contracts. Piero's name was not on the list.

In Tangier, no one checks not because no one cares but because most of those I met there invent themselves; they embellish their past and live with a new identity whose positivity is affirmed by the local ambiance. After all, being a white European is by itself a prestigious status, albeit only in relation to the locals. Within the circle of Europeans, people feel the need to be respected and valued and present themselves in ways they believe will appear interesting to others.

However, it should be noted that not only is this process of self-reinvention motivated by people's need to be held in high esteem, but these same dynamics of self (re)invention also are clearly indicative of individuals' attempts simply to claim an identity. In other words, their residence in Tangier does not make them create narratives of belonging to it or to a larger whole that we call "humanity" as the discourse on normative cosmopolitanism maintains but rather forces them to make new narratives that root them in a specific (faux?) upper-class European background.

Upper-class Europeans, the real ones, in Tangier are not known to hang out with the rest of the Europeans. They may not even really settle in Tangier, despite having homes there. Rather, they appear only occasionally, such as for vacations, and then in exclusive (and invisible) milieus in Tangier, usually on the outskirts of the city, in clubs, luxury hotels, and beaches almost unknown to and unreachable by those outside their circles. During my field-work in the city, I was aware of several names of upper-class Europeans who had houses or villas in the city. But I have never seen or encountered one.[45]

All those I encountered in meetings and at parties, private dinners, or even cafés are seen (and see themselves) differently from how they are seen (and see themselves) in Europe or the United States. Part of this change in image is almost automatic. The West African might have been a soldier, an artisan; he might be a parent, a brother, a Yoruba, but in Tangier, because of the dynamics of postcoloniality, he is the illegal immigrant. His past is behind him. He runs away from it; for him, it is his present (and especially his future) that defines him. In the present, he (and, more rarely, she) is here in Tangier—as a person, strong and adventurous, willing to risk to make it. In the future, he is successful, living in Europe, with a European visa or a European passport, married with European children, returning to Africa as a success, to address the continent, as Rastignac, one of Honoré de Balzac's main characters, addressed Paris after he made it: "Africa is between the two of us now!"[46] But here in Tangier, at the moment, and in the eyes of locals, these migrants are 'azzi, they Africanize the city, they blacken it, they fur-ther "Third Worldize" it. There is nothing they can do about it. Their eyes are on the sea!

Speaking about flexible citizenship, Aihwa Ong notes that "the art of flexibility, which is constrained by political and cultural boundaries, includes sending families and businesses abroad, as well as acquiring multiple pass-ports, second homes, overseas bank accounts, and new habits."[47] Further, she asserts, in the case of Southeast Asian countries, the state, far from losing sovereignty, has often disengaged from taking care of all its citizens; instead, citizenship rights are awarded according to what best contributes to the de-velopment of the country. However, what Ong shows is how capital makes citizenship flexible, not how citizenship has indeed become flexible. Or to say it differently, what we see in Ong's work is the dynamics of capital that have become so important as to bestow rights and privileges on people, regardless of race and national origins. Yet, citizenship can also be flexible, just due to the dynamics of race—even in the utter absence of capital. Europeans in Tangier do not need multiple passports, since an EU or a U.S. passport opens doors, and its holder does not need a visa to cross the national and political boundaries. In Morocco, skin color (European whiteness) also makes citizenship flexible.[48] Many living in Tangier have small incomes, and a few do not have jobs; others create modest livelihoods in antiques, real estate, or bookstores. Some live on remittances or alimony from their families. But the social condition in which they live is undoubtedly one of rights and privileges conditioned by colonial histories, reinforced by European or American institutions within the city. Ong's argument demonstrates that capital has the power, in the age of globalization, to forgo race. However, the power of race (even without capital) also creates great flexibility, unavailable to some, such as the West Africans who share the space of the city (but as "illegal immigrants") with the Europeans.[49] By observing the everyday lives of ordinary European people in a city of the global South such as Tangier, one can see that, in the neoliberal age, they too migrate in search of a better life; they too run away from difficulties, as it becomes increasingly hard in Europe to find a level of comfort and a life of privilege that is the result not of (economic) capital but simply of their European citizenship and their status as "white" men and women in a Moroccan postcolonial society.[50]

Sex in the City

Tangier is reputed to be a city of sex work and drugs. Its bad reputation in Morocco (second only to Marrakesh), in the Middle East, and even in neighboring countries seems to be well earned.

"You see the Europeans who come here," Samir, a Moroccan friend, told me one time, "they don't care about us [meaning they are not here to know us], they only come here for sex and for drugs."

The interest in sex is well known in Tangier among its residents—Moroccans and Westerners alike. Piero, the artist, asked me one time (as if I would know), "Explain to me. Why [do] Moroccan youth go with these old men? Is it for money? I only know one woman who came here for boys, usually it is old men. Most of the men here are for boys," he said. "They stay here for that. I only know one of them who was unsatisfied and left for Taiwan for boys. So, tell me, is it for money?"

I told Piero that I was like him; I did not understand why young men went with older men. I suggested that maybe there was more to it than just money. I wondered to myself whether sexual desire could be produced by money, but I found no answer.

Tangier seems to have a special place in Western gay literature. John Hopkins, a writer and traveler, during his several visits from 1962 to 1979, noticed that he was the only heterosexual writer among Western writers living in Tangier: "They were after boys and drugs. That's what drew them."[51] Mohamed Choukri lamented those many people who "speak or write about it from the angle of their desires, pleasures, and caprices."[52] Some of them see Tangier just as "a brothel, a beautiful beach, or a restful sanatorium."[53] Several figures of the literary avant-garde, such as Jean and Paul Bowles, Williams Burroughs, Truman Capote, Joe Orton, Gore Vidal, Allen Ginsberg, Jean Genet, and Tennessee Williams, made the city, at one point or another in their lives, their home; others visited as tourists.[54] Tangier as a city of sex often appears in their work, as well as in the work of Choukri himself.[55] Even in literature that cannot fall under the label of gay, sexual themes, including gay sex, are frequent. For instance, Tahar Ben Jelloun, who grew up in the city and frequented the same milieu as gay writers such as Jean Genet and Paul Bowles, describes gay sex in what I believe is his most original work, "an essay/novel/poem" all at once, titled *Harrouda* (1973):[56]

The homosexual traveler (often wealthy) who comes to Tangier (because they talked to him about this fairyland where all trespasses are possible) does not know—and cannot possibly know—that even if he exploits an unusual situation where bodies are given for nothing, how he is considered by these bodies:

There is almost no complicity

Shame is on the side of the other, because it is he who comes to these (hot) places for transgression

This traveler brings with him a "meaning" that turns into nothing

He gives himself to the Arab whose poverty is at the origin of the situation

> He has the satisfaction to transgress by sex his own morals at the
> limit of the oriental time whose types of seduction he does not
> know. In fact there is only an illusion of exchange. Nothing
> circulates or passes between the two (only sperm)

But if there is no exchange, there is something else. The young Arab gets his pleasure (and I assume also later his money) by "imposing humiliation on the other,"[57] he violates his "dignity." For "sodomy is considered the ultimate humiliation" in Moroccan society.[58]

Despite its poetic qualities, Ben Jelloun's text expresses a general Moroccan view about same-sex relations between Moroccan and European men—one in which the Moroccan is always represented as masculine, dominant, even in a sense getting some revenge against hegemonic Europe by humiliating the European man through penetration. Such views are narrated by the actors of the sexual encounter themselves and sometimes by other local men when they suspect a friendship between a Moroccan man and a European man. Such sexual encounters, real or imagined, are enacted through narration, endowed with a special meaning of masculinity and conquest, as has been noticed in other Arab contexts.[59] However, other testimonies, especially by Europeans and Americans, tell different and diverse stories[60] that are rather more complicated in ways that at times defy the common imagination.[61] Surely, sex relations between Europeans and locals have layers that shed light not only on the dynamics of gender and race in Moroccan society, but also on the dynamics of colonial and postcolonial relations.

"Several of them found out they were gay, so they just go, and get married to cover it up," Piero told me.

In any case, the European traveler, gay or straight, female[62] or male, possesses, in a racial status, both superiority over the native and freedom in the (post)colony, as Inderpal Grewal points out: "In the European culture of travel, mobility not only came to signify an unequal relation between the tourist/traveler and the 'native,' but also a notion of freedom."[63] Such unequal relations draw their force of possibility from racial ideologies that put the white Westerner on a pedestal in the racial pyramid. Not long ago in the colony, the status of the European was one of power and privilege. Nowadays, Europeans still enjoy this position in the postcolony: as soon as their feet touch its soil, their status magically changes; it becomes one of privilege and status. The individual is no longer primarily defined in terms of class or gender but in terms of race.

The European's privileged status in the city can better be understood in relation to the "native." This relation sets the European apart in a society as an outsider (not a migrant) with a status and power associated with race. His or her status increases in a way that often surprises him or her. The tremendous power of freedom and of status (bestowed by race) does not alter the relation between the gay traveler and the Moroccan man to make it an equal relation. In fact, it may even dramatize the racial inequality. It is not a relation between two marginal individuals, but it is a relation between a man with the power of race and relative wealth and a man with only a sexual organ he puts at work for profit—a profit that often allows him to survive, not to enrich himself. Even in this type of relation, the European traveler or tourist is on top socially even if he may be on the bottom physically. He buys, commands, and changes the status of his sexual "servant." In this sexual realm of human relations, the relation of master/servant is also racially produced. As it has been noticed elsewhere, "the asymmetry of power between European and North American sex tourists and their local or migrant sexual partners is also racialized."[64] The European traveler and the Moroccan man, while in a sexual relation, are what they are: a white man with power and status and a dark postcolonized man turned into a "prostitute."

"I told him don't act arrogant with me, I remember you when you were just a little prostitute," Robert, the gay priest, told me about a Moroccan artist with whom he just had an argument.

In postcolonial times, the unequal relation continues, especially in the form of tourism, a neocolonial industry that creates dependency and exploitation.[65] The European traveler is part of this industry that has always been global: "Tourist industry deployment of difference is gendered, racialized and culturalized. The tourist is often imagined and sought as male—an explorer, adventurer, engaged in action and discovery. The tourist destination is often gendered female, associated with nature, or with passive or erotic female sexuality. These images replay and recharge colonial and racialized images of 'the other,' and so reproduce 'First World'/'Third World' difference yet again. They also function to associate border crossing with sexual temptations or transgressions."[66]

With globalization, the tourist industry boomed even more. Tangier has experienced the age of globalization in its full force: within a single decade (2000–2010), tourism drove it to become the second-largest economy in the country, behind only Casablanca. Globalization means chiefly two things:[67] (1) the subjugation of the nation-state to the world market, which has created misery and suffering among middle-class Europeans[68] who can struggle less by settling in countries where the cost of living is cheaper and (ironically but in some crucial ways) better, and (2) the increased dependency of the state on tourism and on the world market in general, requiring the state to put everything (or almost everything) up for sale, including, for example, its national heritage and its educational system. Because of this set of circumstances (and because of the city's geographical proximity to Europe), Tangier (more than Marrakesh) has increasingly become a destination of European migration and an important city for sex tourism. Closeted and open European gay men (some of them as couples) settle in Tangier because of the relative anonymity it provides. Anonymity and a safe environment are important factors in gay travel.[69] A European, regardless of sexual lifestyle, becomes in Tangier mainly a European, a white man or a white woman—a person with high social status conferred on him or her by a long history of colonial domination (the politics of which have almost been forgotten but the effects of which are deep and long lasting).

Tangier (Tanja) itself is feminized and eroticized, as are other cities of tourism in Morocco: Casablanca (Casa), Marrakesh (the red city). The gendered names of these cities also connote sex work, queerness,[70] licentiousness, and turpitude.[71] As in colonial times, the city is a space of sexual transgression. The city becomes the symbol of a woman—the Arab woman, to be conquered and subdued. Colonial societal grammar plays out in the postcolonial city: the well-to-do European man, the young Moroccan with no income, the young Moroccan woman forced to feed herself and her family by engaging in sex work. The European can do in the former colony not only what he (and sometimes she) cannot do in another European country but also what the Moroccans themselves cannot do in Europe. In fact, sexual frustration and depravation were the lot of the North African migrant in France.[72] Sexual abundance is what the European traveler seeks and finds in the former colony: "Travel between and within affluent countries does not reposition the citizen of an affluent country on economic, gendered, or racial hierarchies of power. But travel to Jamaica or the Dominican Republic or other poor and indebted nations does. In the third world, even the 'third-rate' American or European tourist is king or queen."[73]

It has also been noticed that in Europe itself, sex work is also racialized, with people of color significantly represented. Even the clientele itself is racialized: people of color could be refused the "service" outright. For years as a student in Paris in the 1980s, I used to live not far away from Rue Saint

Denis, a neighborhood notorious for its sex work. I often crossed the street on my way to Center Pompidou, especially during the weekends. Several times, I noticed African and Arab men turned down disparagingly by sex workers. One day I even saw a sex worker scream a resounding no at a black man as he approached her to buy what she was publicly offering for sale. It is possible that the domain of sexuality is the most racialized domain, given how central sex is to life in society and how determinant in the making of the subject. Maybe it is also for these reasons that racial theories were theories about biological production, and thus about sex and sexuality. It is lastly for these reasons, perhaps, that grand philosophical projects of individual liberation focused on the individual's sexuality as the starting point.[74] As Julia O'Connell Davidson and Jacqueline Sanchez Taylor put it:

> The tourist and the local or migrant are simultaneously brought
> together and separated by global inequality. Were it not for the
> huge disparity in terms of political and economic power between
> Europe/North America and Caribbean nations, the average North
> American or European tourist would never even get to Jamaica or
> the Dominican Republic, and those who did venture to the
> Caribbean would not find themselves automatically positioned as
> the local's superior in terms of social, political, and economic
> rights and freedoms. In a different and more equal world, North
> American and European tourists to the Caribbean would find it
> no harder and no easier to make contact (sexual or otherwise)
> with local people than they find it to strike such acquaintances
> with locals when they visit New York, Nice, Seville, or Amalfi.[75]

Tangier is not this different and more equal world. It is a city of sexual inequality. This inequality persists (or appears) even when the sexual act involves the European traveler and the Moroccan male, as in the scene depicted by Ben Jelloun.

Arab societies tend to think of these relationships as such. Sex between men has been considered something someone does, not something someone is.[76] This act involves an active agent (hypermasculine) and a passive recipient (undermasculine, feminine). This is the same view expressed by Ben Jelloun. However, despite the existence of this imagery, same-sex marriage remains a taboo in Moroccan society. Relatively recently, maybe in the last two decades, "gay culture" and "gay activism" within the city and outside it, especially in the cyberspace of the Internet, have changed this common view somewhat, especially among the youth. For the Moroccan youth I spoke to, homosexual acts involve, I was told over and again, both parties, and they involve role-play and not just one comprising heteronormativity. Even among some Moroccan men in Tangier, despite the still dominant homophobic culture, there is a little acceptance of homosexuality, sometimes even discretely expressed in the open. The Finest Pink, a nightclub in Tangier's Corniche frequented by Moroccans and Europeans, is a primary example of this. The idea of homosexuality as an identity—and not only an act—is becoming slowly a reality despite stiff and at times, when such an identity is expressed in the open, violent resistance.

Again, anonymity for a gay person makes Tangier a close and convenient destination for sex tourism. Maybe it is also for the same reasons that well-to-do and conservative families in Europe once sent their gay sons to Tangier, "to get rid of the embarrassment," I was told by Robert the priest. "They are called remittance men," he added. Later, I realized he was, himself, among this group. He is from a conservative Italian family and settled in Tangier twenty-five years back. Tangier offers him not only anonymity but also a new freedom. Now in his mid-sixties, Robert lives with a twenty-six-year-old Moroccan man, Jamal.

"Come, I want to show you something," he told me one day.

He handed me a card and asked me to look at it. It was a card of his young partner. I read the name and the birth date and saw the photo. The card stated testimony that his partner is a Sharif (a proven descendent of the Prophet Muhammad). I could see the signature of the king himself.[77]

"What is this?" I asked.

He replied, "That is a *carte blanche*! I got it for Jamal!"

"How did you get it?" I asked, not hiding my surprise at seeing and touching a card I heard so much about while growing up, its magical power allowing you to do whatever, go wherever, its cachet opening all doors before you. How indeed did this man get it?

"I have my own ways," he responded, conveying his social importance as someone who had reached the highest point of the political pyramid of power in the country.

A relationship between the European gay man and the Moroccan man, as well as a relationship between the Moroccan woman and the European man, is not devoid of a power relation created by racial and class dynamics. As in the Caribbean and in Kenya, the association of a sex worker (male or female) with a white tourist bestows prestige. Writing about Kenya, Wan-johi Kibicho notes that "relationships in Africa were structured around ra-cial and ethnic differences."[78] Kibicho continues, "The force with which the 'superiority' of the white race and values was affirmed in the African colo-nies still evokes feelings of incompleteness among many indigenous Africans in post-independence Kenya. How else can one explain the view that by as-sociating with a white tourist, a CSW [commercial sex worker] feels presti-gious?"[79] This association also extends to a Moroccan male associating with a European gay man, especially because the association, on the surface, does not indicate any sexual relationship and appears as "just friendship."

Piero once told me, "Women don't come here for that. I only knew one woman who came here for that."

Several gay men I encountered have relatively "effeminate" Moroccan boyfriends, sometimes within their age groups. I met Rafael at a Christmas party he attended with his Moroccan boyfriend, who wore a little makeup and most likely assumed I shared the Moroccan stereotypes of homosexu-als. As our discussion progressed, he became more effeminate in his ges-tures as well as his speech, most likely in defiance, and seemed to search for a telling disapproving reaction on my part. In addition to the highly nega-tive stereotypes of gays, the ultimate humiliation is not simply that one is sodomized but rather that an Arab is sodomized by a European—a Moroc-can by a Frenchman. Because sex is such a powerful symbol, the perceived ultimate humiliation is extended from the individual to the family to the entire nation. This adds extra layers to the sense of abject humiliation. But it is unthinkable since, as in Ben Jelloun's narrative, it is always believed that when such an act happens, it is the Moroccan who is inflicting the ultimate humiliation, not the European, whose whiteness and phenotypes, associated with beauty, often signal him as "effeminate." Still, Moroccan society guards itself against sexual transgressions.

It guards itself by reinforcing sexual norms via, of course, a discourse of masculinity. "He is not a man," Mohamed, who lived most of his adult life in Paris (before he settled in Tangier), told me about a Frenchman. "He can-not be a man, and he knows it." The societal mechanism by which society principally controls sexual deviance is precisely in its ingenious distinction between the passive (the "effeminate" gay) and the active (the hypermascu-line). In a society where friendship operates mostly within the same gender, deviance from sexual norms is difficult to spot, unless it comes in the form of clear feminine signs—in which case, it is somehow tolerated and considered a *maskûn* (the person is believed to be inhabited by a spirit against whom he has no power; on the contrary, he himself is only an instrument for the malign spirit). Other than that, the way Moroccan society articulates what it considers deviance from its norm is also (one might say, cleverly or insidiously) reinforced by the masculine, the active, constituting surveillance itself. The hypermasculine agent is further empowered by the fact that he alone can expose the weaker person's sexuality and inflict shame on him. In so doing, his own masculinity is less undermined, for he is the one who does not deviate from his role of an active agent; he is more than a man, "a man-and-half" (*râjal wnas*), as such a man once told me. In short, his masculinity is above suspicion. Because sexuality is also highly racialized even in Moroccan society, the discourse can possibly articulate this relation, but only on the condition that the Moroccan masculinity (*rajla*) is intact. For its transgression by a white man is beyond scandalous; it is one of those few things that remain in the realm of the unthinkable. At the end, rajla becomes this collective thing, this sacred symbol that society values, upholds, and protects against all types of sexual transgression. Rajla is also the power to live up to the moral obligation to protect, without fail, those women under one's protection—mother, wife, sisters, daughters—in short, the same females who also guard one's own honor. Rajla is that concept that allows the societal order to be neatly separated and divided into a realm of men and a realm of women—each with defined gender roles and strict rules of masculinity and femininity. Hence, interracial marriage is not the threat and has become, to a certain degree, accepted, especially in the case of proclaimed conversion. All things considered, the relation between a Frenchman and a Moroccan woman, even outside of marriage, is tolerated, even though it remains part of what Erica Williams calls the specter of tourism,[80] meaning it is always under suspicion for being the local woman's calculated attempt to get papers, to migrate, to get material gains. By contrast, the violation of rajla even among Moroccans is so monstrous that it often remains in the domain of the unspoken. Hence the intensity of the group violence that sometimes explodes at even the suspicion that one has violated it.[81]

However, the unequal relation of power and the racial dynamics do not manifest only in the relationship between the European tourist, or resident, and the Moroccan man. The unequal relation is also seen between the European man and the Moroccan woman. In fact, it is especially in this relation that gender, race, and coloniality display themselves. Gender was instrumental in colonial domination and continues to be so in imperialist policies today.[82] "Power relations among nations and the status of colonial subjects have been made comprehensible (and thus legitimate) in terms of relations between male and female," as Joan Scott put it some time ago.[83] Colonialism did not seek to save colonized women from male oppression but rather sought to make them available for the colonizers, or else how does one explain that some of these men, such as Lord Cromer of Egypt, who were the champions of women's liberation in the colony were also some of the most fervent adversaries of women's liberation in Europe?[84] How can one explain that colonialism, which also exerted a real male domination at home, also fought men and women who sought liberation with the same brutality? The issue is that colonialism was authorized, by virtue of conquest, to put a hold on land, sky, men, plants, and animals. But women seem to have been a red line in most societies, and for Muslim societies, women were in the domain of the inviolable. Hence, a ferocious ideological battle in colonial societies fought over women seems to have continued, under different guises, in some postcolonial societies, most notably France.[85] The liberation of women by colonials was then nothing less than an attempt at their conquest. And that was quickly understood by colonized people.[86]

One of the strongest and more persistent Western images of the Orient is precisely that of lewd sensuality involving voluptuous and submissive women in a world of virile and overmasculine dark men.[87] The conquest and subordination of these women was the necessary condition of the subordination of the land, especially given the colonial (correct) understanding that Arab men invest in their women as carriers of their honor. It was as if the conquest of men had to go through the conquest of women. As Anne McClintock points out, "The imperial conquest of the global [finds] both its shaping figure and its political sanction in the prior subordination of women as a category of nation."[88] When Fanon stated, long ago, that former colonies would become the "brothels of Europe,"[89] he was probably pointing out that power would continue, even after independence, to be played out in the domain of sex and gender.

With women, racial hegemony is even more exaggerated and more acute and involves both racial dynamics and gender dynamics. "It is a site for European and North American men to reenact colonial masculinity."[90] The Moroccan sex worker becomes the "Arab woman" in the presence of the European man, with racial dynamics established between the man and the woman. The European man may often seem more generous, more respectful of the woman, and less judgmental than a Moroccan client. A relation with a European man can also create transnational ties.[91] It can offer the option of migration. For European tourists and residents often do not see the relationship as one of sex work, with a buyer and a seller. On the contrary, they tend to see it as a romantic or semiromantic relationship.

As has been noticed in the Caribbean, "the women are not, in the imaginations of the men, prostitutes who are having sex for money, but are perceived as poor women who genuinely enjoy the sex." This idea "enables tourists to deny any exploitative aspects of their relationship with the Caribbean."[92] Consider the following story.

Daniel is a sixty-five-year-old retired Frenchman, recently divorced, who decided to settle in Tangier because it is close to home and also because women (or rather girls) are "easy to find and fuck," he told me. Initially, he ran into trouble with his landlady, a *hâjja* (that is, she had accomplished the pilgrimage to Mecca, indicating her piety), who asked him to move out because she did not want his *haram* money. She meant that renting her apartment to a man who used it for fornication (*zina*) is like running a brothel. Daniel could not understand why, if he paid his rent, he was not free to do as he pleased in his apartment. He had no choice but to leave and find another one, and he did so rather quickly. By then, he had met a Moroccan "girlfriend" who came to see him whenever he called her. She worked in the sales office at Renault, where she made 2,000 dirhams a month (the equivalent of $200).

"Each time she comes, we eat out, or we order a pizza, and she stays overnight," he explained.

"Do you pay her?" I asked bluntly, because by that time we were becoming friends.

"No, I give her 200 dirhams in the morning."

"Well, it seems like a payment to me," I said.

Looking rather annoyed, he took his hands out of his pockets and gestured in the air as he said, "It does indeed, but what to do?"

The truth of the matter is that it does not seem like a payment. A sex worker in Tangier charges between 1,000 and 1,500 dirhams per night (approximatively $120 and $170). European men, often older, rarely have to resort to short-term female sex workers. Several men I encountered were like Daniel. While they came to Tangier for sexual pleasure, they often had "girlfriends" who they eventually partially or totally supported. While in Europe, age difference is an issue for older men, especially those interested in younger women, in Tangier, it is not a major factor. Their age may be a plus in the relationship, and their status as European is a magnet for young women who may see a "golden chance" to leave for Europe. For *lahrig* is rarely undertaken by Moroccan women. Instead, women cross to Europe via marriage, real or fake. When I started my research in Tangier in 2008, a Moroccan newspaper, *al-Sabâh*, revealed that in that year alone, 7,000 Moroccan women had married Europeans, though it was not clear whether Moroccans with an EU passport were included in the category "European."

Traditionally, Moroccan society has been opposed to its women marrying European men, but was relatively accepting of European wives. The European man, commonly referred to as Christian (*nasrani, gawri*),[93] was believed to be ineligible (from an Islamic point of view) to marry a Muslim woman. However, since the 1990s, society has become more open to it—mainly because it has resolved this issue through the solution of conversion. Of the European husbands of Moroccan women that I have encountered in Morocco, many were Muslim converts.

Marriage between a Moroccan man and a European woman, on the other hand, is not as uncommon and is relatively more acceptable. The man is permitted to marry a non-Muslim (on the condition she is one of "the people of the book," either Christian or Jewish). But marrying a Jewish woman is a rare occurrence for a host of reasons. It is true also that both Muslims and Jews have found it more practical and more convenient to marry close, within their own communities, and often even within their own network of family, relatives, and friends. In Tangier, Jews did not have a mellah (the specifically Jewish quarter found in big Moroccan cities such as Meknès, Fes, and Marrakesh).[94] Yet here, the Jews have also lived as a distinct population[95] bounded by Muslim counterparts (and, since 1844, disconnected from them and more allied with Europe, as Susan Miller shows in one of her studies of the city in the nineteenth century).[96] In recent decades, the conflict in the Middle East has contributed to this rift. Jews may be suspected of being associated with Zionism and thus with Israel.[97]

Most marriages between a European woman and a Moroccan man tend to happen nowadays via the Internet. During my numerous recent stays in Tangier, I did not meet one Moroccan man married to a European woman he had met in the city. Within the city, because of the distance created between locals and Europeans, heterosexual intermarriage is a rare occurrence. Locality exaggerates the Moroccanness of Moroccans in the eyes of Europeans, as it also increases the nationalistic feelings of Europeans. But when such marriages happen, they tend to decrease these nationalistic feelings without necessarily creating a cosmopolitan subject, meaning without the idea of the European embracing the local culture, becoming part of it, resulting in a cultural hybridity that makes of him or her a citizen of the world.

An example follows. Claude was sixty-four years old, with gray hair and short; I secretly doubted he was ever handsome, even in his twenties. He married Jamila, twenty-eight years old. She helped him run a bar in a neighborhood with a bad reputation that has earned it the name of the Quarter of the Devils (Hayy al-Shayâtin). Claude also owns a real estate agency in the same neighborhood. Claude and Jamila were my neighbors, and I could often hear them fight. He approached me one day, heartbroken, almost in tears, telling me she had left him and asking me if I could help him find her. I felt bad for him but did not know how I could help him get his wife back. I politely told him I would help him if he could tell me how. He then said that since I speak the language (meaning Arabic), if I heard something about her whereabouts from the neighborhood, I should tell him. Before I agreed to his request, he almost nonchalantly told me that she was pregnant. I congratulated him and reassured him that since she was pregnant, she would be back. A few days later, I saw them together, and he saluted me as he always did, but from then on he dealt with me in a more reserved way, as if he felt embarrassed that I knew a bit about his domestic problems. Two years later, I saw him often with his daughter, and his family life looked tranquil. Neither his nationality nor even his age was a topic of gossip. He himself joked about his age when he referred to himself as *shibâni* (the old man). His wife was entitled to the respect of what in Morocco is referred to as *mart al râjil* (a husband's wife). She could not be the object of gossip, especially among men, or of harassment from single young men in the street. She is the holder of her husband's honor, and she observes the code of good conduct—reserved, private; even when she is at the bar she helps run, she is in the company of her husband, never alone, and avoids chats with men. She is there to supervise the workers and help her husband run the business. When they closed the bar, Jamila took over the real estate agency and often ran it with her husband around. Claude, by virtue of his marriage to a Moroccan woman, had been included in the Moroccan social system, a position he seemed to enjoy quietly.

Claude was not just an old white Frenchman; he was wealthy yet discrete about his social status. He confided to me that in addition to several businesses he ran in Tangier and in Rabat, he also owned a restaurant in San Francisco managed by his son (from an earlier marriage). He met his current wife, he told me, when she worked for him as a bartender in Rabat. They moved to Tangier as a married couple. Therefore, despite age, Jamila married up, and the hypergamic marriage allowed her to escape the lower-class life of a barmaid—an intensely despised profession that Moroccan society associates with sex work and a host of other vices. Not only did Jamila marry a well-off man, but she also married one whose citizenship and race gave her prestige. She also married a man who accepted a societal condition—conversion—that "indigenizes" the Frenchman.

"Yes, I converted to Islam," Claude said when I asked him, "but I find it hard to fast during Ramadan. I do sometimes, but I cheat. I told my wife I am going to take care of things at the restaurant and secretively eat something there. Fasting during Ramadan is too hard," he said, and I agreed.

Claude was the only European I met who frequently was in touch with Moroccans because he managed a bar attended almost exclusively by Moroccans. I never saw him at one of the events organized by the European community or at any of the Moroccan cultural events. When I last met him in June 2016, he was preparing to go to France for a vacation with his family. He told me he just had a second daughter and bought a Riad (a traditional Moroccan house in the Casbah), which has become a sign of wealth and status among Europeans of Tangier. His two daughters have Moroccan names, Leila and Nejat. Claude's life turned around his family and business.

However, few are those Europeans who, like Claude, are married to Moroccan women. Instead, such encounters occur most often through sex work. Yet, as much as Tangier is a site of sexual colonial encounter between the European man and the Arab woman, as well as between the European man and the Arab man, sexual encounter (in the form of sex work or otherwise) between the European woman and the Arab man is a true rarity. I witnessed only one such relationship, between a slightly younger man, an *assimilè*, and a young French woman. It did not last. The rarity of sex relations between Moroccan men and European women points to the fact that Tangier remains as in colonial times, when these relations were also quasi-absent. When this type of relation occurs, racial inequality is more visible in the couple and is often negotiated as in Jerusalem and in a Turkish village studied by anthropologists.[98] In Tangier local men are generally not sought after by European women, even as Moroccan women, by contrast, are available to European men. Relations between European women and Moroccan men, I was told, are more frequent in the Moroccan desert, where darker men, Touareg or Touareg-like nomads, camel riders, have long alimented the

Western imagination. The Bedouin or the nomad is presented as the quintessence of Arab masculinity, even as sex tourism is also sustained by racial stereotypes.[99] By contrast, Tangier offers urban colonial life, where worlds of Europeans and natives are separated, if only by invisible barriers, and where power relationships manifest themselves maybe most in the realm of sexuality.

All in all, Tangier as a postcolonial space remains also the site of sexual and racial contention. Sexual encounters between European men and Moroccan women (i.e., Arab women) are indeed highly racialized, as they are also in former colonized nations in Africa, Asia, and the Americas. Hotels, casinos, and nightclubs are the main places of these encounters. As in the Caribbean, the European man engaged with a Moroccan sex worker often frames the relation in terms of "my girlfriend."[100] These sex-work relations occur not only between European men and women but also between Moroccan men and Moroccan women, and between Moroccan women and Gulf men, but these are subject to different dynamics, beyond the scope of this study on Europeans in the city.

These sexual encounters are by no means an indication that in the world of sex and sexuality, racial differences are minimized or liquidated. On the contrary, interracial sexuality is itself a domain of racial formation.[101] If colonial conquest established sex as a paradigm of domination and subjugation between Arab man and European man, with women being the ones at stake, postcoloniality preserves that paradigm via sex tourism. This is not to deny that mutual desire does not exist but rather to stress that this desire, when it exists, is structured by "racial stereotypes on both sides."[102] The sides are not of equal power because racial stereotypes themselves are not equal. The inequality itself is the result of violent, tragic colonial history whose effects are still at work in the region and beyond.

Nation-State and Citizenship

White Europeans in the city of Tangier constitute a distinct community—a community with rights and privileges associated with their racial status as *gawri* or *nasrani* and, in some instances, even as *shurfa*. This is not to say they are a homogeneous group, but they do think of themselves as part of the European community, with whom they often share language, race (white), and class status. When I met Paul, he had just moved to Tangier from Paris with his French Algerian wife. His children were in college. As a photographer, fascinated with Morocco (where he had traveled often), he decided to settle in Tangier. He still moves back and forth between the two cities. Like many French residents, he preferred the medina because of its exotic air. I commented, "It must be nice to live there. I spent the summer living in the Casbah."

He did not seem happy with the location of his residence.

"Yes, but there is a class problem with the people in the neighborhood. It is easier with Europeans. We share so much!"

The medina is a popular neighborhood where middle-class, working-class, and poor Moroccans all live together. The neighborhood itself does not create social distinction, but it is rather the house—usually its size, its interior design, and so forth—that creates distinction. Paul felt out of his element in this neighborhood. The Casbah has become more exclusive in recent years and more expensive, and many of its houses were already occupied by those lucky ones (like Piero) who purchased early.

However, the issue was not that Paul occupied a different class background from that of his Moroccan neighbors but rather there is often a distance between Europeans and Moroccans (with the exception of the high class of évolués, the same as assimilés). Europeans do "share so much" in common, as Paul cogently observed. For this "sharing" to occur, a racial background needs to be cultivated to survive, develop, and grow. To reproduce themselves as a community, Europeans develop a sense of community by participating in cultural events. These numerous encounters allow for the creation of a social habitus that also creates and reinforces the idea of a community among Europeans. It is this idea of a sense of community that not only helps one settle into a new country but also integrates newcomers while excluding "others," who either cannot perform such cultural rites of passage or are unwilling to develop this performance into a habit. What is created, then, is not a cosmopolitan culture but a diasporic culture of a community. This community is also made possible by the history that has instituted Europe as a realm of privileged citizenship. The true mark of this citizenship is "whiteness." This is also to say that cosmopolitanism is not always or not necessarily, as its critics such as David Harvey argue, "an ethical and humanitarian mask for hegemonic neoliberal practices of class domination and financial and militaristic imperialism."[103] Cosmopolitanism is also another face of the postcolonial privileges of white Euro-Americans in a postcolonial space.

The European population I studied was not of the business class or part of a corporate elite but rather of modest means. Such was the case of Eric, whose claim of being a psychologist Juliette had questioned.

He was a middle-aged man and had arrived in Tangier by the end of the spring of 2011. He looked distressed, sad, poor, and he had no place to stay except with one of his friends. He later explained to me that he had recently divorced in France and his wife kept the house and the children. It was hard for him, and he came to Tangier to take a break. A few weeks later, he was able to make other connections, mainly thanks to Anne-Marie, a French woman in her late thirties who opened a bar in Tangier. He stayed with other French female friends and eventually had a French girlfriend he stayed with for a few more weeks until, he said, he could not stand her racist comments about Moroccans: "She told me one day, 'A Moroccan is just a piece of walking meat with a bit of hair.' My father is Kabyle.[104] Her racist comments were appalling to me."

He went back to staying with friends. He was short of money and complained to me. I insisted on lending him money and told him he could give it back any time he wanted. That was just a few weeks before I left in December 2011. I came back in May 2012 and saw him again. We talked over the phone, and he told me he wanted to introduce me to someone. I waited for him at Café Comedia II, and he soon arrived with a girlfriend, an *assimilée*, a Moroccan woman with fair skin, of his age (in her late forties), well dressed and exuding self-confidence. She had graduated from a prestigious art school in Paris and was from a well-to-do family from Tangier. I was surprised and, as a friend, happy to see in his appearance a near-total transformation. He was well dressed and clean shaven, with a classy raincoat and shiny maroon shoes; he looked like a real monsieur. He told me Lycée Regnault had offered him a job as a psychologist because of his expertise working with teenagers in France. Soon, however, I noticed his attitude of unkindness toward Moroccans in the streets, especially toward those who would ask him for a cigarette—something that people frequently do in both France and Morocco, and one is typically given over without a fuss. He, however, would say, "Go away [*casse-toi*]!" making a hand gesture without looking at them. Soon I noticed his attitude even toward me had changed. On several occasions, he was quick to remind me of something I never forget— namely, my Moroccan origins. If someone from the European community did not respond to my Facebook request, he would reply, "Yes, because you are Moroccan." If I were not invited to an event, he would say, "You were not invited because you are Moroccan." Within less than two weeks, he stopped calling me and did not want to meet when I called. In short, the friendship that had occurred in his moment of distress died in his moment of "cosmopolitan" revival. He could see that, despite everything, there are two worlds that separate us in Tangier: the world of white Europeans (with its complementary component of *assimilés*), and the world of the brown/black natives.

In the period of colonization, many Europeans and Americans migrated to the city, existed, and coexisted—though not without tensions and frictions, springing mainly from the conflictual European and American colonial policies. It is this diversity of European and American ways of life that gave the city its reputation for being cosmopolitan. However, in its postcolonial times, when the city joined Morocco politically, it automatically became part of the francophone zone. Lycée Regnault is a French high school of great repute in the francophone world, founded by a French officer who gave it its name. The French Institute of Tangier is also there, serving the cause of the Francophonie. The French Consulate occupies a strategic place at the top of the Boulevard, facing Gran Café de Paris, expressing (by its location and its European, majestic, white, and rather refined architecture) the place the French enjoy in the city and reflecting (or should I say projecting), by and large, their place in Morocco. These places—the Lycée, the French Cultural Center, and the consulate—all offer opportunities for cosmopolitan performance. So, too, do coffee shops, as places where French cultural activities unfold, such as the Café de Paris, a meeting place of francophone writers and artists. Most recently, Cinema Rif, both a coffee shop and a theater reinvented by a French Moroccan and an international artist to boot—Yto Barrada—has come on the scene. French itself is the lingua franca spoken in Tangier with different degrees of fluency and a variety of accents. All those I met—Americans, English, and Spanish residents of the city, as well as ordinary Moroccans, not to mention the Moroccan elites of the city and their children, who usually attend Lycée Regnault—spoke fluent French.

In comparison, the Spanish presence (even though solidly rooted in the city) seems to be overshadowed, especially since the late 1990s. The Spanish have the Cervantes Institute in Marshan, a historic modern neighborhood for old and influential Muslim and Jewish families distinguished by their last names (as are all the historically elite Moroccan families). The Cervantes Gallery also sits at the top of the Boulevard, almost facing the French

Consulate, emphasizing the closeness to Spain and the strong presence of Spanish-born residents in Tangier from different generations. The Spanish and the French seem to be old acquaintances and have clearly learned how to cohabitate in the city. Yet, again, the French presence is stronger and more privileged, with several companies (including Renault) having established themselves in the city. Spanish companies seem to be more prevalent in the construction domain. But American institutions, such as Lycée American, Tangier American Legation Museum (TALIM), the American Cultural Center, and (most recently) a campus of the University of New England, all make a significant American contribution to the diversity of the city.

This is to say that the Europeans are not in a space devoid of the power of the Western nation-state. Those places are institutions in and of themselves, and each exerts its cultural power on its citizens and even harbors ambitions to extend that to others, especially Moroccans. The nation-state exists not only within the parameters of the national territory but also within the territories of other nation-states. In a postcolonial space where colonial powers have long shaped spaces and selves, the concept of the nation-state, especially of a powerful one in the West, extends beyond its own limits to operate with full force in any territory it once governed, including via institutions practicing the politics of culture.

I ran into the French consul several times at private dinners and parties. Though I dined with him multiple times, he continually ignored me and, when I saw him one morning following a dinner, would not return my greeting. During the dinners, I often overheard him lament the absence of culture. This act was neither racist (as an American friend understood it) nor an ignorance of Moroccan cultures (as I initially thought). The consul complained in fact about the absence of a *certain* culture, one that he recognized, one that deserved the name, and one that he, as a consul of France, had a mandate to spread and encourage, especially in the face of the rising influence of American culture. What he missed was *la culture*, whose correct English translation is "high French culture."

During my interview with Piero at the Madame Porte café, mentioned above, he told me that whenever he runs into problems with a Moroccan, his friends "explain the problems with some bizarre nationalist language and say this [is because] he is Moroccan. I tell them, I have no problems with your culture." At that point Robert chimed in, "Just with your religion!" Such an attitude of indifference, distance, and at times an open sense of superiority and disdain toward Moroccans (seen by and large as a group, as in Piero's statement) is common. "They [the Moroccans] are angry at themselves because they feel inferior," a young Spanish resident told me as I listened to her in utter dismay that, because of my position as an ethnographer, I felt unable to respond. I kept the same smile and continued to take notes.

Part of the lack of openness and engagement between "Westerners" and Moroccans lies in the quasi-general unwillingness among Americans and Europeans living in Tangier to learn either Arabic or Moroccan Arabic.[105] Among the entire Euro-American population I met, only two people spoke some Moroccan Arabic. In his study of Mexican migrants in Chicago, Nicholas de Genova argues that the "foreigner" is assimilated into American culture and thus "the US nation-state likewise subjugates his foreignness and triumphs over the foreignness of all nations beyond its borders."[106] One can argue that in postcolonial nation-states such as Morocco, not only is there no such project of assimilation, but rather the French nation-state, as a postcolonial power that has largely assimilated local Moroccan elites, indisputably still triumphs over Moroccan culture and even, to a certain extent, over all other "foreignness" (including the other European ones such as Spanish and English). French reigns supreme as the language of "high culture" in Tangier, as it does in the rest of Morocco and even the larger Maghreb.[107] All the non-French Europeans I met spoke French with different degrees of fluency—and awkwardness always showed among those who were not adequately fluent.

Nowadays, some scholars argue that cosmopolitanism is not the monopoly of the elite. Homi Bhabha and Kwame Anthony Appiah speak about vernacular, marginal, or patriotic cosmopolitanism to designate a way of life open to and embracing the world as a home.[108] Others, whose work is inscribed in the same perspective, view cosmopolitanism as "rising social relations that do not negate cultural, religious, or gendered difference, but see people as capable of relationships of experimental commonalities despite difference."[109] However, such scholars do not speak about this kind of cosmopolitanism without questioning whether it is ever possible (in this day and age) to meet its sine qua non requirements, which are "self-doubt and reflexive distanciation" as well as "an awareness of the existence and equal validity of other cultures, other values, and other mores."[110] If there is such a vernacular cosmopolitanism, it is surely not in Tangier. There is less engagement, less openness to others (especially to the hosts). Among those I interviewed, I did not encounter one European who believed Moroccan cultures were as valid as French culture. Actually, it is rare to find that idea even among many Moroccans (whose condition today is one of postcoloniality—marked by a strong colonial legacy that has instituted French as a high, indeed superior, culture).

Performing "High Culture"

Once a small city, Tangier is becoming, by Moroccan standards, a big city with a population of 947,952, making it the third-largest city in Morocco after Casablanca and Fes. The Boulevard, once called Pasteur, today called Mohammed V, is the center and heart of the city. Members of the European communities see each other often on the Boulevard, save for the elusive and reclusive elite. The rest of the community meets on a regular basis at events organized for them at the French consulate, L'Institut Français de Tanger, the American school, and TALIM, and also in bookstores such as Les Insolites and Les Colonnes, and even at Cinema Rif. Well managed, these places often organize art exhibits, film projections, and readings by authors. For instance, Cinema Rif projects films designated for Western audiences every week. Authors' readings are bimonthly at Les Insolites and monthly at Les Colonnes. This is to say that the European community has developed hubs of European cultures in the city—a milieu of learning, entertainment, as well as places to meet friends and make new acquaintances. Readings of novels and poetry in bookstores and institutes, as well as art exhibits in galleries, not to mention projection of films in cinemas, are also cultural performances. Cultural performances, Deborah Kapchan notes, are "patterns of behavior, ways of speaking, manners of bodily comportment," the repetition of which structures "individual and group identities."[111] The cultural performances in Tangier (because of their regularity) are indeed crucial ways of creating—and cementing—the social tissue of a heterogeneous white European and American population as a community distinct from the Moroccan milieu in which it finds itself.

I would like to examine one such event I attended to demonstrate how the performance of "high culture" participates in the making of the European community of Tangier. The event in question was a reading from texts by New York Times best-seller Tahir Shah, a native Brit who moved to and settled in Casablanca with his family. He too confessed, when I asked him, that he knew neither Arabic nor Moroccan Arabic—and did not intend to

learn either. Nevertheless, he writes about everyday life in the city, mixing
fiction with his observations, creating a literary mélange of the hyperrealist
type.

Organized by the bookstore Les Colonnes, the reading took place in the
most luxurious room of TALIM. The entire room was crowded and several
people (including myself) could find no seat and were left to stand at the
back, along the wall. Most of the audience showed up to the event in formal
wear. The director of TALIM himself introduced the author and spoke about
the event to convey its importance. The performance must have been prepared ahead of time and probably rehearsed. Shah appeared in formal dress
behind a large rectangular table covered with red cloth. His books were ar-
ranged by most recent, from his left. At his right, a young, blond, slim lady
stood respectfully, in a formal-looking dress, hands crossed in front of her.

Shah chose to read from his work on Morocco, mostly from his book
Caliph's House. Each time he prefaced the readings, speaking about how "we
in the West" do this and think this, he then contrasted those Western norms
with those of Morocco (implicitly the East, despite its etymology that literally means the West). Not at one point did Shah say "here" or "here in Morocco"; rather he said "in Morocco," as if the country were somewhere else
(and he not in it). And in fact, it is somewhere else, outside TALIM (which
is an American cultural center and a museum and thus legally part of U.S.
territory). TALIM is located in an old house (bought originally by George
Washington in 1821). In it, on that day of the reading, everything was indeed "Western"—the audience, of course, but also the very organization of
the room with its beautiful mahogany chairs and tables, not to mention its
sophisticated American and European impressionist works of art hanging
on the walls.

Once Shah finished the preface to a particular passage, he subtly gestured to the young lady, who proceeded to read in a way that combined so-
lemnity and a British feminine accent, further giving the performance what
seemed to be intended as an air of distinguished elegance and grace. The
chosen passage described in vivid, well-crafted prose the scenes of the slaugh-
tering of lambs in the streets of Casablanca. The slaughter turned the
streets into rivers of blood. The scenes described by Shah, read by the young
woman, were violent. The images of the animals on the streets were
gruesome; the color of blood everywhere conveyed the sense of a macabre
culture. It was interesting to see what seemed to be a discrepancy in this
performance—between a violent scene, most disorderly, most gruesome, and

the well-organized, well-behaved, calm, and graceful ambiance of the room. But this was by no means a discrepancy. These are complementary scenes: one of the Here (the West as Shah reminded his audience time and again) and the Elsewhere, the East (Morocco). This is by no means specific to this context. It has been noticed that in experiences of migration, especially non-forced migration, the "here" may be an emotional "there" and the "there" an emotional "here."[112] However, in the case at hand, the performance (with all its components that also included people and space as well as reading and listening) transformed the "there" into "here" and the "here" into "there." Both are imaginary spaces as the "there" is nothing but a hyper-Europe, "whose geographical referents remain somehow indeterminate,"[113] and the "here" is also an imaginary space, part of a larger one called the Orient with its dispersed, unconnected, and ambiguous referents made possible only by imagination of the very discourse that makes its existence possible.

This specific reading caught the attention of the audience, including me. It conveyed images of death, blood, and cruelty. Shah did not use the term "sacrifice" to name what he described; neither did he use the concept of ritual. As the readings went on, I looked at the audience to gauge their reactions. They seemed to be absorbed, fascinated indeed by the descriptions that conveyed to them the utter "otherness" of Moroccans—an otherness that mirrored their own positive image. The few Moroccan youth standing along the wall also listened with great interest. If someone observed me, they must have read my discomfort with the descriptions—that were meant to be "barbaric"—of the Sacrifice Feast (*Eid al-Adha*).[114] Shah was conveying to his audience something they were already so familiar with: Orientalist themes, which constitute an important dimension of Western culture, as Edward Said demonstrated in his classic work *Orientalism*.[115] However, the images were not at all exotic images of sensuality and mystery but specifically ones of death, blood, and cruelty—all tropes of unmodern, non-Western, and even primitive life. One would recognize here the "savage slot" that constitutes the "geography of Western imagination" and that helped transform Christendom into the West.[116] It might have become outdated in ethnography, but it is undoubtedly alive and well in travel literature and media reports.[117]

It should be noted, however, that in his description, Shah did not mention Islam or indicate that the killing of the lamb is an Islamic ritual. In fact, Shah did not need to mention it—not because the Islamic character of the sacrifice is explicit in its very name and its story is shared, despite variations between Christians and Jews, but rather because the audience (as informed coauthors by virtue of their residency) knew Shah was describing Islamic culture. The very use of the term "West" by Shah implies the concept of the East, but also connotes the secular West.[118] Religiosity is a feature of the East. Consequently, that the East is Muslim did not need to be mentioned to the audience. What Jorge Luis Borges said mistakenly about camels in Arabia applies here about Islam in the world of Shah and his audience: Islam is too present in Morocco; Morocco is Islam and thus there is no reason to "emphasize" it as Borges would say.[119]

The silence in the room, the great attention each person seemed to focus while listening to the images expressed in the "Queen's English" made the author, the reader, and the audience part and parcel of the same performance. Orientalism has a unique power: through repetition of its themes, Shah was able to reaffirm the existence, here and now, of the imaginary already constituted in diametrical opposition to another imagined community, that of Moroccans as Orientals. Shah's performance created a reality that his work claims to represent. Small wonder the audience members, many of whom had lived in the country for thirty years, could not see that the sacrifice of the lamb in an Islamic society, rooted in an Abrahamic tradition, is never accomplished in the streets. In the Morocco I know, you never see blood running, never in plain sight, never in the presence of children or even women. Since the ritual is a reenactment of a foundational time, it is accomplished with the utmost veneration, including of the lamb itself (which replaced the child).[120] The ritual is often accomplished in the living room or roof of a private home, never in public in Morocco.[121]

Performances such as this one were frequent in Tangier. Not only do they create a community, as performances do, but, by their frequency and regularity, they also solidify the community, they define its social contours, and function as an important means to integrate newcomers, making them part of the community. Unlike the "festival sacred" described by Kapchan in Fes, where performance of sacred music creates a transnational community,[122] the local performances in Tangier create local ones. They create a local European community whose distinctive features, manifest in the very performances themselves, set them apart from the rest of Moroccan society.

As I left TALIM that evening after Shah's reading and walked the narrow streets of the medina in the glimmering light, passing old traditional houses, I felt I left an entire world (of Europeans) and entered another one (of Moroccans). I walked down the busy and noisy street toward the Boulevard, which was even busier and noisier. For the first time, I saw the Boulevard as a female space. I was not sure it was like that every evening. There were more women than men, more girls than boys. But what was most intriguing to me was something I did not pay attention to before. The female dress was varied. Older women wore traditional robes (*djellabas*) with a scarf or a veil. Younger women wore blue jeans, skirts, dresses. Some of them wore jeans with a veil. Sometimes the same group of women (usually a family) combined the same variety of dress, with one or two with djellabas, one with jeans and a scarf, another with jeans without a scarf, and a third with a dress without a scarf. But what intrigued me most was not this variation. Rather, it was the fact that those same French authorities who had banned the veil in defense of secularism and to protect national identity could not see that French dress had become standard attire. Could a law be issued to ban jeans and dresses as a sign of French secularism that undermines the national identity of Morocco? I thought to myself, quite a few groups believe that with certainty nowadays, especially with the strong influence of Wahhabism in the country. But the opposite—the banning of the veil—is a similar measure that falls (despite its inherent biases) within the norms of state conduct. In Tangier, as well as in the rest of Morocco, jeans and dresses have been integrated into local culture and (despite their foreign import) become part and parcel of Moroccan women's lives. They are seen and experienced as a possibility—one of many possibilities—not exclusive of other forms of attire. If there is indeed cosmopolitanism, it is here, "in one of these new cities," as Derrida says: "At the limit of these cities, these new cities that are other things than 'new cities,' a certain idea of cosmopolitanism, another, has perhaps not yet arrived. And if it has . . . then, we have not yet recognized it."[123]

While commenting on Kant, Derrida also espouses the idea that the condition of cosmopolitanism is hospitality: "By defining, in full rigor, hospitality as a right (which is in many regards a progress), Kant assigned to it the conditions that make it dependent on the sovereignty of the state, especially when there is a right to residency . . . the hospitality of the city or private hospitality are dependent on, and controlled by the law and by the police of the State."[124]

However, neither Derrida nor those who have discussed cosmopolitanism in recent years, such as Pheng Cheah, Bruce Robbins, Martha Nussbaum, Kwame Anthony Appiah, and even, to a certain extent, Harvey,[125] have paid attention to an aspect of hospitality of crucial importance to Kant and whose existence would undoubtedly reinvent cosmopolitanism, if such a shift were even possible. Hospitality, as in the quote above but also in an entire book about hospitality by Derrida, is understood only as a "natural right" of those who come, those who visit, those who reside, but not as a right of those who host, those who welcome, and those with whom we reside. Indeed, in his discussion of hospitality as a condition of cosmopolitanism, Kant laments that "the inhospitable conduct of the civilized states of our continent, especially the commercial states, the injustice which they display in visiting foreign countries and peoples (which in their case is the same as conquering them) seems appallingly great."[126]

The question for us in the context of this discussion about Tangier is the following: given the postcolonial relation between Europe and Africa, between North and South, between former colonial powers and former colonial subjects—is an equal relation possible? Posing this question also implies that it is not equal right now. It will be when the African (Moroccan or Nigerian) can likewise move without a visa to Europe and when the Pakistani can settle in England the way an Englishman can settle in Tangier—with ease. Positing the question itself suggests the remote possibility of such a condition in the foreseeable future.

Conclusion

The concept of cosmopolitanism is a key aspect of globalism (the ideology of globalization), one that masks the inequality of movement and mobility. Those who can easily move and settle outside the territory of their nation-state, who often enjoy postcolonial status, are called expats and cosmopolitans.[127] They are often white Europeans and Americans from the middle classes. However, they remain fundamentally patriots. If anything, their condition in Tangier intensifies their national belonging—and not only in relation to the local population at which they tend to look askance. It is their attachment to their countries that allows them to enjoy a condition of status and privilege that they may not enjoy at home. There is no pressure to learn the local language, not only because French is present (which is a postcolonial fact) but also, most important, because the languages of the locals are devoid of cultural capital in this postcolonial city and are thus not worth learning—especially because one can get away with speaking French wherever one goes.

Compare this linguistic situation with English in London or New York. I have met French, Spanish, and Italian men and women who were able to "pick up" English within a year in New York. But for two exceptions, I was unable to meet Europeans who had an interest in the local language of the people of Tangier with whom, or rather among whom, they had lived for years—up to thirty-five years in some cases. Often times, one can see the embarrassment of a Moroccan struggling to express himself or herself in French and simultaneously see the confidence of a French speaker, even if he is Moroccan, enjoying the awkwardness of his interlocutor.

Europeans are absent in national and local festivals that are frequent, especially during the summer. They have no interest in their hosts (Kant's forgotten partner in hospitality)—neither in the language nor in the culture that many of them deem absent (and it is indeed absent, for you can only be aware of what you learn through experience). They do not engage in local cultures, and they keep their interactions with Moroccans to the necessary minimum.

One can only wonder whether the face of the cosmopolitan is not in fact the face of the old colonial. If it is not, the so-called cosmopolitan herself is the heir of that Janus-faced settler—despised because of her illegitimate entitlement, her ability to move in and out freely, her ability to settle in and prosper easily, yet simultaneously respected because of the colonial power that made that entitlement possible. Neither the cosmopolitan nor the local is responsible for a historical condition from which one benefits and the other suffers—but none has the ability to change.

Epilogue

Notes on the Migrant Condition

We wanted to rebuild our lives, that was all.
—Hannah Arendt

I confess that my reason to return to Tangier was not only to pursue this study on migration to and from Europe. There was another important reason for my return. As much as I was committed to this project, I went to Tangier to test the idea of my definitive return to Morocco, the country of my birth, where I have all my memories of my childhood and teenage years. The idea had been in my mind ever since I had left three decades before. I chose Tangier to test my ability to reintegrate in my country of birth and end a tiring and painful life of exile and estrangement. Despite having spent more years in the United States than in my native country, I never felt settled, for reasons that are not relevant to the discussion here. And so, I was back "home" in Tangier, hoping to gain back my lost home.

I am not a native of Tangier. But I thought the city would allow me to keep my sense of foreignness while still giving me a taste of home. Tangier would help me to make the transition, adjust gradually, and hopefully settle.

In Tangier on a rainy day, the smell of the moist air, the color of the street, the sound of the rain were familiar to me and brought back precious memories of childhood and youth. It was the similarities I noticed first: the Moroccan language, of course, and people's manners and small gestures; there was also that thing you can feel but cannot point to, that ineffable quality that makes you know you are in Morocco and not in England or even Tunisia or Egypt. Elements that made the city foreign to me were also there, but I decided not to see them and instead busied my mind, my spirit, and my body with what I wanted. I was back home and I wanted to stay or at least try to stay. Between the time of my departure and return, an entire generation had passed. Could I undo exile, that "unhealable rift forced between a human being and a native place"?[1] And there were other questions that I attempted to tackle through the experiences of others: Why choose migration over staying home, challenges over comfort, familiarity over estrangement? Is home still home once it has been left for long? Is one still oneself after exile, which is a search for another home? Can one ever return home?

My own narrative of exile started in 1981. Tangier was then, as it is today, the main gate to Europe, especially at a time when traveling by air was a luxury that few could afford. The last Moroccan city one saw before leaving the country was Tangier. The city looked modest, even poor, with visible signs of misery. Only the beach, located downtown, was intriguing. When the train crossed the port and neared the ferry gate, all of a sudden one found oneself in a currency market, surrounded by men offering French francs and Spanish pesetas. What I saw confirmed the city's reputation as a magnet for contraband and dealers of all types.

On a hot day during Ramadan, as I left the country and the sweetness of my own home for the first time (though not the last), the city looked painfully impoverished.

Words cannot describe the devastating emotional rupture I experienced as I left home. Whenever the train from Meknès to Tangier stopped at an intervening station, the urge I felt to get off and go back was overwhelming, matched only by the fear that I would be mocked as a "wimp" if I dared return. Once inside the port of Tangier, that urge left me, though the pain worsened. Not that I feared the unknown. Rather, I was being uprooted at a vulnerable age that was neither young enough to quickly forget and adjust nor old enough to help me withstand the duress of leaving. Even now I vividly remember, and have many times relived, that rupture. From that moment, I developed a genuine dislike for train stations—all of them. Now I firmly believe that getting off would have been in itself a courageous decision. But I did not think that at that moment. And in the years since, I have imagined, with deep sadness, what life would have become had I decided to stay instead of leaving. I am convinced that it would have been sweeter and more comforting. No matter what they say about migration and exile, the condition of the migrant is perhaps often not only one of inner conflict but also one of constant pain—a life of otherness, foreignness, and depending on the context, it can also be one of constant suspicion and even sporadic acts of hostility—overt and covert. In this day and age, it is awfully difficult to be a foreigner even if one enjoys great privileges in employment and social status. The discourse on globalization often celebrates what are commonly called "easy mobility" and a "flat world" but rarely states the fact that this increase in movement is also accompanied by an increase in xenophobia and racism of all types. Social status does not prevent one from experiencing their effects. If anything, it may make them more acute. This feeling is well captured in a statement of a colleague who was teaching at an Ivy League school: "Here I feel I am walled in. I understand everything, but nothing speaks to me: not this magnificent, chilly campus, not my colleagues, not the trees everywhere, not this society so often given to competition and violence. And on top of all this—contempt for Arabs."[2]

Contempt for just Arabs or for Muslims? Contempt for Muslims or for anybody deemed unacceptably foreign? There is surely a variety of types of foreignness in a given society. There is a foreignness that signals difference that is espoused and embraced because it is supposed to create distinction; there is difference that is accepted, there is difference that is tolerated, and there is surely a difference that is perceived as threatening, dangerous, and against which one, consciously or subconsciously, guards oneself. Foreignness, or the condition of being foreign, is also historical and circumstantial. What used to be foreign and threatening once may be relatively accepted today, and what is not accepted now may one day become familiar. Other forms of foreignness may emerge. Foreignness is also relative, and this relativity plays out in everyday life through small and big acts, visible and trivial gestures, through furtive gazes and hostile stares. It is these acts, gestures, and gazes that remind one that no matter how long one has lived in a land of migration, one may still feel and be felt as foreign. Shahram Khosravi describes his migrant condition in Sweden in terms of "unreachable borders." These borders, he says, are "invisible" and "intractable," yet "the wounds they inflict [are] no less real."[3] He too uses a spatial metaphor to express his sense of alienation: "I have survived crossing many borders between nation-states in dangerous places, surviving bandits, corrupt border guards, statelessness and lack of status, but these invisible borders have, since my arrival in Sweden more than two decades ago, pushed me into a corner."[4]

In Morocco also, migrants (including Moroccans from the underclass) live a hellish life made of daily acts of *hogra*. These migrants, of low status, different phenotypes, foreign accents, different cultures, different faiths, are also cornered and walled, but their corner is too small, and their walls are thicker and more solid than those of middle-class migrants in Europe and in the United States. Their corners and walls are not just metaphors: they are as much symbolic as they are physical. Think of the small corner of the port next to the mosque, or the gray wall that guards and protects the port. The people whose lives I have discussed in this book are without privilege. For many of them, the street is their home. Most of them moved from home to Tangier in hope of crossing to Europe for an array of reasons that are complex. The desire to turn a page, to rebuild a life, to run away from one, to reinvent oneself is common among all the migrants I encountered in Tangier and beyond.

Saskia Sassen argues that "the flows of immigrants and refugees" are not a matter of a "search of better opportunities in a rich country." Instead, she continues, "migrations are highly selective processes; only certain people leave, and they travel on highly structured routes to their destinations, rather than gravitate blindly towards any rich country they can enter. The reason migrations take this highly structured form has to do with the interactions and interrelations between sending and receiving countries."[5]

In this epilogue, I attempt to show how the pattern of African emigration has changed within one generation. Today the African migrant intends to go toward "any rich country," but in his imagination, the rich ones are in Europe. The United States is out of reach. It is not material wealth per se that motivates the migrants I encountered, but rather a certain life of which material life is only a part. The French anthropologist Sylvie Bredeloup also noticed the same thing when she wrote, "The decision to leave does not systematically result in 'costs-advantages calculations' but can also result in a pressing urge to change lifestyle, to invent new ways of life, to explore far-off lands, real or imaginary. If seen in this way, migration is also similar to a moral experience."[6] (And, as she points out, migration within Africa itself is often overlooked by outside analysts. African migrants move to other African countries, too, where they can reinvent themselves.) As I have attempted to show in this book, the decision of the West African youth or the Moroccan child to leave a hometown is in itself an act of courage, a refusal to accept a destiny of injustice and fairness, an expression of a spirit that "wills his own will," to use Nietzsche's words,[7] a heroic act of the exercise of freedom—freedom of movement and freedom to build a new life at all costs, including the costs of dying, which the *harraga* believe is a shared destiny; no human can decide the moment of its happening.

All things considered, this also holds true as much for the African migrants as it does for the European migrants who settle in Tangier, or in any part of Morocco for that matter. Morocco, until the early 1990s, was a tourist destination for Europeans. Europeans then sought to live "an elitist life or one that looks like an elitist one," as Henri Lefebvre put it, describing their life in the "underdeveloped countries that border the Mediterranean."[8] A French youth struggling to make a living or a middle-class divorced woman from Spain or a gay man embarrassed by his sexuality can also rebuild a life, an elite life, in Tangier, and invent a new self—one not chosen by the accident of birth. "In Tangier," a European resident once told me, "you can become whatever you want." He was speaking about Europeans, not about me. European migrants in the city see their status change for the better. And that change itself brings with it an attitude of superiority over "others." Often, this superiority manifests itself as contempt.

The condition of the West African migrants is not, of course, the condition of the French migrants. History, that is, the making of the modern world with its central event of colonialism, decided which route each one can take for the drastic change they seek. It is history indeed that makes one route relatively easy and another incredibly difficult. It is also history that makes one guest accepted and valued in Tangier and another one a pariah—unwanted and often despised. It is history that associates whiteness with status, prestige, and power; and blackness with poverty, misery, disease, and illegality. Race, as I argued, is an important analytical category for understanding the dynamics of migration in Tangier, including the fact that European migration is not even called migration, let alone considered illegal. This migration is, instead, associated with development, and the presence of Europeans endows the city with its character, its cosmopolitanism—that is, its diversity, albeit with obvious inequality among migrant communities.

Because of the dreadful condition of the West African migrants in the city, they are determined to cross, to get out, even when offered "papers" to regularize their legal status.[9] Legal or illegal, the way the Moroccan state sees the West African migrant affects neither his day-to-day life in the city nor his determination to cross. In addition to whatever reasons why the migrant left his country, say Mali or Ghana, he has reason to leave Morocco. When I met Melissa, a young lady from Nigeria, she was dressed in the traditional Moroccan style with a green *djellaba* and a white headscarf. As we walked the Boulevard Mohammed V, I asked her why she did not find a job in Morocco instead of attempting to cross. She said, "There are no jobs in

Morocco and Moroccans do not want to hire blacks. In Europe, there are all kinds of jobs I can do."

"What kind of jobs would you do?"

"They will not hire me here, but in Europe I can do a lot."

"Like what?"

"I know how to bake, I know how to do hair, I can make dreadlocks. There are a lot of things I know how to make."

The condition of West Africans is shared to a great extent with the condition of Moroccan harraga. The city is as hostile to the first as it is to the second. In modern times, the greatest exoduses were caused first by extreme hostile conditions in one's own country, as Hannah Arendt explains in the case of the large number of Jewish refugees who left Europe.[10] Nowadays, this holds, mutatis mutandis, for the large number of African migrants who are "leaving" the continent,[11] not to mention the millions of Iraqi and Syrian refugees who are fleeing war zones. These migrants are leaving, or "burning," as the expression goes, not only in search of "better opportunities" but to run away from something—generally from a life in which they were born, by accident, and now that they are conscious of it, want to refuse and change, or exchange.

None of the hundreds of migrants I interviewed and spent time with, or the dozens I befriended, told me that they wanted to go to Europe to become "rich." Rather, they wanted to go to Europe to live a different life. Europe offers that "different life" the migrant wants to live, the way Morocco offers the European migrant a different life. The first is highly attractive for its modern elements; the second is equally attractive for its traditional, exotic, colonial-like characteristics, which also come with the high prestige associated with being a white European. For both populations, "home" does not satisfy their wants, does not fulfill their dreams; it is abroad, an elsewhere, that hails them. The appeal of this elsewhere is also a product of history: for African migrants, it is where the magic thing called modernity resides; for the Europeans, it is where an outdated prestige lives on. Each believes that the space of the destination, once reached, will transform him or her for the better. The migrant condition is, after all, about exchanging home for another home even if that home turns out to be exile.

However, the categories by which we measure space (such as home and abroad) are intellectual efforts to think, perceive, and understand what may be inherently absurd. As a product of migration and exile, the only home I left was in my imagination, in the form of memories of places and people in places and experiences in places that no longer exist except in recollections. But the ability to remember allows us to relive the experience, to make something absent present, as Paul Ricœur would say.[12] In exile, I have always felt my recollections of past events and experiences as acute. I can remember the details of feelings, discussions, objects, and even faces of passengers at the port, in the boat, at the airport, and in the airplane. In another symptom of this obsession not to let time pass, which would mean to accept the time in exile, I almost pathologically cling to all objects from this past—clothes, postcards, gifts, papers, notes, and even boxes of things that I put together purposely to throw away and have never been able to. But paradoxically, these same objects of the past turn out to prove to me, to tyrannically remind me, of time past, of that which prevents me from liberating myself, if that is ever possible, from the condition of exile.

In the 1980s when I left home, the frontier of Europe seemed porous; Spanish customs agents could care less whether one was a migrant or tourist as long as one had a valid passport. Spain itself, in the aftermath of Franco's rule, seemed like a Third World country and was indeed a poor cousin of Europe until much later, when it became a democracy, part of the European Union. But in these times of the first postcolonial migration, Spain was a land like ours, so much so that on the train from Madrid to France, the Moroccan migrants mixed well with the Spanish ones, who were leaving the country for a more prosperous Europe. Thus, Spanish customs was in a way not the border itself but just a continuation of Moroccan customs. The wait used to be long, tiring, amid migrants and would-be migrants and a few students, like me, heading to Europe. The French customs agents, on the other hand, were a bit more concerned but not obsessively. They would ask you questions such as, "Why are you traveling to France?" and if you said tourism, then they would ask you to show proof that you could sustain yourself. Usually, 600 francs would let you pass. If you were a student, you would be asked to show proof of registration, but a preregistration was good enough.

At that time, the responsibility for controlling mobility (or migration, as it was already called) lay on the shoulders of the nation-state, of the sending countries. For instance, in Morocco, passports, though considered in the constitution a civil right, were given perniciously. It was difficult to get a passport. One needed to show proof of employment or evidence of a certain salary, or one could bribe the official who decided whether or not your dossier would be sent to the *wilâya* (city hall). Migration was not a dream then.

The country of Morocco held only 16 million people when I was growing up. Illiteracy was high already, and thus those who were schooled could
be assured that they were going to get jobs. Most of the teachers in my high
school were Europeans, especially from France. Europe and, more specifically, France still had its colonial attraction—mainly, its language, culture,
and material modernity. But the idea of abandoning one's country and seeking exile (*ghorba*) was far from most people's minds.

There was something even shameful about being an immigrant in the
1970s. One could be insulted for living abroad because that meant one was
in need and could not even make it in one's own country. Migration was also
associated, to a large degree, with the countryside and the shantytowns, as
well as generally from the so-called *Maroc inutile*—poor areas such as the
Rif and the Sous areas.[13] French recruiters actively sought "solid" human
labor in campaigns that looked sometimes like "slave markets."[14] Lack of education, poverty, and uncouthness were stereotypes associated with the status
of migrants.[15]

In the 1970s, these migrants, often not highly respected and even mocked,
came back during the summer and, to counter the mocking, indulged in
excessive spending. The minimum wage in France allowed them to appear
well off, though of course they had also concentrated on saving up to show
off once they were back home. They wanted to show they had succeeded. Cars
were a luxury in Morocco, and most if not all of the migrants came back
with French cars such as Peugeots. Real estate prices were low, and migrants
who once lived in the countryside or a shantytown now moved to a city—a
sign of wealth and even a certain class. New houses, half traditional and half
modern, were constructed on the outskirts of cities and towns for the
immigrant, the nouveau riche, with a house, a car, new clothes, pompous weddings, and money to spend and share with family members.

Gradually, the culture of migration was instilled in Morocco. The migrant turned his (unknown) condition into a social status to be envied and
even sought after. The hidden face of migration could not possibly be seen
by those who stayed back at home; only the signs of success were displayed.
The postcolonial subaltern conditions—low-level jobs, daily racism, ghetto-
like housing—were in many ways the "dirty secrets" of the migrant who returned and may even have displayed an attitude of arrogance toward those
who had stayed back. Tensions and mutual condescension started forming
between the two. Migrants would call the country *lablâd* (from the highly
pejorative, racist *bledar* for the less civilized, poor, uneducated). Those who

had stayed would refer to migrants as *facance* (from *vacance*): those who come back during the summer for vacation and are unable to even pronounce the word "*vacance*" that they use so arrogantly. The peasants or rather "hicks" (*a'rûbiya*) were unable to make a living at home and had to migrate to make one abroad. Even the term "*immigré*" itself, when pronounced in Moroccan, "*zmâgri*," has nothing flattering about it. It evokes an attitude of boasting behind which a life of misery is difficult to cover.

One night, while chatting on the fishermen's nets, I asked a group of kids, "Why would you like to cross?"

"We want to have a life there, live well."

"What makes you think you can live well there?"

"We know, we see Moroccans back here, and they are well off."

"Do you know that they don't like us?"

"What do you mean?"

"Arabs and Muslims are generally not liked in Europe."

"Even you, they don't like you, *ustâdh*?"

"Even me," I quickly responded, "they don't discriminate in discriminating against us."

I purposely used that generalization. I wanted to convey to them the general feeling in Europe today and wanted to communicate that dislike and discrimination await them when they cross. In short, I wanted to communicate that they will exchange a local (national) form of hogra for an extra-national one. I am not sure which one is worse.

I resisted lecturing them on how difficult life is in Europe. But sometimes, the question of racism and xenophobia came into the discussion. Thus, one day I was talking with two Nigerians about daily racism in Morocco. At one point, I said, "You want to go to France? You know well there is so much racism there against African immigrants?"

"Yes, but we are not going to France; we are going to Italy. Italians are not racists."

In Tangier, I had several lives: with the harraga at night when they gathered at the port, played cards, and spoke about their lives and their dreams; with Europeans at social events; and during lonely days and nights, bored to tears in a city where I felt a foreigner. Yet, each of these lives enhanced my understanding of the condition of my own exile that I often feel to be a curse, despite the advantages it has provided. For those advantages also come with a price, and I am never sure whether they are worth the price I pay daily for them. Often, I feel they are not.

With the Moroccan kids, I could relate because once upon a time, I was one of them. With the West Africans, I was unable to relate or even to understand, let alone experience, the extraordinary condition of wretchedness. With the Europeans, I could return to the position of the postcolonial "other" that I had once known in France. The "racism" that arrived with the colonial Europeans in 1860 seems to have persisted. If anything, it has flourished, especially in recent years, with the rise of militant Islam and the sporadic terrorist attacks that have been hitting Europe and the United States.

Neither the Moroccan harraga nor the West African migrants feel that "home" is home. The hostility of the environment, sometimes intense, makes them feel they are not home, if being at home is "the question of affects," as Sara Ahmed put it, a matter of "how one feels or how one might fail to feel."[16] Hence also, in large part, the spur to leave. Leaving a homeland almost becomes a necessity for the harraga: "I wanna burn because it is fucked up here" or "I wanna burn because this country gave us nothing." The West Africans I met expressed the same feelings—that their countries had failed them, that there is nothing to do, no future. It is this urge to leave that Amin Maalouf, also a migrant, captures in his novel, *Les désorientés*: "First of all it is your country that needs to have a number of commitments towards you. You will need to be treated like a first-class citizen and not to be subject to oppression or discrimination or unwanted deprivations. Your country and its leaders have the duty to guarantee you this; otherwise you owe them nothing—no attachment to the soil, no saluting the flag. The country where you live, head up: give it everything, sacrifice everything for it, even your own life. The country where you live, head down: give it nothing regardless whether it is your adoptive country or your native one."[17]

A harrag told me in 2008 that he was willing to "sign a contract to give up his nationality"; he does not feel a citizen. Between him and the state, there is no contract. He has no rights to education or even to safety—the safety a state should give you even if you are not its citizen. It is not surprising, then, that he wants to make a deal somewhere else. I also heard other reasons: "we wanna see the world" (*bghinâ namchîw nchûfu dâk aldanyâ*), or as a Nigerian youth once told me, "I need to move; it is movement that makes history." The truth for him, for them, and for me as well is that feeling that one should refuse to be "caged" in one place at the beginning of life, seeing the same thing every day, and doing the same thing every day, such that one sees oneself in the future unchanged and unchanging. In other words, one refuses to live without hope or without a dream. While it has been said that "to be rooted is perhaps the most important and least recognized need of the human soul,"[18] the idea of freedom may be more important to some than the idea of being rooted. Without freedom, the idea of being rooted becomes synonymous with imprisonment. The harraga, children and adults alike, and the West African migrants also feel that mobility is more important than the need to be rooted. Even if we assume that the endeavor of the harrag is suicidal, suicide itself may be "the last supreme guarantee of human freedom."[19] Unlike many Moroccan harraga (who may feel rooted by virtue of being "there"), the West Africans I met all stayed in touch with their families, whom they called on a regular basis. This is to say that "being rooted," having a home, is not necessarily being in the place where one was born (by accident); rather, "home is the reflection of our subjectivity."[20]

At night, while talking to a group of kids gathered, sitting on fishing nets hopping with all sorts of bugs, I tried to see their lives in the future. At the moment, despite the condition of exile at home, they seemed to be genuinely happy. They seemed almost unaware of how miserable their lives were. I strangely didn't doubt their happiness. I had no reason to. They laughed, they played cards, they joked, they shared stories, they shared food. After all, they had hope.

There were times when I arrived and no one was there; the entire place was strangely deserted. The following day, they were all back again.

"Where were you last night?"

"We went to watch a music band in Malabata."

Age has a big part to do with the insouciance that enables their happiness: "'Hope' is the thing with feathers," writes Emily Dickinson.[21] The dreams of some of them may come true. Some migrants will create that new home that is called the family. And some will try to come back home, like myself, but they will not find it. Home is lost in time and in space at every departure. It exists only in recollection, and so the longing for home becomes progressively more acute, more painful, making the migrant's condition one of unbearable suffering.

Notes

INTRODUCTION

1. Michael Crawford and Benjamin Campbell, *Causes and Consequences of Human Migration: An Evolutionary Perspective* (Cambridge: Cambridge University Press, 2012); Joseph Conrad, *Heart of Darkness and Selections from The Congo Diary* (New York: Modern Library, 1999).

2. Saskia Sassen, *Globalization and Its Discontents* (New York: New Press, 1998), 56.

3. Tayeb Saleh, *Season of Migration to the North* (New York: New York Review of Books, 2009).

4. For a history of these forms of mobility, see Saskia Sassen, *Guests and Aliens* (New York: New Press, 1999). See also Catherine Wihtol de Wenden, *La question migratoire au XXIe siècle: Migrants, réfugiés et relations internationales* (Paris: Presses de Sciences Po, 2010).

5. For the history of migration to France, see Jacques Dupaquier, *Histoire de la population française* (Paris: Presses Universitaires de France, 1995); Gérard Noiriel, *Le creuset français. Histoire de l'immigration XIXe–XXe siècles* (Paris: Le Seuil, 1988). See also Patrick Weil, *La France et ses étrangers: L'aventure d'une politique de l'immigration de 1938 à nos jours* (Paris: Gallimard, 2005).

6. David Harvey, *Cosmopolitanism and the Geographies of Reason* (New York: Columbia University Press, 2009).

7. On what makes a city postcolonial, Garth Myers observes that "the biggest spatial impact of European colonization lies in the location of so many of Africa's eventually major cities along the coast or in close proximity to sites of resource extraction." See Garth Myers, *African Cities: Alternative Visions of Urban Theories and Practice* (London: Zed Books, 2011), 51.

8. See Karim Bejjit, *English Colonial Texts on Tangier, 1661–1684: Imperialism and the Politics of Resistance* (New York: Routledge, 2016); Jean-Louis Miège, "Les refugiés politiques à Tanger, 1796–1875," *Revue Africaine* 1–2 (1957): 129–46; Edouard Michaux-Bellaire, *Tanger et sa zone* (Paris: Ernest Leroux, 1921).

9. See Lawdom Vaidon, *Tangier: A Different Way* (London: Scarecrow Press, 1977).

10. Bejjit, *English Colonial Texts on Tangier*, 9.

11. Ibid., 7.

12. Ibid.

13. Ibid.

14. Claire Spencer, "The Zone of International Administration of Tangier (1923–1935)" (PhD diss., University of London, SOAS, 1993).

15. Graham Stuart, *The International City of Tangier* (Stanford, Calif.: Stanford University Press, 1955), 38.

16. Ibid.

17. Jean-Louis Miège, *Le Maroc et l'Europe (1830–1894)*, vol. 2 (Paris: Presses Universitaires de France, 1961), 170.

18. Ibid., 172, 474.

19. Miège, "Les réfugiés politiques à Tanger," 131–46.

20. Susan Gilson Miller, "The Beni Ider Quarter of Tangier in 1900: Hybridity as a Social Practice," in *The Architecture and Memory of the Minority Quarter in the Muslim Mediterranean City*, ed. Susan Gilson Miller Mauro Bertagnin (Cambridge, Mass.: Harvard University Press, 2010), 146.

21. I owe this remark to Fayre Makeig.

22. Edmondo de Amicis, *Morocco: Its Peoples and Places* (Philadelphia: Coates & Co., 1897).

23. Mark Twain, *The Innocents Abroad or the New Pilgrims' Progress*, vol. 1 (New York: Harper & Brothers, 1869), 64.

24. Ibid., 78.

25. Ibid., 79.

26. Ibid., 79.

27. Ibid., 65.

28. Alexandre Dumas, *Tangier to Tunis*, trans. A. E. Murch (London: Peter Owen, 1959), 24.

29. Ibid.

30. Stuart, *The International City of Tangier*, 37.

31. For more on this accord, see ibid., 43–44.

32. Ibid., 44–45.

33. On the treaty of Algeciras, see Anthony F. Eastman, "The Algeciras Conference, 1906," *Southern Quarterly* 7, no. 1 (1969): 185–205; Heather Jones, "Algeciras Revisited: European Crisis and Conference Diplomacy, 16 January–7 April 1906," EUI Working Papers, MWP 2009/01, Max Weber Programme, 2009, http://diana-n.iue.it:8080/bitstream/handle/1814/10527/MWP_2009_01.pdf?sequence=1&isAllowed=y.

34. Graham Stuart, "The Future of Tangier," *Foreign Affairs*, July 1945.

35. Stuart, *The International City of Tangier*; Spencer, "The Zone of International Administration of Tangier."

36. Spencer, "The Zone of International Administration of Tangier."

37. Paul Rabinow, *French Modern: Norms and Forms of the Social Environment* (Cambridge, Mass.: MIT Press, 1989).

38. Paul Bowles, *Let It Come Down* (London: John Lehmann, 1952).

39. Stuart, *The International City of Tangier*, 170.

40. See Daniel Schroeter, "Philo-Sephardism, Anti-Semitism, and Arab Nationalism: Muslims and Jews in the Spanish Protectorate of Morocco During the Third Reich," in *Nazism, the Holocaust, and the Middle East*, ed. Francis R. Nicosia and Boğaç A. Ergene (New York: Berghan, 2018).

41. Mohamed Choukri, *Jean Genet in Tangier*, trans. Paul Bowles (New York: Ecco Press, 1974).

42. Frantz Fanon, *The Wretched of the Earth* (New York: Grove, 1963).

43. Mohamed Choukri, *For Bread Alone*, trans. Paul Bowles (London: Saqi, 2006).

44. As was reported to me by a European man during my fieldwork, upper-class and well-to-do Europeans used to send their gay relatives to Tangier because they were too ashamed of them. Family members paid their way "to get rid of the embarrassment."

45. Barry Miles, *Call Me Burroughs: A Life* (New York: Twelve, 2014).

46. Fanon, *The Wretched of the Earth*.

47. See the collective volume, *Abd el-Krim et la république du Rif* (Paris: Maspero, 1976).

48. The history of postcolonial Tangier has yet to be written.

49. Choukri, *Jean Genet in Tangier*.

50. See Luiza Bialasiewicz, "Tangier, Mobile City: RE-Making Borders in the Straits of Gibraltar," in *Borderities and the Politics of Contemporary Mobile Borders* ed. Anne-Laure Amilhat-Szary and Frédéric Giraut (London: Palgrave Macmillan, 2015).

51. See Myers, *African Cities*.

52. Henri Lefebvre, *La production de l'espace* (Paris: Anthropos, 2000), 66.

53. This is not unique to Tangier. The Casbah of Marrakesh has also been westernized, with the entirety of its population from Europe. See Rachida Saigh Bousta, "New Forms of Migration: Europeans in Marrakech," in *Going Abroad: Travel, Tourism, and Migration*, ed. Christine Geoffrey and Richard Sibley (Cambridge: Cambridge Scholars, 2007), 158–266; Anton Escher and Sandra Petermann, "Neo-Colonialism or Gentrification in the Medina of Marrakesh," *ISIM Newsletter* 5, no. 1 (2000): 34.

54. For a different view of Tangier, see Luiza Bialasiewicz and Lauren Wagner, "Extraordinary Tangier: Domesticating Practices in a Border Zone," *GeoHumanities* 1, no. 1 (2015): 131–56.

55. Ibid.

56. Gisella Williams, "A Fabled City of the Dissolute Gets Shine," *New York Times*, December 19, 2008, http://www.nytimes.com/2008/12/21/travel/21next.html.

57. Olivier Piot, "Tanger, La mille et une ville," *Le Monde*, April 27, 2010, http://www.lemonde.fr/voyage/article/2009/09/01/tanger-la-mille-et-une-ville_1339691_3546.html.

58. Matt Gross, "Lost in Tangier," *New York Times*, September 9, 2010, http://www.nytimes.com/2010/09/12/travel/12Lost.html.

59. Andrew O'Hagan, "The Aesthetes," *New York Times*, April 11, 2014.

60. Ibid.

61. Joseph Conrad, *Lord Jim* (Edinburgh: Blackwood's Magazine, 1900).

62. Tahar Ben Jelloun devoted much of his writings to the city. Tahar Ben Jelloun, *Jour de silence à Tanger* (Paris: Seuil, 1990); Tahar Ben Jelloun, *Partir* (Paris: Seuil, 2007). Choukri's acclaimed novel/autobiography takes place mostly in Tangier. See Choukri, *For Bread Alone*.

63. Oliver Piot, "Tanger. La mille et une ville." The only *Le Monde* article that mentions the harraga uses an exaggerated collectivity, "*des milliers de harraga*" (thousands of harraga).

64. Especially with the emergence of new literature consisting mainly of autobiographical narratives by French women and by young Moroccans about their experience in Tangier. See examples in Veronique Bruez, *La Terrasse des Paresseaux* (Clamecy: Éditions Leo Scheer, 2011); Stephanie Gaou, *Capiteuses* (Casablanca: al Manar, 2012).

65. Maurice Merleau-Ponty, *Éloge de la philosophie et autres essais* (Paris: Gallimard, 1965), 23.

66. See Abdelmajid Hannoum, "The (Re)Turn of the Native: Anthropology, Ethnography, and Nativism," in *The Anthropologist and the Native: Essays for Gananath Obeyesekere*, ed. H. L. Seneviratne (Firenze: Società Editrice Fiorentina, 2009), 423–70.

67. Clifford Geertz, "Deep Hanging Out," *New York Review of Books*, October 22, 1998.

68. Robert Desjarlais and C. Jason Throop, "Phenomenological Approaches in Anthropology," *Annual Review of Anthropology* 40 (2011): 87–102.

69. I follow the old wisdom to consider Maghrebi studies as part of Middle Eastern studies.

70. Abdelmalek Sayad, *La double absence: Des illusions de l'émigré aux souffrances de l'immigré* (Paris: Seuil, 2014).

71. In English, Laurie Brand, *Citizens Abroad: Emigration and the State in the Middle East and North Africa* (Cambridge: Cambridge University Press, 2006). In French, there seems to be an increased interest in migration, but it generally remains oriented toward security and policy studies. Some of the most notorious examples include the work of Abdelkrim Belguendouz, "Le Maroc: Vaste zone d'attente?" *Plein Droit* 57 (2003): 35–40; Abdelkrim Belguendouz, "Expansion et sous-traitance des logiques d'enfermement de l'Union Europeenne: L'example du Maroc," *Cultures & Conflicts* 57 (2005): 155–220; Mehdi Lahlou, "Morocco's Experience of Migration as a Sending, Transit, and Receiving Country" (15 Working Papers, Instituto Affari Internazionali, September 30, 2015). See also Mehdi Lahlou, *Les migrations irrégulières entre le Maghreb et l'Union européenne: Évolutions récentes*, CARIM Research Report 2005/03 (Florence: European University Institute, 2005), http://cadmus.eui.eu/bitstream/handle/1814/6278/?sequence=1 (accessed June 6, 2017).

72. Michel Wieviorka, ed., *Racisme et modernité* (Paris: La Découverte, 1993), 7.

73. Hannah Arendt, *The Origins of Totalitarianism* (New York: Harcourt, 1966).

74. Susan Miller, "Watering the Garden of Tangier: Colonial Contestations in a Moroccan City," in *The Walled Arab City in Literature, Architecture, and History: The Living Medina*, ed. Susan Slyomovics (London: Routledge, 2001), 26.

75. Michel Foucault, *Il faut défendre la société* (Paris: Seuil, 1997).

76. Claude Lévi-Strauss, *Race et histoire* (Paris: UNESCIM, 1952; reprint, Denoël, 1987). Already in his text to UNESCO in 1952, Lévi-Strauss evokes genetics to dismiss the concept as anthropologically relevant and instead uses a Boasian conception (and even ideas) to tackle the question of human diversity.

77. See Kamala Visweswaran, "Race and the Culture of Anthropology," *American Anthropologist* 100, no. 1 (1998): 70–83.

78. Magali Bessone, *Sans distinction de race? Une analyse critique du concept de race et de ses effets pratiques* (Paris: VRIN, 2013), 86 and passim.

79. See Visweswaran, "Race and Cultural Anthropology."

80. Paul Gilroy, *There Ain't No Black in the Union Jack: The Cultural Politics of Race and Nation* (London: Hutchinson, 1987), 149.

81. For a discussion, see Abdelmajid Hannoum, "Notes on the (Post)Colonial in the Maghreb," *Critique of Anthropology* 29, no. 3 (2009): 324–44.

82. Ibid.

83. See especially Thomas Glick, *Islamic and Christian Spain in the Early Middle Ages* (Princeton, N.J.: Princeton University Press, 1979).

84. For the case of Muslim Spain, see Glick, *Islamic and Christian Spain*. See also the sociological categories of Ibn Khaldun in Mohamed Abed al-Jabri, *al-Asabiyya ad-dawla: ma ' âlim nazariyya khalduniyya fî t-târikh al-islâmi* (Casablanca: al-Markaz dirâsât al-wahda al 'arabiya, 1971). For how these categories have been transformed into racial categories, see Abdelmajid Hannoum, "Translation and the Colonial Imaginary: Ibn Khûldun, Orientalist," *History and Theory* 42, no. 1 (2003): 61–81.

85. For a discussion of the race theories of Gobineau and their impact on racial thinking into the first half of the twentieth century, see Arendt, "Race-Thinking Before Racism."

86. Lévi-Strauss, *Race et histoire.*

87. Paul Gilroy, "One Nation Under a Grove: The Cultural Politics of 'Race' and Racism in Britain," in *Anatomy of Racism*, ed. David Goldberg (Minneapolis: University of Minnesota Press, 1990), 265.

88. Ibid., 264.

89. David Goldberg, *Racist Cultures: Philosophy and the Politics of Meaning* (Oxford: Blackwell, 1993), 78.

90. The existence of race shows itself not only in slurs and negative statements but also in positive statements conferring to a group highly positive characteristics that ipso facto imply that "we" or "others" do not have those qualities. I give the example of being a white European in Morocco.

91. Fredrik Barth, *Ethnic Groups and Boundaries: The Social Organization of Culture Difference* (Oslo: Universitetsforlaget, 1969).

92. Ibid., 78.

93. Léon Poliakov, "Racism from the Enlightenment to the Age of Imperialism," in *Racism and Colonialism: Essays on Ideology and Social Structure*, ed. Robert Ross (Hague: Martinus Nijhoff, 1982), 55–64.

94. Dipesh Chakrabarty, *Provincializing Europe: Postcolonial Thought and Historical Difference* (Princeton, N.J.: Princeton University Press, 2000).

95. Fassi does not just mean a resident of the city of Fes but rather a member of a specific group that is distinguished by its Andalusian heritage. By and large, Fassis represent the traditional Moroccan bourgeoisie. Known for their dress, cuisine, and distinct accent, they could also be identified by their last names of Bannouna, Fassi, Benchekroun, Sqalli, and so on. Therefore, a Fassi remains a Fassi even when born in another city. By contrast, a Jebli (plural *Jbala*) is from the poor area of the Rif in northern Morocco; they are Arabized Berbers.

96. Chouki El Hamel, *Black Morocco: A History of Slavery, Race, and Islam* (Cambridge: Cambridge University Press, 2014).

97. "The Republic does not recognize race or skin colour," President Hollande said, implying by the same phrase that there is no racism. See Laure Bretton, "François Hollande: 'La République ne connaît pas de races ni de couleurs de peau,'" *Libération*, October 8, 2015, http://www.liberation.fr/france/2015/10/08/la-republique-ne-connait-pas-de-races-ni-de -couleurs-de-peau_1400069.

98. For the discursive invisibility of race and the visibility of racism in France, see Didier Fassin and Eric Fassin, eds., *De la question sociale a la question raciale* (Paris: La Découverte, 2006); Didier Fassin, *Enforcing Order: An Ethnography of Urban Policing* (Cambridge: Polity, 2013); Ann Laura Stoler, *Duress: Imperial Durabilities in Our Times* (Durham, N.C.: Duke University, 2006); Sadri Khiari, *Pour une politique de la racaille* (Paris: Textual, 2006).

99. For black Moroccans, see Chouki El Hamel, *Black Morocco.*

100. See Belguendouz, "Le Maroc, vaste zone d'attente?"; Belguendouz, "Expansion et sous-traitance."

101. See Nicholas de Genova, "Migrant 'Illegality' and Deportability in Everyday Life," *Annual Review of Anthropology* 31 (2002): 419–47.

102. Ibid.

103. Michel Foucault, *Surveiller et punir: Naissance de la prison* (Paris: Gallimard, 1975), 285.

104. Ibid.

105. Didier Fassin, "Policing Borders, Producing Boundaries: The Governmentality of Immigration in Dark Times," *Annual Review of Anthropology* 40 (2011): 222.

106. See Nina Glick Schiller and Noel Salazar, "Regimes of Mobility Across the Globe," *Journal of Ethnic and Migration Studies* 39, no. 2 (2013): 183–200.

107. Nancy Scheper-Hughes and Carolyn Sargent, eds., *Small Wars: The Cultural Politics of Childhood* (Berkeley: University of California Press, 1998), 13–14.

108. De Genova, "Migrant, 'Illegality' and Deportability in Everyday Life"; Fassin, "Policing Borders."

109. Geertz, "Deep Hanging Out."

110. George Marcus, "The Uses of Complicity in the Changing Mise-en-Scène of Anthropological Fieldwork," *Representations* 59 (1997): 85–108.

111. This was also noticed by Lahlou, *Les migration irrégulières.*

112. For the routes of sub-Saharan Africans to Europe, see map in *Le Monde*, "les routes africaines de l'immigration clandestine," August 24, 2004, http://www.lemonde.fr/inter national/infographie/2004/08/24/les-routes-africaines-de-l-immigration-clandestine_628348 _3210.html. See also Lucie Bacon, Olivier Clochard, Thomas Honoré, Nicholas Lambert, Sarah Mekdjian, and Philippe Rekacewicz, "Cartographier les mouvements migratoires," *Revue européenne des migrations internationales* 3, no. 32 (2016): 185–214.

113. European media use the term "sub-Saharan African migrants" to refer to all those who arrive to its shore from western, central, and eastern Africa. Francophone Moroccan media reproduce the same name when in fact most of those who seek to cross from Morocco are from western Africa. It is true that French does not have a category for West African the same way it has for North African. Arabophone media commonly use the name "African" (*afârikqa*). The concept of West African does not seem to exist in French or in Arabic the way the category North African does.

CHAPTER 1

1. See video at https://www.youtube.com/watch?v=Vxr7gwYrj0k (accessed March 10, 2011).

2. *Ghalba*, to dominate someone even from the same social class or with equal power; *dsara* (often used for children and youth), the act of daring to challenge someone or some group even if they are from a higher social class or hold more power.

3. Precolonial European travel literature cites frequent cases of *hogra* by the *makhzen* against the population. See, for example, de Amicis, *Morocco*; Charles de Foucauld, *Reconnaissance au Maroc 1883–84* (Paris: Editions d'aujourd'hui, 1888 [1985]).

4. Janet Abu-Lughod, *Rabat: Urban Apartheid in Morocco* (Princeton, N.J.: Princeton University Press, 1981).

5. Frantz Fanon, *Les damnés de la terre* (Paris: Éditions Maspero, 1961).

6. Since the 1990s, the medina and Casbah have increasingly become luxury spaces for postcolonial European migration. This is more so for Tangier and Marrakesh, where Europeans "rediscovered" the "authentic Morocco" and started moving to settle in it. See Saigh Bousta, "New Forms of Migration."

7. Boris Gobille, "L'événement Mai 68: Pour une histoire du temps court," *Annales: Histoire et sciences sociales* 2 (2008): 321–49.

8. Michel de Certeau, *La prise de la parole: Et autres écrits politiques* (Paris: Seuil, 1994).

9. Polisario, Popular Front of the Liberation of Saguia el-Hamra and Rio de Oro, is a self-declared national movement for the independence of the Sahara, which has had disputes with Morocco since 1975. Morocco considers it a separationist movement that would not have existed without the support of Algeria, the national enemy of Morocco.

10. See Facebook website, http://fr-fr.facebook.com/Movement20.

11. The United Nations Conventions on the Rights of the Child, https://downloads .unicef.org.uk/wp-content/uploads/2010/05/UNCRC_united_nations_convention_on_the _rights_of_the_child.pdf?_ga=2.226260956.757105074.1520257041-1665287845.1520166244.

12. Ernest Bloch, *The Principle of Hope* (Cambridge, Mass.: MIT, 1986).

13. For this topic, see Aomar Boum, *Memories of Absence: How Muslims Remember Jews in Morocco* (Stanford, Calif.: Stanford University Press, 2013). Boum argues that the reason many youth hold negative attitudes toward Jews (which contrasts with the positive attitudes of the older generation) may be because they have never lived with one or met one. But there are other reasons, in my opinion, that fuel these negative attitudes. For instance, the Internet has become a major source of anti-Semitic views and conspiracy theories, especially in times of grand tragedies such as 9/11, the Iraq war of 2003, the conflict in Israel/Palestine, and most recently the wars in Gaza.

14. Jean Comaroff and John Comaroff, "Reflections on Youth: From the Past to the Post-colony," in *Makers and Breakers: Children & Youth in Postcolonial Africa*, ed. Filip De Boeck and Alcinda Honwana (Trenton, N.J.: Africa World Press, 2005), 27.

15. Giorgio Agamben, *Homo Sacer* (Stanford, Calif.: Stanford University Press, 1996).

16. See http://fr-fr.facebook.com/Mouvement.du.9.mars?sk=info.

17. These accusations are not random. They echo important debates in Moroccan society about fundamentalism, about homosexuality, and about the right not to fast during Ramadan and to eat publicly as a form of civil freedom. These issues are highly contested.

18. Vincent Courcelle-Labrousse and Nicolas Marmié, *La guerre du Rif: Maroc (1921–1926)* (Paris: Seuil, 2008).

19. Henry Munson Jr., *Religion and Power in Morocco* (New Haven, Conn.: Yale University Press, 1993); Malika Zeghal, *Les Islamistes marocains: Le defi de la monarchie* (Paris: Éditions La Découverte, 2005).

20. On May 18, Casablanca was the object of an unprecedented terrorist attack by a small group of young people, presumably members of al Qaeda. As a consequence, the government launched a very robust campaign against Islamists, including those of the outlawed "Justice and Charity" movement.

21. Mawazine is an annual summer musical festival that takes place in Rabat. The performers are international artists. The festival, organized by the Ministry of Culture, was called the Festival of the King because it was under the direction of the king's private secretary, Mounir Al Majidi. It is highly popular, attracting millions of fans, but it is also critiqued because of its high cost.

22. The Istiqlal Party (Hizb al-Istiqlal) was founded in 1943 to demand independence from France. Istiqlal, headed by Allal al-Fasi, was then very popular. Among Moroccans, al-Istiqlal is perceived as a bourgeois party in service of the monarchy.

23. The man was addressing the reputation of the city. For a long time and even today, Tangier has had the reputation of being a city of drug dealers, prostitution, and, recently, real estate dealers.

24. The two notorious ones are Youssouf Qardawi, an Egyptian religious scholar and a mufti who was frequently quoted by Al Jazeera as supporting all the uprisings with the exception of Morocco's, which, for him, was blessed by a king who "anticipated events" and introduced real reforms. The second one is the Francophone Moroccan writer Tahar Ben Jelloun, who applauded all the revolutions yet defended the Moroccan monarchy as being nondictatorial and thus exceptional. See statements on his website: http://www.taharbenjelloun .org/index.php?id=61&tx_ttnews%5Btt_news%5D=268&cHash=2d5ddcf01ca70b2f258930 31451d7f67 (accessed June 6, 2017).

25. See Ursula Lindsey, "Morocco's Rebellious Mountains Rise Up Again," *New York Times*, June 28, 2017, https://www.nytimes.com/2017/06/28/opinion/morocco-protest -monarchy.html (accessed March 5, 2018); Celian Mace, "Colere du Rif: Le fosse se creuse entre les deux Maroc," *Libération*, May 30, 2017, http://www.liberation.fr/planete/2017/05/30 /colere-du-rif-le-fosse-se-creuse-entre-les-deux-maroc_1573426 (accessed March 5, 2018).

26. See "Sit-in de soutien au Hirak d'Al Hoceima dans plusieurs villes, un journaliste algérien interpellé," *Tel Quel*, May 29, 2017, http://telquel.ma/2017/05/29/journaliste-algerien -interpelle-al-hoceima_1548377; "Marruecos opta por la represión en el Rif: Intenta decapitar la rebellion," *El Confidencial*, May 27, 2017, http://www.elconfidencial.com/mundo/2017 -05-27/marruecos-opta-por-la-represion-intenta-decapitar-a-la-rebelion-del-rif_1389824/. For the arrest of the leader, see "Maroc: Arrestation de Nasser Zefzafi, leader de la contestation dans le Rif," *Middle East Eye*, May 29, 2017, http://www.middleeasteye.net/fr/reportages /maroc-arrestation-de-nasser-zafzafi-leader-de-la-contestation-dans-le-rif-183852197.

27. They are called *'Ayâsha* in reference to the slogan, "Long Live the King" (*'Asha al malik*), which this group tends to shout or write on social media whenever there is any mention of the king or any critique of the makhzen. The name has been recently invented and is highly sarcastic.

28. Since independence, Algeria has surfaced as the national enemy of Morocco. The two countries went to war over borders in 1964. In 1974, they started another one via the Polisario supported by Algeria. Differences in their political regimes—one socialist republican and pro-Soviet and the other monarchist, capitalist, and pro-U.S.—did not help to bring the two countries together.

29. See Hisham Aidi, "Is Morocco Headed Toward Insurrection?" *Nation*, July 13, 2017, https://www.thenation.com/article/is-morocco-headed-toward-insurrection/ (accessed October 1, 2018).

30. See Rosa Moussaoui, "Maroc: Les rebelles du Rif dans le viseur du roi Mohammed VI," *L'Humanité*, May 30, 2017, http://www.humanite.fr/maroc-les-rebelles-du-rif-dans-le -viseur-du-roi-mohammed-vi-636710.

31. Brand, *Citizens Abroad*, 47.

32. Saeed Kamali Dehghan, "Morocco's Gag on Dissent in Rif Region Fuels Exodus to Europe," *Guardian*, November 1, 2017, https://www.theguardian.com/world/2017/nov/01 /moroccos-gag-on-dissent-in-rif-region-fuels-exodus-to-europe (accessed October 1, 2018).

CHAPTER 2

1. An estimated 500,000 migrants cross to Europe from North African shores every year. Most of them use "death boats." An estimated 200 die and an estimated 8,804 are ex-

pelled every year (*Le Monde*, November 23, 2006). The number of deaths has increased drastically in the years since this research was undertaken. In 2014 alone, 3,500 died in the sea; in 2015, 3,771; and in early 2016, 2,814 deaths had been counted. Between 2014 and 2016, more than 10,000 died in the Mediterranean Sea. See "Migrants: Plus de 10 000 morts en Méditerranée depuis 2014, selon l'ONU," *Le Monde*, June 7, 2016, http://www.lemonde.fr /international/article/2016/06/07/migrants-plus-de-10-000-morts-en-mediterranee-depuis -2014-selon-l-onu_4940967_3210.html. For 2018, 138,882 have already arrived in Europe against 186,768 arrivals in 2017. The number of deaths between 1993 and 2017 is estimated at 33,293 according to the German newspaper *Der Tagesspiegel*. "Liste von 33.293 registrierten Asylsuchenden, Geflüchteten und Migrant*innen die aufgrund der restriktiven Politik der Festung Europas zu Tode kamen," *Der Tagesspiegel*, June 15, 2017, http://www.tagesspiegel .de/downloads/20560202/3/listeentireberlinccbanu.pdf (accessed July 1, 2018).

2. Allison James, Chris Jenks, and Alan Prout, *Theorizing Childhood* (Cambridge: Polity, 1998); Sarah Holloway and Gill Valentine, eds., *Children Geographies: Playing, Living, Learning* (London: Routledge, 2000).

3. Mary Bucholtz, "Youth and Cultural Practice," *Annual Review of Anthropology* 31 (2002): 531.

4. For these two concepts, see de Certeau, *La prise de la parole*.

5. This passage is taken verbatim from Abdelmajid Hannoum, "The Harraga of Tangiers," *Encounters: International Journal of the Study of Culture and Society* 1, no. 1 (2009): 231–46.

6. Philippe Ariès, *L'enfant et la vie familiale sous l'Ancien Régime* (Paris: Seuil, 1975).

7. Michel Foucault, *Histoire de la folie à l'âge classique* (Paris: Gallimard, 1976).

8. Deborah Durham, "Disappearing Youth: Youth as a Social Shifter in Botswana," *American Ethnologist* 31, no. 4 (2004): 589–605; see also her introduction, "Youth and the Social Imagination in Africa: Introduction to Parts 1 and 2," *Anthropological Quarterly* 73, no. 3 (2000): 114.

9. Since the family is not a nuclear family, unless it is an upper-class family, there are always high expectations, especially of those who have migrated.

10. Schooling is obligatory from ages seven to thirteen in Morocco according to a law issued in 1963. Despite progress, primary schooling is still "limited and volatile," according to a UNICEF report. The percentage of the population who had completed primary schooling increased steadily from 38 percent in 1960–61 to 77 percent in 1999–2000 to 86 percent in 2002–3. See Abderrahmane Berrada Gouzi and Noureddine El Aoufi, "La non scholarisation au Maroc" (UNICEF, 2006). However, these numbers are very uneven across the country. The rate of schooling varies across regions, and it also varies according to gender and class. In the countryside (and countryside-like areas) where harraga mostly originate, schooling is more restricted. It is also more restricted among girls than among boys.

11. See Rachel Newcomb, *Women of Fes: Ambiguities of Urban Life in Morocco* (Philadelphia: University of Pennsylvania Press, 2010), 135 and passim of chap. 6 for women and spatial restrictions.

12. Rahma Bourquia, "Habitat, femmes et honneur: Le cas de quelques quartiers populaires d'Oujda," in *Femmes, culture et societies au Maghreb*, ed. Rahma Bourquia, Mounira Charrad, and Nancy Gallagher (Paris: Afrique-Orient, 1996), 19.

13. Ibid. For more on the concept of honor in Arab societies, see Lila Abu-Lughod, *Veiled Sentiments: Honor and Poetry in a Bedouin Society* (Berkeley: California University Press,

1986); Bourqiua, "Habitat, femmes et honneur"; Deborah Kapchan, *Gender on the Market: Moroccan Women and the Revoicing of Tradition* (Philadelphia: University of Pennsylvania Press, 1996).

14. *Hchouma*, often translated as "shame," refers instead to being modest and reserved, what in French is called *pudeur*. See Soumaya Naamane-Guessous, *Au delà de toute pudeur: La sexualité féminine au Maroc* (Paris: Karthala, 1991); Newcomb, *Women of Fes*.

15. Cited in Olivier Piot, "Tanger, la mille et une ville."

16. Ariès, *L'enfant et la vie familiale*.

17. Ibid.

18. Michel Peraldi, *Les mineurs migrants non accompagnés: Un défi pour les pays européens* (Paris: Karthala, 2014), 7.

19. Robert Montagne, "Perspectives marocaines," *Politique étrangère* 16, no. 3 (1951): 266.

20. Robert Montagne, *Revolution au Maroc* (Paris: France Empire, 1953). See also Robert Montagne, *Naissance du prolétariat marocain: Enquete collective 1848–1950* (Paris: Peyronnet, 1964).

21. Pierre Bourdieu, "L'école conservatrice. Les inégalités devant l'école et devant la culture," *Revue française de sociologie* 7 (1966): 325–47.

22. For cooperation in education and the agreements signed between Morocco and France in 1957 and 1972, see Henri Aron, "Au Maroc: Des coopérants enseignants pour quoi faire?" *Revue Tiers Monde* 51 (1972): 559–73.

23. *Hâlat al maghrib 2011–2010* (Rabat: Matbaʿat al-najar al jadida, 2011), 167.

24. Ibid.

25. Jean Comaroff, *Body of Power, Spirit of Resistance: The Culture and History of a South African People* (Chicago: University of Chicago Press, 1985); Mark Schloss, *The Hatchet's Blood: Separation, Power, and Gender in Ehing Social Life* (Tucson: University of Arizona Press, 1988); Durham, "Youth and the Social Imagination in Africa," 115.

26. Riccardo Lucchini, *Sociologie de la survie: L'enfant dans la rue* (Paris: Presses Universitaires de France, 1996), 12.

27. Sharon Stephens, "Children and the Politics of Culture," in the *Global History of Childhood Reader*, ed. Heidi Morrison (London: Routledge, 2012), 381. Also, to survive, street children organize themselves in gangs and indulge in crimes—not the harraga, who create networks of friends, not gangs. See James Diego Vigil, "Urban Violence and Street Gangs," *Annual Review of Anthropology* 32 (2003): 225–42.

28. Philippe Ariès, "L'enfant et la rue, de la ville à l'anti-ville," *Urbi* 2 (1979): III.

29. The invention of the passport.

30. This remark is based on a tape recording of the boulevard I undertook in the summer of July 2011.

31. Natalia Ribas-Mateos, *The Mediterranean in the Age of Globalization: Migration, Welfare, and Borders* (New Brunswick, N.J.: Transaction, 2005).

32. Often, in Moroccan parlance, Europe is referred to as *khàrijî*, the outside.

33. Hannoum, "The Harraga of Tangiers."

34. The current ruling dynasty. It came to power in 1631 when it was founded in the southern region of Tafilal by Moulay Ali Cherif, believed to be a descendant of the Prophet Muhammad. However, the dynasty extended to the rest of Morocco thanks to Moulay Rashid, the son of Moulay Ali Cherif. After the death of Moulay Rashid in 1672, he was succeeded by his brother Moulay Ismail, who consolidated the power of the dynasty.

35. I use "global city" in the sense given by Saskia Sassen, *The Global City* (Princeton, N.J.: Princeton University Press, 2013).

36. Stephens, "Children and the Politics of Culture," 381; Joy Boyden, "Childhood and the Policy Makers: A Comparative Perspective on the Globalization of Childhood," in *Constructing and Reconstructing Childhood: Contemporary Issues in the Sociological Study of Childhood*, ed. Allison James and Alan Prout (London: Falmer, 1997), 187 and passim.

37. Boyden, "Childhood and the Policy Makers," 189.

38. "And ever has it been known that love knows not its own depth until the hour of separation," as Kahlil Gibran wrote in *The Prophet* (New York: Penguin, 2002), 8.

39. See Hannoum, "The Harraga of Tangiers."

40. See, for instance, Nashaat Hussein, *Street Children in Egypt: Group Dynamics and Subcultural Constituents* (Cairo: American University in Cairo Press, 2005); Tobias Hecht, *At Home in the Street: Street Children of Northeast Brazil* (Cambridge: Cambridge University Press, 1998).

41. Jean-Claude Quentel, "Penser la différence de l'enfant," *Le Débat* 132 (2004): 18.

42. Because the topic is taboo, there is no study on sex tourism in Morocco. Yet, the topic comes up frequently in literary works, especially those related to Tangier, as well as in some autobiographies.

43. Ian Hacking, *Rewriting the Soul: Multiple Personality and the Sciences of Memory* (Princeton, N.J.: Princeton University Press, 1995), 55.

44. See also Hannoum, "The Harraga of Tangiers."

45. Ibid., 21.

46. Boyden, "Childhood and the Policy Makers."

47. Tayeb Saleh, *Mawsim al-hijra ilâ al-shamâl* (Beirut: Dâr al-maʿârif, 1981), 71.

48. "Culture is the ensemble of stories we tell about ourselves," wrote Clifford Geertz in *The Interpretation of Cultures* (New York: Vintage, 1979), 452.

49. The sea seems to inspire storytelling. It was out at sea that important European myths and fiction developed. On the case of Captain Cook, see Gananath Obeyesekere, *The Apotheosis of Captain Cook: European Mythmaking in the Pacific* (Princeton, N.J.: Princeton University Press, 1992). For the case of Joseph Conrad, see Robert Rubin, *Travel, Modernism, and Modernity* (New York: Ashgate, 2015).

50. Comaroff and Comaroff, "Reflections on Youth," 21 and passim.

CHAPTER 3

1. On the port of Tanger-Med, see the report by César Ducruet et al., "Maghreb Port Cities in Transitions: The Case of Tangier," *Portus Plus*, 2016, http://retedigital.com/wp-content/themes/rete/pdfs/portus_plus/1_2011/Tem%C3%A1ticas/La_ciudad_portuaria_contempor%C3%A1nea/07_C%C3%A9sarDucruet_FatimaZohraMohamedCh%C3%A9rif_Najib Cherfaoui.pdf (accessed March 18, 2018). For an idea about *lahrig* from Tanger-Med, see Sarah Przybyl and Youssef Ben Tayeb, "Tanger-Med, un espace hautement securise mais non moins attractif," *Hommes et migrations: Revue française de référence sur les dynamiques migratoires* 1304 (2013): 41–48.

2. Jill Korbin, "Children, Childhood, and Violence," *Annual Review of Anthropology* 32 (2003): 431–46; Bucholtz, "Youth and Cultural Practice."

3. Even though they are synonymous, these names are not equivalent: *drari* means children, *awlad* refers to sons, and *barhouch* means a child but also a young adult who displays immaturity and is incapable, most of the time, of making sound decisions.

4. See Peraldi, *Les mineurs migrants non accompagnes.*

5. Núria Empez Vidal, "Social Construction of Neglect: The Case of Unaccompanied Minors from Morocco to Spain" (MPIDR working paper WP 2007-007, Max Planck Institute for Demographic Research, 2007), http://www.demogr.mpg.de/papers/working/wp-2007-007.pdf.

6. Stefania Pandolfo, "'The Burning': Finitude and the Politico-Theological Imagination of Illegal Migration," *Anthropological Theory* 7, no. 3 (2007): 329–63.

7. Arthur Kleinman, "The Violence of Everyday Life: The Multiple Forms and Dynamics of Social Violence," in *Violence and Subjectivity*, ed. Veena Das, Arthur Kleinman, Mamphela Ramphele, and Pamela Reynolds (Berkeley: University of California Press, 1998), 227. For the concept of structural violence, see Nancy Scheper-Hughes, *Death Without Weeping: The Violence of Everyday Life in Brazil* (Berkeley: University of California Press, 1992); Paul Farmer, "On Suffering and Structural Violence: A View from Below," *Daedalus* 125, no. 1 (1996): 261–83.

8. Pierre Bourdieu, *Domination masculine* (Paris: Seuil, 1998).

9. See Robert Montagne, *Les Berbères et le makhzen dans le sud du Maroc; Essai sur la transformation politique des Berbères sédentaires (groupe chleuh)* (Paris: Alcan, 1930); Clifford Geertz, *Islam Observed: Religious Development in Morocco and Indonesia* (Chicago: University of Chicago Press, 1968); Abdallah Hammoudi, "The Reinvention of Dar al-Mulk in Rahma Bourquia," in *Shadow of the Sultan: Culture, Power, and Politics in Morocco*, ed. Susan Miller (Cambridge, Mass.: Harvard University Press, 1999), 133–38.

10. Hammoudi, "The Reinvention of Dar al Mulk."

11. See ibid., 139. For more on these practices, see Montagne, *Revolution au Maroc*, 101–2. Robert Montagne documents a number of cases between the sultan and disgraced Amghars (Berber Qaids, leaders of regions) of the south who are given the choice between "the cage or the cup of tea." The cage consists of public humiliation before execution. The disgraced Amghar is put in a cage and circulated in the streets to maximize humiliation. The cup of tea is poisonous. All those that Montagne mentioned chose the cup of tea. See Montagne, *Les Berbères et le makhzen dans le sud du Maroc.* The last case of cage humiliation happened in 1981, when a leader by the name of Zaitouni disobeyed King Hassan II. In another incident, one of the closest members of the *makhzen* to the monarchy, Driss Bassri, fell into disgrace after the death of Hassan II when he complained in an interview about his exclusion and even denial of his right to a passport. In a voice struggling to fight tears (a recognizable sign of the *mahgur*), he said, *"A'ibâd Alla, ashnou had lhogra?"* (Oh people, what is this *hogra?*). See video at http://www.dailymotion.com/video/xr977 (accessed March 23, 2018).

12. The immunity of the king is inscribed in the constitution; Driss Maghraoui, "The Dualism of Rule and the Immune Monarchy" (Paper presented at the conference "Rethinking the 'Arab Spring' in the Maghreb," Aga Khan University, April 28, 2018).

13. See also Hammoudi, "The Reinvention of Dar al-Mulk," 133–38. For the concept of the center, see Geertz, *Islam Observed.*

14. Irene Bono, "L'emploi comme 'revendication sectorielle': La naturalization de la question sociale au Maroc," in *L'état d'injustice au Maghreb*, ed. Irene Bono, Béatrice Hibou, Hamza Meddeb, and Mohamed Tozy (Paris: Karthala, 2015), 279–80.

15. Hence the fact that these ceremonies, which are after all ceremonies of power, were also targeted during the Arab Spring by the protesters of the February 20 movement. These ceremonies are not just a display of power but they are power in and of themselves. For an analysis of ceremonies as power, see Clifford Geertz, *Negara* (Princeton, N.J.: Princeton University Press, 1980). For an analysis of the case of Morocco, see Jocelyne Dakhlia, "La symbolique du pouvoir itinérant," *Annales: Histoire et sciences sociales* 43, no. 3 (1988): 735–60.

16. Abdallah Hammoudi, *Master and Disciple* (Chicago: University of Chicago Press, 1997); see also Hammoudi, "The Reinvention of Dar al-Mulk."

17. To my knowledge, there is no ethnography on the subject. However, Moroccan literature may support this thesis. See the autobiography of Choukri, *For Bread Alone*. See also Driss Chraibi, *Le passé simple* (Paris: Enoeil, 1954).

18. Tayeb told me that once three harraga wanted to meet the king, who often comes to Tangier. So, they knew he was in town and somehow managed to find out where he was going be. They hid, and then—there he was, walking on the beach with several European men. The harraga came out of their hiding places to salute the king (and ask him to do something for them). The king was mad and said, "How were these guys able to reach me?" They were arrested and sent to jail.

19. There are many studies of the makhzen, but they tend to analyze the system in and of itself, separate from its surroundings and, astonishingly, overlook the popular base upon which it derives its legitimacy not only by an ideology (sherfism) but also by violence. See Robert Montagne, *Les Berbères et le Makhzen dans le sud du Maroc: Essai sur les transformation sedentaires des Berbères sédentaires (groupe chleuh)* (Paris: Alcan, 1930); John Waterbury, *The Commander of the Faithful* (New York: Columbia University Press, 1982); Geertz, *Islam Observed*; Leveau, *Le fellah marocain défendeur du trône* (Paris: Presses de la Fondation Nationale des Sciences Politiques, 1985); Hammoudi, "The Reinvention of Dar al-Mulk."

20. Yet, the 2014 report on human trafficking, especially of women and children, makes no mention of the Moroccan harraga. It speaks more about "sub-Saharan Africans" and mentions only one child victim of human trafficking. One can only wonder how thorough the report was. Joy Ngozi Ezeilo, "Report of the Special Rapporteur on Trafficking in Persons, Especially Women and Children," April 1, 2014, http://www.ohchr.org/en/professionalinterest/pages/crc.aspx (accessed March 23, 2018).

21. Al Jazeera paid special attention to this phenomenon and, as a consequence, ran into problems with the Moroccan government. In December 2010, Al Jazeera was expelled from Morocco for a host of reasons, most having to do with reporting that upset the Moroccan government.

22. With the exception of Darna, an organization in Tangier that was devoted to helping minors by hosting them and even schooling them. But it was short-lived.

23. See Agnes Heller and Sonja Puntscher Riekmann, eds., *Biopolitics: The Politics of the Body, Race and Nature* (Aldershot: Avebury, 1996).

24. Michel Foucault, *Histoire de la sexualité* (Paris: Gallimard, 1984).

25. "In Morocco, four out five unemployed people are aged 15 to 34," according to the minister of labor, Abdeslam Seddiki. See Abdeslam Seddiki, "In Morocco Youth Unemployment Is Driving Up Inequality," *Guardian*, August 20, 2014, https://www.theguardian.com/global-development-professionals-network/2014/aug/20/youth-unemployment-interactive-abdeslam-seddiki-morocco (accessed June 4, 2017).

26. See Irene Bono, "La démographie de l'injustice sociale au Maroc," in *L'état d'injustice au Maghreb*, ed. Irene Bono, Béathrice Hebou, Hamza Meddeb, and Mohamed Tozy (Paris: Karthala, 2015).

27. An estimated 26.5 percent of urban youth in 2016–17, according to a report of du Haut Commissariat au Plan, https://www.hcp.ma/Chomage_r70.html (accessed March 19, 2018).

28. Nicholas de Genova, *Working the Boundaries: Race, Space, and "Illegality" in Mexican Chicago* (Durham, N.C.: Duke University Press, 2005).

29. William Julius Wilson, *The Truly Disadvantaged: The Inner City, The Underclass, and Public Policy* (Chicago: University of Chicago Press, 1987.

30. Georges Bataille, *La part maudite* (Paris: Hachette, 1949), 25.

31. Karl Marx, *Capital, Volume I: A Critique of Political Economy* (New York: Dover, 2011), 255–330.

32. Ibid.

33. Scheper-Hughes, *Death Without Weeping.*

34. This is common knowledge among Moroccans. They know, for instance, that the *moqaddam* (a state official in every district of every city or town) is a spy (*bargâg*).

35. de Genova, *Working the Boundaries.*

36. Indeed, see the sophisticated facilities that welcome these children in Europe, especially in France. The European Union deploys resources to school them and train them. Upon successful completion of the training, they are given papers and a probation period to find work in order to formalize their status as "permanent" residents.

37. There is an entire literature about violence and the state and even about violence and the foundation of states. Some of these are classics and include the work of Marx, Weber, Pareto, Gramsci, and others.

38. The literature on the topic is not negligible, even though most of it is dispersed under different themes. See Benedict Anderson, "The Goodness of Nations," in *The Specter of Comparison: Nationalism, Southeast Asia, and the World* (London: Verso, 1998).

39. Camille Bordenet and Madjid Zerrouky, "Méditerranée: Chiffres et carte pour comprendre la tragédie," *Le Monde*, April 20, 2015, http://www.lemonde.fr/les-decodeurs/article/2015/04/20/en-2015-un-migrant-meurt-toutes-les-deux-heures-en-moyenne-en-mediterranee_4619379_4355770.html (accessed March 19, 2018).

40. Ibid.

41. Cited in "Migrants: Plus de 10 000 morts en Méditerranée depuis 2014, selon l'ONU," *Le Monde*, June 7, 2016, http://www.lemonde.fr/international/article/2016/06/07/migrants-plus-de-10-000-morts-en-mediterranee-depuis-2014-selon-l-onu_4940967_3210.html.

42. Michel Foucault, "Faire vivre et laisser mourir: La naissance du racism," *Les Temps modernes*, February 1991, 48.

43. Ibid., 53, 55.

44. Anderson, "The Goodness of Nations," 149–50.

45. Jacques Berque, "L'idée de classe dans l'histoire contemporaine des Arabes," *Cahiers internationaux de sociologie* 38 (1965): 55–70. For the case of Algeria, where many of the dynamics are similar to Morocco, see Marnia Lazreg, *The Emergence of Classes in Algeria: A Study of Colonialism and Socio-political Change* (Boulder, Colo.: Westview, 1976).

46. Pierre Bourdieu, "Dévoiler et divulguer le refoulé," in *Algérie—France—Islam*, ed. Joseph Jurt (Paris: L'Harmathan, 1997).

47. Etienne Balibar and Immanuel Wallerstein, *Race, Nation, and Class: Ambiguous Identities* (London: Verso, 1991), 21.

48. This is for historical reasons as well as societal ones. Unlike Algeria, Morocco kept its feudal-like class system protected and did not know a popular revolution against colonialism.

49. About difference, bodies, and pollution, see my discussion of West Africans in Chapter 4.

50. Indeed, in Spain, an entire cemetery is devoted exclusively to these harraga, graves without names. See Al Jazeera, "Tahta al mijhar: Nuʿushun fi Lajjat al Bahr," November 22, 2012, https://www.youtube.com/watch?v=vAO_X2Qw5hM (accessed March 23, 2018).

51. A form of discipline that used to be practiced in schools and homes and that consists of tying a boy and beating him on his feet with a stick or a belt.

52. For freedom and mobility, see Bartholomew Dean, "Freedom," in *Keywords of Mobility: Critical Engagements*, ed. Noel Salazar and Kiran Jayaram (New York: Berghahn, 2016), 55–68.

53. As has been noticed in other contexts of transgressive actions among youth; see Bucholtz, "Youth and Cultural Practice," 531.

54. Hannah Arendt, *Men in Dark Times* (New York: Harcourt Brace, 1970), 9.

55. Rogier Van Reekum and Willem Schinkel, "Drawing Lines, Enacting Migration: Visual Prostheses of Bordering Europe," *Public Culture* 29 (2016): 38.

56. See Vincenzo Brove and Tobias Bohmelt, "Does Immigration Induce Terrorism?" *Journal of Politics* 78, no. 2 (2016): 572–88.

57. For an example of the connection between jihadism and engineering studies, see Diego Gambetta and Steffen Hertog, *Engineers of Jihad: The Curious Connection Between Violent Extremism and Education* (Princeton, N.J.: Princeton University Press, 2016).

58. In this regard, hope and repetition are not always separated, as they are in the thinking of Kierkegaard, but there is the hope of repetition as there is repetition of hope. While Tayeb and a few others live the first predicament, most of the harraga live the second predicament. See Søren Kierkegaard, *Fear and Trembling/Repetition* (Princeton, N.J.: Princeton University Press, 1983).

59. Boris Cyrulnik and Gérard Jorland, eds., *Résilience: Connaissances de base* (Paris: Odile Jacob, 2012), 8.

60. Marie Anaut, *Les thérapies familiales: Approches systémiques et psychanalytiques* (Paris: Armand Colin, 2012), 66.

61. Catherine Panter-Brick, "Street Children, Human Rights, and Public Health: A Critique and Future Directions," *Annual Review of Anthropology* 31, no. 1 (2002): 163.

62. Sigmund Freud, *The Freud Reader* (New York: Norton, 1989), 782.

63. Vincent Crapanzano, "Reflections on Hope as a Category of Social and Psychological Analysis," *Cultural Anthropology* 18, no. 1 (2003): 15.

64. Ibid.

65. Hannah Arendt, *The Human Condition* (Chicago: University of Chicago Press, 1998), 247.

66. Ibid.

67. Mary Douglas, *Risk and Blame: Essays in Cultural Theory* (New York: Routledge, 1992), 41.

68. Martin Heidegger, *Qu'est ce que la métaphysique?* (Paris: Gallimard, 1938).

69. Douglas, *Risk and Blame*, 118.

70. Kierkegaard, *Fear and Trembling*, 132.

71. Ibid.

72. L'Espérance voit ce qui n'est pas encore et qui sera/Elle aime ce qui n'est pas encore et qui sera. Charles Péguy, *Le porche du mystère de la deuxième vertu* (Paris: Gallimard, 1929).

73. See Henri Desroche, *The Sociology of Hope* (London: Routledge & Kegan Paul, 1979), 16.

CHAPTER 4

1. William Burroughs, *Interzone* (New York: Viking, 1989), 49.

2. Moroccans commonly do not think of themselves as Africans, and even geographically, they think of themselves as part of the geography of the Middle East and somehow tend to forget that Morocco, as well as the entire region, is part and parcel of Africa. However, this view is also largely shared in a perception of Africa as a black continent, such that North Africa is not part of Africa. This view is common in African studies departments and centers in the United States, for instance, where North Africa is absent; it is present instead in Middle Eastern studies departments, where it occupies a minimal space.

3. As evidenced by the thousands of entries in newspapers, including the *New York Times*, the *Guardian*, and *Le Monde*, not to mention footage on YouTube and social media.

4. Ribas-Mateos, *The Mediterranean in the Age of Globalisation*; Pandolfo, "'The Burning'"; Ruben Anderson, *Illegality, Inc.: Clandestine Migration and the Business of Bordering Europe* (Berkeley: University of California Press, 2014).

5. For the case of Gambia, for example, see Paolo Gaibazzi, "Visa Problem: Certification, Kinship, and the Production of 'Ineligibility' in the Gambia," *Journal of the Royal Anthropological Institute* 20, no. 1 (2014): 38–55.

6. Emmanuel Dongala, *Les petits garçons naissent aussi des étoiles* (Paris: Editions Le Serpent à plumes, 1998), 14.

7. Ibid.

8. See, for example, Janet Roitman, "A Successful Life in the Illegal Realm: Smugglers and Road Bandits in the Chad Basin," in *Readings in Modernity in Africa*, ed. Peter Geschiere, Birgit Meyer, and Peter Pels (Bloomington: Indiana University Press, 2008); Janet Roitman, "The Ethics of Illegality in the Chad Basin," in *Law and Disorder in the Postcolony*, ed. Jean Comaroff and John Comaroff (Chicago: University of Chicago Press, 2006); Janet Roitman, "New Sovereigns? Regulatory Authority in the Chad Basin," in *Intervention and Transnationalism in Africa: Global-Local Networks of Power*, ed. Thomas Callagy, Ronald Kassimir, and Robert Latham (Cambridge: Cambridge University Press, 2001), 240–66; Carolyn Nordstrom, *Global Outlaws: Crime, Money, and Power in the Contemporary World* (Berkeley: University of California Press, 2007).

9. Philippe Bourgois, *In Search of Respect: Selling Crack in El Barrio* (Cambridge: Cambridge University Press, 1995).

10. Nordstrom, *Global Outlaws*; Roitman, "The Ethics of Illegality."

11. Leo Chavez, *Shadowed Lives: Undocumented Immigrants in American Society* (New York: Harcourt Brace Jovanovich College, 1992), 45.

12. For a view of the different routes to Europe from Africa, see Bacon et al., "Cartographier les mouvements migratoires."

13. Agamben, *Homo Sacer*. For an interesting discussion of this book, see Veena Das and Deborah Poole, "State and Its Margins: Comparative Ethnographies," in *Anthropology in*

the Margins of the State, ed. Veena Das and Deborah Poole (Santa Fe, N.M.: School of American Research Press, 2004).

14. Agamben, *Homo Sacer.*

15. Cecilia Menjívar and Daniel Kanstroom, *Constructing Immigrant "Illegality": Critiques, Experiences, and Responses* (Cambridge: Cambridge University Press, 2014), 9.

16. Since 2008, when I first started working on the topic, the deaths of migrants in the desert have been reported only twice. One was on October 31, 2013. See Laura Smith-Spark and Arwa Damon, "Sahara Desert Deaths: 92 Migrants Perish in Niger After Vehicle Breakdowns," CNN, October 31, 2013, http://www.cnn.com/2013/10/31/world/africa/niger-bodies. The second time was on June 16, 2016, when the deaths of forty-three people in the desert on the border of Algeria were reported. See "Niger Says 34 Migrants Found Dead in Sahara Desert," BBC, June 16, 2016, http://www.bbc.com/news/world-africa-36545015 (accessed March 20, 2018).

17. Henrik Vigh, *Navigating Terrains of War: Youth and Soldiering in Guinea-Bissau* (Oxford: Berghahn, 2006), 106.

18. Fatou Diome, *Dans Le ventre de l'Atlantique* (Paris: Editions Anne Carrière, 2003); Saleh, *Season of Migration to the North*; Ben Jelloun, *Partir* (Paris: Seuil, 2006).

19. Omar Abdi Farah, "Le rêve européen dans la littérature négro-africaine d'expression française" (PhD diss., Universite de Bourgogne).

20. See Jennifer Cole and Christian Groes, *Affective Circuits: African Migrations to Europe and the Pursuit of Social Regeneration* (Chicago: University of Chicago Press, 2016, 4.

21. See Vigh, *Navigating Terrains of War*, 106; Charles Piot, *Nostalgia for the Future: West Africa After the Cold War* (Chicago: University of Chicago Press, 2010), 85.

22. Dean, "Freedom."

23. See, for example, Roitman, "A Successful Life"; Roitman, "The Ethics of Illegality"; Roitman, "New Sovereigns?" See also Nordstrom, *Global Outlaws.*

24. Roitman, "The Ethics of Illegality," 249.

25. Philip Abrams speaks of "the legitimizing of the illegitimate" as "the cardinal activity involved in the serious presentation of the state." See Philip Abrams, "Notes on the Difficulty of Studying the State," *Journal of Historical Sociology* 1, no. 1 (1988): 76. Yet, outside of the realm of the state, the process of legitimizing the "illegitimate" is also possible.

26. Max Weber, *Economy and Society: An Outline of Interpretive Sociology*, vol. I (Berkeley: University of California Press, 1978), 33.

27. Foucault, *Surveiller et punir*; de Genova, "Migration, 'Illegality' and Deportability in Everyday Life"; Menjívar and Kanstroom, *Constructing Immigrant "Illegality."*

28. Abrams, "Notes on the Difficulty of Studying the State," 76.

29. "Everyone has the right to leave any country, including his own, and to return to his country." To leave one country to where? The declaration does not specify where. This right conflicts with the rights of countries to control their borders.

30. See Bergson Lendja Ngnemzue, *Les étrangers illégaux à la recherche de papiers* (Paris: L'Harmattan, 2008); Marie-Thérèse Tétu-Delange, *Clandestins au pays des papiers: Expériences et parcours de sans-papiers algériens* (Paris: La Découverte, 2009). For the case of Senegalese in Italy, see Donald Carter, *State of Grace: Senegalese in Italy and the New European Immigration* (Minneapolis: Minnesota University Press, 1997).

31. Weber, *Economy and Society*, 31.

32. Ibid., 32.

33. Ibid.

34. Noel Salazar, "Keywords of Mobility, What's in a Name?" in *Keywords of Mobility: Critical Engagements*, ed. Noel Salazar and Kiran Jayaram (New York: Berghahn, 2016); Dean, "Freedom."

35. Dean, "Freedom."

36. Belguendouz, "Le Maroc."

37. Chavez, *Shadowed Lives*; de Genova, *Working the Boundaries*; Menjivar and Kanstroom, *Constructing Immigrant "Illegality."*

38. I have met hundreds of migrants just in Tangier since 2008. Until 2016, I saw many of them. From time to time, I heard that one or a few had crossed. Of the ones who crossed, I heard no more news about them from their friends, which opens up the door to all possibilities. They may have successfully crossed or they may have died in the sea.

39. Belguendouz, "Expansion et sous-traitance."

40. Marie-ThérèseTétu-Delange, *Clandestins au pays des papiers Expériences et parcours de sans-papiers algériens* (Paris: Le Découverte, 2009).

41. Chouki El Hamel, *Black Morocco*.

42. Didier Fassin, *Humanitarian Reason: A Moral History of the Present* (Berkeley: University of California Press, 2011), 112.

43. Arabized, meaning they see themselves as Arabs and may even call other West Africans names such as '*azzi*. But Moroccans generally tend to "other" the Moroccan blacks, as evident by a whole range of racist names such as *drawi*, *hartani*, and *zraq*, meaning blue and so forth.

44. Mary Douglas, *Purity and Danger* (London: Routledge, 1966).

45. Victor Turner, *Forest of Symbols: Aspects of Ndembu Ritual* (Ithaca, N.Y.: Cornell University Press, 1967), 97.

46. Catherine Therrien, ed., *La question du "chez-soi" au Maroc: les représentations des migrants français confrontées aux points de vue des Marocains* (Rabat: Association Marocaines d'Etudes et de Recherches sur les Migration [AMERM], 2014).

47. On the phenomenology of whiteness, see Sara Ahmed, "A Phenomenology of Whiteness," *Feminist Theory* 8, no. 2 (2007): 149–68.

48. Edward Said noticed a long time ago that Arabs are perceived as a collectivity. Edward Said, *Orientalism* (New York: Vintage, 1979).

49. Even sub-Saharan students, athletes, and sometimes diplomats are mistaken for "illegal" immigrants. I was told that taxi drivers may not stop to take them.

50. For a recent example, see the testimony of Malick Ndiaye, which was unfortunately based on a very short stay of one week in Tangier. See Malick Ndiaye, *Un nègre à Tanger* (Tangier: Khbar Bladna, 2013).

51. Geertz, *Islam Observed*; Waterbury, *The Commander of the Faithful*; Leveau, *Le fellah marocain défenseur du trône*.

52. De Amicis, *Morocco*; de Foucauld, *Reconnaissance au Maroc*.

53. James Clifford, *Routes: Travel and Translation in the Late Twentieth Century* (Cambridge, Mass.: Harvard University Press, 1997), 257.

54. Abdelmalek Sayad, *L'immigration ou les paradoxes de l'alterité* (Paris: De Boeck, 1992).

55. Judith Butler, *Excitable Speech: A Politics of the Performative* (New York: Routledge, 1997), 35.

56. Henri Bergson, *Oeuvres* (Paris: Presses Universitaires de France, 1970), 431.

57. Bergson argues in comic situations the roles are inversed, such as a child pretending to educate his parents, which provokes laughter. Bergson, *Oeuvres*, 431.

58. Chouki El Hamel, *Black Morocco*, 301.

59. For perceptions and attitudes toward the Jews, see Boum, *Memory of an Absence*.

60. Sara Ahmed, "A Phenomenology of Whiteness," 155.

61. David Harvey, *The Urban Experience* (Baltimore: Johns Hopkins University Press, 1989), 182; Lefebvre, *La production de l'espace*; Sophie Body-Gendrot, *Ville et Violence: l'Irruption de nouveaux Acteurs* (Paris: Presses Universitaires de France, 1993).

62. Harvey, *The Urban Experience*, 182.

63. See Jamal Amiar, "Tanger: Manifestation anti-subsahariens et montée du racism," *Medias24*, December 8, 2013, http://www.medias24.com/SOCIETE/7096-Tanger-manifes tation-anti-subsahariens-et-montee-du-racisme.html.

64. Allen Feldman, *Formations of Violence: The Narrative of the Body and Political Terror in Northern Ireland* (Chicago: University of Chicago Press, 1991), 28.

65. See, for example, "Nouveaux affrontements entre Marocains et Subsahariens à Tanger," *Tel Quel*, June 23, 2014, http://telquel.ma/2014/06/23/nouveaux-affrontements -marocains-subsahariens-tanger_139883. See also "A Tanger, le racisme tue," *Tel Quel*, September 7, 2014, http://telquel.ma/2014/09/07/tanger-racisme-tue_1415366.

66. "Meurtre d'un Sénégalais au Maroc: Deux personnes interpellées," *Afrik.com*, September 1, 2014, http://www.afrik.com/meurtre-d-un-senegalais-au-maroc-deux-personnes -interpellees; "Maroc: Un sénégalais egorgé avec deux autres africains tués," *Senenews*, August 30, 2014, https://www.senenews.com/2014/08/30/maroc-un-senegalais-egorge-par-des -marocains-avec-deux-autres-africains-tues_88909.html.

67. This is not very common and happens in case of conflict. The most well-known campaign in favor of West Africans was in June 2014, after the protest of people from the Irfan neighborhood. The second one was in May 2017.

68. See Aisha Deme, "Au Maroc, Scènes de racisme ordinaire contre les noirs," *Le Monde*, January 6, 2015, http://www.lemonde.fr/afrique/article/2015/01/06/le-maroc-du-reve-a-l -amertume_4550079_3212.html.

69. Mohammed Nafaa, "Les pauvres riches de Rabat," *Le Reporter.ma*, November 1, 2014, http://www.lereporter.ma/actualite/a-la-une/3801-reportage-les-pauvres-riches-de-rabat.

70. Paul Stoller, *Money Has No Smell: The Africanization of New York City* (Chicago: University of Chicago Press, 2002).

71. Bruce Whitehouse, *Migrants and Strangers in an African City: Exile, Dignity, Belonging* (Bloomington: Indiana University Press, 2012).

72. It is understood as a voluntary charity that increases one's piety.

73. Adam Sabra, *Poverty and Charity in Medieval Islam: Mamluk Egypt 1250–1517* (Cambridge: Cambridge University Press, 2000), 67.

74. Ibid, 50.

75. de Genova, *Working the Boundaries*.

CHAPTER 5

1. Paul Bowles, "View from Tangier," *Nation*, June 30, 1956. Reprinted under the title *The Death of a Cosmopolitan City*, in *Travels: Collected Writings 1950–1993* (New York: HarperCollins, 2010).

2. Ibid.

3. Ibid.

4. Ibid.

5. Immanuel Kant, *Political Writings* (Cambridge: Cambridge University Press, 1997), 106.

6. Ibid.

7. Mimoun Hillali, "Le cosmopolitanisme à Tanger: Mythe et réalité," *Horizons maghrébins* 31–32 (1996): 11–16.

8. Jacques Derrida, *De l'hospitalité* (Paris: Calmann-Levy, 1997), 4.

9. Martha Nussbaum, *For Love of Country* (Boston: Beacon, 1996), 4.

10. Amanda Anderson, "Cosmopolitanism, Universalism, and the Divided Legacies of Modernity," in *Cosmopolitics: Thinking and Feeling Beyond the Nation*, ed. Pheng Cheah and Bruce Robbins (Minneapolis: University of Minnesota Press, 1998), 265.

11. See a critique of this premature announcement by Partha Chatterjee, "Beyond the Nation? Or Within?" *Social Text* 56 (1998): 57–69.

12. Aihwa Ong, *Flexible Citizenship: The Cultural Logics of Transnationality* (Durham, N.C.: Duke University Press, 1999); Nussbaum, *For Love of Country*.

13. See, for instance, Arjun Appadurai, *Modernity at Large: Cultural Dimensions of Globalization* (Minneapolis: University of Minnesota Press, 1996); Kwame Anthony Appiah, *Cosmopolitanism: Ethics in a World of Strangers* (New York: Norton, 2006).

14. Jean-Paul Sartre, "Introduction," in *Orphée Noir* (Paris: Presses Universitaires de France, 1948), IX.

15. See Jean Cassaigne, *La situation des Français au Maroc depuis l'indépendance, 1956–1964* (Paris: Presses de Sciences Po, 1964). For more recent studies about the French in Morocco, see Catherine Therrien, ed., *La question du "chez-soi" au Maroc: Les représentations des migrants français confrontées aux points de vue des Marocains* (Rabat: Association Marocaines d'Etudes et de Recherches sur les Migration [AMERM], 2014).

16. *Assimilés* or *évolués*, what Geertz calls mimic Frenchmen or what is known as the brown Frenchman (his counterpart, the brown British man), is a figure that is found early on with colonialism. Generally, they speak French, behave like the French, and have an exaggerated negative view of the natives. In the city of Tangier, *les assimilés* were always included in the statistics along with the French. See, for example, Hillali, "Le cosmopolitanisme à Tanger."

17. See Abdelmajid Hannoum, "Qu'est-ce qu'un Maghrebin," *Awal: Cahiers d'études berbères* 43 (2011): 75–87.

18. Clifford Geertz, *Local Knowledge: Further Essays in Interpretive Anthropology* (New York: Basic Books, 1985), 65–66.

19. See Barth, *Ethnic Groups and Boundaries*.

20. Indeed, Tangier has also been greatly affected by this world event since it was reported that it was the first Moroccan city to provide recruits to the Islamic State of Iraq and Syria (ISIS).

21. See, for this history, Abdelmajid Hannoum, "Colonialism and Knowledge in Algeria: The Archives of the Arab Bureau," *History and Anthropology* 12, no. 4 (2001): 343–79.

22. Geertz, *Local Knowledge*.

23. See Hannoum, "Qu'est-ce qu'un Mahrebin?"

24. Especially by a party called Parti indigène. See Nicholas de Genova, "The European Question: Migration, Race, and Postcoloniality in Europe," *Social Text* 34, no. 3 (2016): 75–102; Abdelmajid Hannoum, "Memory at the Surface: Colonial Forgetting in Post-Colonial France," *Interventions: Journal of Postcolonial Studies* 21, no. 3 (2019): 367–91.

25. See Abdelmajid Hannoum, "Cartoons, Secularism, and Inequality," *Anthropology Today* 31, no. 5 (2015): 21–24.

26. de Genova, "The European Question," 79.

27. For more details about racism in France, see Joan Scott, *The Politics of the Veil* (Princeton, N.J.: Princeton University Press, 2007), chap. 2, 42–89.

28. See the report by Will Sanders and Travis Hodges, "The Aesthetes: Expats in Tangier," *New York Times Magazine*, April 11, 2014, http://tmagazine.blogs.nytimes.com/2014/04/11/the-aesthetes/?mcubz=0&_r=0.

29. *Shurfa* refers to the Muslim nobility, or descendants of the Prophet Muhammad. Moroccans sometimes refer to Europeans as such mainly because of a popular perception that Europeans are more honest, straightforward, and even more polite. One reason for this perception, I contend, is precisely that Moroccans rarely enter into deep interactions with Europeans who, again, tend to live in their own community and have minimal contact with Moroccans. In several interviews with Europeans, they conveyed to me that before they moved to Morocco, they were advised to keep an attitude of distance with Moroccans usually by people who had lived in the country.

30. Mona Khaled, "Perceptions marocaines de la migration française au Maroc," in *La question du "chez soi" au Maroc: Les representations des migrants francais confrontées aux points de vue des Marocain-es*, ed. Catherine Therrien (Rabat: AMERM, 2014), 114.

31. Scott, *The Politics of the Veil*, 160.

32. Escher and Petermann, "Neo-Colonialism or Gentrification in the Medina of Marrakesh."

33. Bourdieu, *Domination masculine*, 13.

34. See Stoler, *Duress*.

35. Frantz Fanon, *Peau noir, masques blancs* (Paris: Éditions du Seuil, 1952).

36. Such as in the highly influential work of Gobineau, *Essai sur les inégalités des races*.

37. Fanon, *Peau noir, masques blancs*.

38. William Edward B. Du Bois, *The Souls of Black Folk* (New York: New American Library, 1995), 54.

39. Sartre, "Introduction," IX.

40. Anton Escher and Sandra Petermann, "Marrakesh Medina: Neocolonial Paradise of Lifestyle Migrants?" in *Contested Spatialities, Lifestyle Migration, and Residential Tourism*, ed. Michael Janoschka and Heiko Haas (London: Routledge, 2013), 31.

41. Gaston Bachelard, *La poétique de l'espace* (Paris: Les Presses Universitaires de France, 1957), 28.

42. Maurice Merleau-Ponty, *Phénoménologie de la perception* (Paris: Gallimard, 1945), 290.

43. Ibid., 291.

44. This thinking and describing of space by European residents can be also found in writing, photography, or painting. For writing, see Stephanie Gaou, *Capiteuses* (Casablanca: Al Manar, 2012); Veronique Bruez, *La Terrasse des Paresseux: Carnets marocains* (Clamecy: Editions Léo Scheer, 2011).

45. They only came twice or so a year. See interview with Pierre Bergé in *Zamane*, November 10, 2015, http://zamane.ma/fr/pierre-berge-%E2%80%89le-maroc-est-devenu-notre-second-pays%E2%80%89/.

46. Honoré de Balzac, *Le Père Goriot* (Paris: Gallimard, 1999).

47. Ong, *Flexible Citizenship*, 214.

48. Catherine Therrien and Chloe Pellegrini, "French Migrants in Morocco: From a Desire for Elsewhereness to an Ambivalent Reality," *Journal of North African Studies* 20, no. 4 (2015): 605–21; Escher and Petermann, "Marrakesh Medina."

49. See Chapter 4.

50. Indeed, this is why even anthropologists in Morocco would still overlook the race dimension and freely speak of cosmopolitanism. See Susan Ossman, *Moving Matters: Paths of Serial Migration* (Stanford, Calif.: Stanford University Press, 2013); Stephen Foster, *Cosmopolitan Desire: Transcultural Dialogues and Antiterrorism in Morocco* (New York: AltaMira, 2006). For an excellent op-ed about the status of the "immigrant" and the one of the "expat," see Mawuna Remarque Koutonin, "Why Are White People Expats When the Rest of Us Are Immigrants?" *Guardian*, March 13, 2015. Yet, Moroccan scholars tend to use the term "migrants" to describe this population. See Saigh Bousta, "New Forms of Migration"; Khaled, "Perceptions."

51. According to an interview conducted by Richard Hamilton, cited in BBC, October 12, 2014, https://www.bbc.co.uk/news/magazine-29566539 (accessed June 28, 2018).

52. Mohamed Choukri, "Paul Bowles *wa ʿuzlat Tanja*," in *Al-Aʿmâl al Kâmila*, vol. 2 (Casablanca: Al Markaz al-Thaqafi al-ʿArabi, 2008), 221.

53. Ibid.

54. Brian T. Edwards, *Morocco Bound: Disorienting America's Maghreb, from Casablanca to the Marrakech Express* (Durham, N.C.: Duke University Press, 2005); Michael Walonen, *Writing Tangier in the Postcolonial Transition: Space and Power in Expatriate and North African Literature* (New York: Routledge, 2016); Ralph Coury and Kevin Lacey, eds., *Writing Tangier* (New York: Peter Lang, 2009).

55. See his *For Bread Alone.*

56. Tahar Ben Jelloun, *Harrouda* (Paris: Denoël, 1973), 145–46.

57. Ibid.

58. Ibid.

59. Glenn Bowman, "Fucking Tourists: Sexual Relations and Tourism in Jerusalem's Old City," *Critique of Anthropology* 9, no. 2 (1989): 77–93.

60. Miles, *Call Me Burroughs.*

61. Ibid.

62. Among LGBT people, only gay men are somewhat visible in the European community of Tangier. Lesbian sexuality is invisible within the domain of the sex industry and in Moroccan society by and large. The most well-known relationship between a white woman and a Moroccan woman, often mentioned by the European residents of Tangier today, is that between writer Jane Bowles and Cherifa, described by Jane as an "illiterate but powerful peasant girl." See Negar Azimi, "The Madness of Queen Jane," *New Yorker*, June 12, 2014.

63. Inderpal Grewal, *Home and Harem: Nation, Gender, Empire, and the Cultures of Travel* (Durham, N.C.: Duke University Press, 1996), 136.

64. Julia O'Connell Davidson and Jacqueline Sanchez Taylor, "Travel and Taboo: Heterosexual Sex Tourism to the Caribbean," in *Regulating Sex: The Politics of Intimacy and Identity*, ed. Elizabeth Bernstein and Laurie Schaffner (New York: Routledge, 2005), 86.

65. J. Brohman, "New Directions in Tourism or Third World Development," *Annals of Tourism Research* 23, no. 1 (1996): 48–70.

66. Jan Jindy Pettman, "Sex Tourism: The Complexities of Power," in *Culture and Global Change*, ed. Tracey Skelton and Tim Allen (London: Routledge, 1999), 113.

67. So much has been written on globalization; for a history and a general view, see David Harvey, *A Brief History of Neoliberalism* (Oxford: Oxford University Press, 2007).

68. For testimonies of these men and women, see Pierre Bourdieu, *La misère du Monde* (Paris: Seuil, 1993).

69. Howard Hughes, "Holidays and Homosexual Identity," *Tourism Management* 18, no. 1 (1997): 5.

70. Edwards, *Morocco Bound.*

71. While undertaking Hajj, the Muslim duty of pilgrimage to Mecca, Abdellah Hammoudi was insistently asked by two Saudi men, "Which city is the most impure in Morocco? Casablanca or Tangier?" "I do not know what you mean . . ." "I mean the place where there is the most vice, the most turpitude and lust." See Hammoudi, *A Season in Mecca: Narrative of a Pilgrimage* (New York: Hill and Wang, 2006), 267.

72. Ben Jelloun, *La prière de l'absent.*

73. Ibid.

74. Some of the most notorious examples include the work of Sigmund Freud, Michel Foucault, and Judith Butler.

75. O'Connell Davidson and Sanchez Taylor, "Travel and Taboo," 87.

76. Joseph Massad, "Re-Orienting Desire: The Gay International and the Arab World," *Public Culture* 14, no. 2 (2002): 361–85, reprinted in *Desiring Arabs* (Chicago: University of Chicago Press, 2007); Steven Seidman, "The Politics of Cosmopolitan Beirut: From the Stranger to the Other," *Theory, Culture, and Society* 29, no. 2 (2012): 3–36; Jared McCormick, "Transition Beirut: Gay Identities, Lived Realities: The Balancing Act in the Middle East," in *Sexuality in the Arab World,* ed. Samir Khalaf and John Gagnon (London: Saqi, 2006).

77. I heard it was a real industry, and there is traffic in these *cartes blanches* issued for those who have the right connection or who can afford the price to pay for them.

78. Wanjohi Kibicho, *Sex Tourism in Africa: Kenya's Booming Industry* (Farnham: Ashgate, 2009), 135.

79. Ibid.

80. Erica Williams, *Sex Tourism in Bahia* (Urbana: University of Illinois Press, 2013).

81. Little of such violation and violence has made the news. One incident involves suspicion of a gay marriage in the city of Ksar al-Kabir in February 5, 2007; the second is the arrest and beating of a man dressed like a woman in the city of Fes in June, 2015.

82. Leila Ahmed, *Gender and Women in Islam* (New Haven, Conn.: Yale University Press, 1992); Lila Abu-Lughod, *Do Muslim Women Need Saving?* (Cambridge, Mass.: Harvard University Press, 2013).

83. Joan W. Scott, "Gender: A Useful Category of Historical Analysis," *American Historical Review* 91, no. 5 (1986): 1073.

84. See the case of Lord Cromer discussed by Leila Ahmed, *Women and Gender in Islam.*

85. See Scott, *The Politics of the Veil.*

86. Fanon, *The Wretched of the Earth.*

87. Said, *Orientalism;* Leila Ahmed, *Women and Gender in Islam;* Joseph Massad, *Desiring Arabs* (Chicago: University of Chicago Press, 2007); Jessica Jacobs, *Sex, Tourism and the Postcolonial Encounter: Landscapes of Longing in Egypt* (Farnham: Ashgate, 2010); Grewal, *Home and Harem.*

88. Anne McClintock, cited by Steven Gregory, "Men in Paradise: Sex Tourism and the Political Economy of Masculinity," in *Race, Nature, and the Politics of Difference,* ed. Donald Moore, Jake Kosek, and Anand Pandian (Durham, N.C.: Duke University Press, 2003), 326.

89. Fanon, *The Wretched of the Earth.*

90. Kamala Kempadoo, *Sexing the Caribbean: Gender, Race, and Sexual Labor* (London: Routledge, 2004), 138–39.

91. See, for the case of the Dominic Republic, Denise Brennan, *What's Love Got to Do with It? Transnational Desires and Sex Tourism in the Dominican Republic* (Durham, N.C.: Duke University Press, 2004), 170–71; Erica Williams, *Sex Tourism in Bahia,* 159–63.

92. Kempadoo, *Sexing the Caribbean*, 123–24.

93. There is, however, a common erudite explanation saying that *gawri* is from the Turkish word "*giouri*," meaning "infidel," and *giouri* itself originates from the Arabic term "*kafir*," which means "infidel," according to one of the earliest explanations of Edward Daniel Clarke, *Travels to Europe, Asia, and Africa* (London: Fay & Company, 1813).

94. See Miller, "The Beni Ider Quarter in 1900."

95. According to Daniel Schroeter, the Jews of Tetouan, Larache, and Tangier developed an identity "connected to the nation-state of Spain since Spanish occupation of northern Morocco in 1860"; see Schroeter, "Philo-Sephardism, Anti-Semitism, and Arab Nationalism," 183.

96. Susan Gilson Miller, "Crisis and Community: The People of Tangier and the French Bombardment of 1844," *Middle Eastern Studies* 27, no. 4 (1991): 592.

97. The issue is complicated and not yet studied. Marriage between a Muslim woman and a non-Muslim man (Jewish or Christian) is illegal in Morocco unless the man converts. A Muslim man is allowed to marry a Christian or Jewish woman without need of conversion. Marriage between a Muslim man and a Jewish woman may cause great anxiety in the Jewish community, especially in regard to children. I owe these remarks to Daniel Schroeter.

98. Hazel Tucker, *Living with Tourism: Negotiating Identities in a Turkish Village* (London: Routledge, 2003); Bowman, "Fucking Tourists."

99. Jacobs, *Sex, Tourism and the Postcolonial Encounter.*

100. Kamala Kempadoo, *Sexing the Caribbean: Gender, Race, and Sexual Labor* (London: Routledge, 2004).

101. For the case of the Bahia in Brazil, see Erica Williams, *Sex Tourism in Bahia*, 62.

102. Susan Frohlick, "Sex of Tourism? Bodies Under Suspicion in Paradise," in *Thinking Through Tourism*, ed. Julie Scott and Tom Selwyn (New York: Beg, 2010), 66.

103. Harvey, *Cosmopolitanism and the Geographies of Freedom*, 84; see also the same view expressed by Paul Gilroy, *Postcolonial Melancholia* (New York: Columbia University Press, 2005), 58–59.

104. The Kabyle is a Berber ethnic group from the northern part of Algeria.

105. Arabic is a standardized, literary language written and also spoken in the media all over the Arab world. Moroccan Arabic is the daily language of the masses in Morocco; it is a dialect (*darija*) specific to Moroccans and easily understood by Maghrebis, who speak similar dialects.

106. de Genova, *Working the Boundaries*, 86.

107. Hannoum, "Notes on the (Post)Colonial in the Maghreb."

108. Homi Bhabha, "Unsatisfied: Notes on Vernacular Cosmopolitanism," in *Text and Nation*, ed. Laura Garcia-Morena and Peter C. Pfeifer (London: Camden House, 1996), 191–207; Appiah, *Cosmopolitanism*.

109. Nina Glick Schiller, Tsypylma Darieva, and Sandra Gruner-Domic, "Defining Cosmopolitanism Sociability in a Transnational Age: An Introduction," *Ethnic and Racial Studies* 34, no. 3 (2011): 403.

110. Pnina Werbner, "Vernacular Cosmopolitanism," *Theory, Culture, and Society* 23, nos. 2–3 (2006): 496–98.

111. Deborah Kapchan, "Performance," *Journal of American Folklore* 108, no. 430 (1995): 479.

112. J. P. Winner (1979), cited in Veena Daas, "Composition of the Personal Voice: Violence and Migration," *Studies in Histories* 7, no. 1 (1991): 65–77.

113. Chakrabarty, *Provincializing Europe*, 27.

114. Eid al-Adha, or the day of sacrifice, happens once a year, on the tenth day of the Muslim month of Muharram. It is a commemoration and a celebration of Abraham's attempted sacrifice of his son, Ishmael for the Muslim. The sacrificed lamb is thus a repetition of the Patriarch's original sacrifice. It is thus a story rooted in Judeo-Christian tradition.

115. Said, *Orientalism*.

116. Michel-Rolph Trouillot, "Anthropology and the Savage Slot: The Poetics and Politics of Otherness," in *Global Transformations: Anthropology and the Modern World* (New York: Palgrave, 2001), 7–28.

117. Even though it has vanished from the discipline of anthropology, the savage slot, I contend, is alive and well in the media, and in travel and other entertainment literature, where it is more readable than many of the esoteric anthropological narratives.

118. I use the concept of the West in the sense that Michel-Rolph Trouillot describes: an imaginary construction, the product of the Western imagination of geography, the other face of which is the Elsewhere. Trouillot, "Anthropology and the Savage Slot."

119. The reference here is to Borges's theory of representation. For him, because the camel is so present in Arabia, there is no mention of it in the Quran. The point he wants to make is that one does not represent that which is omnipresent, since it needs no representation. The theory is interesting except that the example Borges gives is not a good one. The Quran is full of references to the camel. See Jorge Luis Borges, *The Argentine Writer and Tradition* (Richmond, Va.: Latin American and European Literary Society, 1961).

120. Abdellah Hammoudi, *A Season in Mecca*; Elaine Combs-Schilling, *Sacred Performance: Islam, Sexuality, and Sacrifice* (New York: Columbia University Press, 1989).

121. There are local variants, of course. In Côte d'Ivoire, the sacrifice can happen in a public space. I owe this remark to Alma Gottlieb.

122. Deborah Kapchan, "The Promise of Sonic Translation: Performing the Festive Sacred in Morocco," in *Practicing Sufism: Sufi Politics and Performance in Africa*, ed. Abdelmajid Hannoum (London: Routledge, 2016), 150–74.

123. Derrida, *De l'hospitalité*, 58.

124. Ibid., 56.

125. Pheng Cheah, "The Cosmopolitical—Today," in *Cosmopolitics: Thinking and Feeling Beyond the Nation*, ed. Pheng Cheah and Bruce Robbins (Minneapolis: University of Minnesota Press, 1998); Bruce Robbins, "Actual Existing Cosmopolitanism," in *Cosmopolitics: Thinking and Feeling Beyond the Nation*, ed. Pheng Cheah and Bruce Robbins (Minneapolis: University of Minnesota Press, 1998); Nussbaum, *For Love of Country*; Appiah, *Cosmopolitanism*; Harvey, *Cosmopolitanism*.

126. Kant, *Political Writings*, 106.

127. The racial dimension of so-called cosmopolitanism is often ignored. One of the few who remind us of its strong presence is Koutonin, "Why Are White People Expats?" *Guardian*, March 13, 2015, https://www.theguardian.com/global-development-professionals-network/2015/mar/13/white-people-expats-immigrants-migration (accessed March 23, 2018).

EPILOGUE

1. Edward Said, *Reflections on Exile and Other Essays* (Cambridge, Mass.: Harvard University Press, 2000), 173.

2. Hammoudi, *A Season in Mecca*, 13.

3. Shahram Khosravi, *'Illegal' Traveler: An Auto-Ethnography of Borders* (New York: Palgrave Macmillan 2011), 75.

4. Ibid.

5. Sassen, *Guests and Aliens*, 2.

6. Sylvie Bredeloup, "The Figure of the Adventurer as an African Migrant," *Journal of African Cultural Studies* 25, no. 2 (2013): 170–82. A similar view is also expressed by Lahlou, *Les migrations irrégulieres*.

7. Friedrich Nietzsche, *Thus Spoke Zarathustra* (Oxford: Oxford University Press, 2005), 26.

8. Lefebvre, *La production de l'espace*, 145.

9. The Moroccan government, in part because of EU pressure and in part because of human rights organizations, and also as a diplomatic gesture toward its African partners, offered to "regularize" African migrants. For more on the first campaign, in which 25,000 migrants were "regularized," see "Le Maroc lance une campagne de régularization des sans-papiers," *Afrique*, January 3, 2014, http://www.rfi.fr/afrique/20140103-le-maroc-lance-une-campagne-regularisation-papiers. In the second campaign, 20,000 applications were submitted; see "Campagne des régularisations des migrants: Ce qu'il faut savoir," *Tel Quel*, December 13, 2016, http://telquel.ma/2016/12/13/campagne-regularisation-migrants-ce-quil-faut-savoir_1527188; "Régularisation des migrants: où en est la deuxième campagne?" *Tel Quel*, April 17, 2017, http://telquel.ma/2017/04/17/deuxieme-campagne-regularistaion-migrants-en-on_1543585.

10. Hannah Arendt, "We Refugees," in *Altogether Elsewhere*, ed. Marc Robinson (London: Faber and Faber, 1994), 110–19.

11. On April 2, 2017, the *Guardian* reported that one million Africans were on their way to Europe from Libya alone. Patrick Wintour, "1m African Migrants May Be En Route to Europe, Says Former UK Envoy," *Guardian*, April 2, 2017, https://www.theguardian.com/uk-news/2017/apr/02/1m-african-migrants-may-be-en-route-to-europe-says-former-uk-envoy.

12. Paul Ricœur, *La mémoire, l'histoire et l'oubli* (Paris: Seuil, 2000).

13. Brand, *Citizens Abroad*, 47.

14. As it was reported to me by several interlocutors in the area of the Rif who, in the 1970s, stood in long lines waiting for their turn to be examined by French recruiters. "They were checking out our bodies as if we were beasts" (*kayqalbuna bhâl labhâyim*), one person told me. "I left," he said.

15. Sayad, *La doubleabsence*. Testimonies about that period by first-generation French citizens started to emerge. One of the most poignant is the novel, now a film, by Sophia Azzedine, *Mon père est femme de ménage* (Paris: Editions 84, 2014). Also, see the early work of Ben Jelloun, *La prière de l'absent*.

16. Sara Ahmed, "Home and Away: Narratives of Migration and Estrangement," *International Journal of Cultural Studies* 2, no. 3 (1999): 341.

17. Amin Maalouf, *Les désorientés* (Paris: Grasset, 2012), 66.

18. Simone Weil, cited in Said, *Reflections on Exile*, 183.

19. Arendt, "We Refugees," 113.

20. Aviezer Tucker, "In Search of Home," *Journal of Applied Philosophy* 2, no. 2 (1994): 184.

21. Emily Dickinson, "Poem 254" in *Final Harvest: Emily Dickinson's Poems*, ed. Thomas H. Johnson (New York: Little, Brown), 34.

Bibliography

PERIODICALS AND NEWS ORGANIZATIONS

Afrik.com
Afrique
Al Jazeera
BBC
CNN
Der Tagesspiegel
El Confidencial
El Pais
Guardian
Jeune Afrique
Libération
Le Monde
Le Monde Diplomatique
L'Humanité
Medias24
Nation
New York Times
New Yorker
Al-Sabâh
Senenews
Tel Quel
Zamane

REPORTS AND DECLARATIONS

Hâlat al maghrib 2011–2010 (Rabat: Matbaʿat al-najâr al jadida, 2011).
Report of du Haut Commissariat au Plan, Maroc (2017).
Report, United Nations, OM's Global Migration Data Analysis Centre (2016, 2017, 2018).
Report UNICEF, la non scholarisation au Maroc (May 2006).
Report UNICEF, Les enfants non scholarisés (October 2014).
Report, UNICEF, Migration en Espgne des enfants non accompagnés: cas du Maroc (February, 2007).

United Nations Human Rights, Office of the High Commissioner, "Convention on the Rights of the Child" (November 20, 1989).

Universal Declaration of Human Rights (1948).

OTHER WORKS

Abd el-Krim et la république du Rif (Paris: Maspero, 1976).

Abdi Farah, Omar. "Le rêve européen dans la littérature négro-africaine d'expression française" (PhD diss., Universite de Bourgone, 2015).

Abrams, Philip. "Notes on the Difficulty of Studying the State." *Journal of Historical Sociology* 1, no. 1 (1988): 58–89.

Abu-Lughod, Janet. *Rabat: Urban Apartheid in Morocco* (Princeton, N.J.: Princeton University Press, 1981).

Abu-Lughod, Lila. *Do Muslim Women Need Saving?* (Cambridge, Mass.: Harvard University Press, 2013).

Abu-Lughod, Lila. *Veiled Sentiments: Honor and Poetry in a Bedouin Society* (Berkeley: California University Press, 1986).

Agamben, Giorgio. *Homo Sacer* (Stanford: Stanford University Press, 1998).

Ahmed, Leila. *Gender and Women in Islam* (New Haven: Yale University Press, 1992).

Ahmed, Sara. "Home and Away." *International Journal of Cultural Studies* 2, no. 3 (1999): 341.

Ahmed, Sara. "A Phenomenology of Whiteness." *Feminist Theory* 8, no. 2 (2007): 149–68.

Aidi, Hisham. "Is Morocco Headed Toward Insurrection?" *Nation*, July 13, 2017, https://www.thenation.com/article/is-morocco-headed-toward-insurrection/ (accessed October 1, 2018).

Aidi, Hisham. *Music Rebel: Race, Empire, and the New Muslim Culture* (New York: Vintage, 2014).

Al Jazeera. "Nuʿushun fi Lajjat al Bahr," a documentary, November 22, 2012, https://www.youtube.com/watch?v=vAO_X2Qw5hM (accessed March 23, 2018).

Amiar, Jamal. "Tanger: Manifestation anti-subsahariens et montée du racism." *Medias24*, December 8, 2013, http://www.medias24.com/SOCIETE/7096-Tanger-manifestation-anti-subsahariens-et-montee-du-racisme.html.

Anaut, Marie. *Les thérapies familiales: Approches systémiques et psychanalytiques* (Paris: Armand Colin, 2012).

Anderson, Amanda. "Cosmopolitanism, Universalism, and the Divided Legacies of Modernity." In *Cosmopolitics: Thinking and Feeling Beyond the Nation*, ed. Pheng Cheah and Bruce Robbins (Minneapolis: University of Minnesota Press, 1998).

Anderson, Benedict. *The Specter of Comparison: Nationalism, Southeast Asia, and the World* (London: Verso, 1998).

Anderson, Ruben. *Illegality, Inc.: Clandestine Migration and the Business of Bordering Europe* (Berkeley: California University Press, 2014).

Appadurai, Arjun. *Modernity at Large: Cultural Dimensions of Globalization* (Minneapolis: University of Minnesota Press, 1996).

Appiah, Kwame Anthony. *Cosmopolitanism: Ethics in a World of Strangers* (New York: Norton, 2006).

Arendt, Hannah. *The Human Condition* (Chicago: University of Chicago Press).

Arendt, Hannah. *Men in Dark Times* (New York: Harcourt Brace, 1970).

Arendt, Hannah. *The Origins of Totalitarianism* (New York: Harcourt, 1966).

Arendt, Hannah. "We Refugees." In *Altogether Elsewhere*, ed. Marc Robinson (London: Fabre and Fabre, 1994).

Ariès, Philippe. "L'enfant et la rue, de la ville à l'anti-ville." *Urbi* 2 (1979): III.

Ariès, Philippe. *L'enfant et la vie familiale sous l'Ancien Régime* (Paris: Seuil, 1975).

Aron, Henri. "Au Maroc: Des coopérants enseignants pour quoi faire?" *Revue Tiers Monde* 51 (1972): 559–73.

Azimi, Negar. "The Madness of Queen Jane." *New Yorker*, June 12, 2014.

Azzedine, Sophia. *Mon père est une femme de ménage* (Paris: Editions, 2014).

Bachelard, Gaston. *La poétique de l'espace* (Paris: Les Presses Universitaires de France, 1957).

Bacon, Lucien, Olivier Clochard, Thomas Honoré, Nicholas Lambert, Sarah Mekdjian, and Philippe Rekacewicz. "Cartographier les mouvements migratoires." *Revue européenne des migrations internationales* 3, no. 32 (2016): 185–214.

Balibar, Etienne, and Immanuel Wallerstein. *Race, Nation, and Class: Ambiguous Identities* (London: Verso, 1991).

Balzac, Honoré. *Le Père Goriot* (Paris: Gallimard, 1999).

Barth, Fredrik. *Ethnic Groups and Boundaries: The Social Organization of Culture Difference* (Oslo: Universitetsforlaget, 1969).

Bataille, George. *La part Maudite* (Paris: Hachette, 1949).

Bejjit, Karim. *English Colonial Texts on Tangier, 1661–1684: Imperialism and the Politics of Resistance* (New York: Routledge, 2016).

Belguendouz, Abdelkrim. "Expansion et sous-traitance des logiques d'enfermement de l'Union Europeenne: L'example du Maroc." *Cultures & Conflicts* 57 (2005): 155–220.

Belguendouz, Abdelkrim. "Le Maroc: Vaste zone d'attente?" *Plein Droit* 57 (2003): 35–40.

Ben Jelloun, Tahar. *Harrouda* (Paris: Denoël, 1973).

Ben Jelloun, Tahar. *Jour de Silence à Tanger* (Paris: Seuil, 1990).

Ben Jelloun, Tahar. *La prière de l'absent* (Paris: Seuil, 1981).

Ben Jelloun, Tahar. *Partir* (Paris: Gallimard, 2006).

Bergson, Henri. *Oeuvres* (Paris: Presses Universitaires de France, 1970).

Berque, Jacques. "L'idée de classe dans l'histoire contemporaine des arabes." *Cahiers internationaux de sociologie* 38 (1965): 55–70.

Berrada Gouzi, Abderrahmane, and Noureddine El Aoufi. "La non scholarisation au Maroc." UNICEF, 2006, https://www.unicef.org/morocco/french/La_non_scolarisation_au _Maroc.pdf (accessed July 1, 2018).

Bessone, Magali. *Sans distinction de race? Une analyse critique du concept de race et de ses effets pratiques* (Paris: Vrin, 2013).

Bhaba, Homi. "Unsatisfied: Notes on Vernacular Cosmopolitanism." In *Text and Nation*, ed. Laura Garcia-Morena and Peter C. Pfeifer (London: Camden House, 1996).

Bialasiewicz, Luiza. "Tangier, Mobile City: RE-Making Borders in the Straits of Gibraltar." In *Borderities and the Politics of Contemporary Mobile Borders*, ed. Anne-Laure Amilhat-Szary and Frédéric Giraut (London: Palgrave Macmillan, 2015).

Bialasiewicz, Luiza, and Lauren Wagner. "Extra-ordinary Tangier: Domesticating Practices in a Border Zone." *GeoHumanities* 1, no. 1 (2015): 131–56.

Bloch, Ernest. *The Principle of Hope* (Cambridge, Mass.: MIT Press, 1986).

Body-Gendrot, Sophie. *Ville et Violence: l'Irruption de nouveaux Acteurs* (Paris: Presses Universitaires de France, 1993).

Bono, Irene. "La démographie de l'injustice sociale au Maroc." In *L'état d'injustice au Maghreb*, ed. Irene Bono, Béathrice Hibou, Hamza Meddeb, and Mohamed Tozy (Paris: Karthala, 2015).

Bono, Irene. "L'emploi comme 'revendication sectorielle': La naturalization de la question sociale au Maroc." In *L'état d'injustice au Maghreb*, ed. Irene Bono, Béathrice Hebou, Hamza Meddeb, and Mohamed Tozy, 279–80 (Paris: Karthala, 2015).

Bordenet, Camille, and Madjid Zerrouky. "Méditerranée: Chiffres et carte pour comprendre la tragédie." *Le Monde*, April 20, 2015, http://www.lemonde.fr/les-decodeurs/article /2015/04/20/en-2015-un-migrant-meurt-toutes-les-deux-heures-en-moyenne-en -mediterranee_4619379_4355770.html (accessed March 19, 2018).

Borges, Luis. *The Argentine Writer and Tradition* (Richmond, Va.: Latin American and European Literary Society, 1961).

Boum, Aomar. *Memories of Absence: How Muslims Remember Jews in Morocco* (Stanford, Calif.: Stanford University Press, 2013).

Bourdieu, Pierre. "Dévoiler et divulguer le refoulé." In *Algérie—France—Islam*, ed. Joseph Jurt (Paris: L'Harmathan, 1997).

Bourdieu, Pierre. *Domination masculine* (Paris: Seuil, 1998).

Bourdieu, Pierre. *La misère du Monde* (Paris: Seuil, 1993).

Bourdieu, Pierre. "L'école conservatrice. Les inégalités devant l'école et devant la culture." *Revue française de sociologie* 7 (1966): 325–47.

Bourgois, Philippe. *In Search of Respect: Selling Crack in El Barrio* (Cambridge: Cambridge University Press, 1995).

Bourquia, Rahma. "Habitat, femmes et honneur: Le cas de quelques quartiers populaires d'Oujda." In *Femmes, culture et societies au Maghreb*, ed. Rahma Bourquia, Mounira Charrad, and Nancy Gallagher, 15–34 (Paris: Afrique-Orient, 1996).

Bowles, Paul. *The Death of a Cosmopolitan City*. In *Travels: Collected Writings 1950–1993* (New York: HarperCollins, 2010).

Bowles, Paul. *Let It Come Down* (London: John Lehmann, 1952).

Bowles, Paul. "View from Tangier." *Nation*, June 30, 1956.

Bowman, Glenn. "Fucking Tourists: Sexual Relations and Tourism in Jerusalem's Old City." *Critique of Anthropology* 9, no. 2 (1989): 77–93.

Boyden, Joy. "Childhood and the Policy Makers: A Comparative Perspective on the Globalization of Childhood." In *Constructing and Reconstructing Childhood: Contemporary Issues in the Sociological Study of Childhood*, ed. Allison James and Alan Prout (London: Falmer, 1997).

Brand, Laurie. *Citizens Abroad: Emigration and the State in the Middle East and North Africa* (Cambridge: Cambridge University Press, 2006).

Bredeloup, Sylvie. "The Figure of the Adventurer as an African Migrant." *Journal of African Cultural Studies* 2, no. 25 (2013): 170–82.

Brennan, Dennis. *What's Love Got to Do with It? Transnational Desires and Sex Tourism in the Dominican Republic* (Durham, N.C.: Duke University Press, 2004).

Bretton, Laure. "François Hollande: 'La République ne connaît pas de races ni de couleurs de peau.'" *Libération*, October 8, 2015, http://www.liberation.fr/france/2015/10/08/la -republique-ne-connait-pas-de-races-ni-de-couleurs-de-peau_1400069.

Brohman, J. "New Directions in Tourism or Third World Development." *Annals of Tourism Research* 1, no. 23 (1996): 48–70.

Brove, Vincenzo, and Tobias Bohmelt. "Does Immigration Induce Terrorism?" *Journal of Politics* 78, no. 2 (2016): 572–88.

Bruez, Veronique. *La Terrasse des Paresseaux* (Clamecy: Éditions Leo Scheer, 2011).

Bucholtz, Mary. "Youth and Cultural Practice." *Annual Review of Anthropology* 31 (2002): 531.

Burroughs, William. *Interzone* (New York: Viking, 1989).

Butler, Judith. *Excitable Speech: A Politics of the Performative* (New York: Routledge, 1997).

"Campagne des régularisations des migrants: Ce qu'il faut savoir." *Tel Quel*, December 13, 2016, http://telquel.ma/2016/12/13/campagne-regularisation-migrants-ce-quil-faut -savoir_1527188.

Caraës, Marie-Haude, and Jean Fernandez. *Tanger La dérive littéraire* (Paris: Publisud, 2002).

Carter, Donald. *States of Grace: Senegalese in Italy and the New European Immigration* (Minneapolis: University of Minnesota Press, 1997).

Cassaigne, Jean. *La situation des Français au Maroc depuis l'indépendance, 1956–1964* (Paris: Presses de Sciences Po, 1964).

Chakrabarty, Dipesh. *Provincializing Europe: Postcolonial Thought and Historical Difference* (Princeton, N.J.: Princeton University Press, 2000).

Chatterjee, Partha. "Beyond the Nation? Or Within?" *Social Text* 56 (1998): 57–69.

Chavez, Leo. *Shadowed Lives: Undocumented Immigrants in American Society* (New York: Harcourt Brace College, 1992).

Cheah, Pheng. "The Cosmopolitical—Today." In *Cosmopolitics: Thinking and Feeling Beyond the Nation*, ed. P. Cheah and B. Robbins (Minneapolis: University of Minnesota Press, 1998).

Chouki El Hamel. *Black Morocco: A History of Race, Slavery, and Islam* (Cambridge: Cambridge University Press, 2014).

Choukri, Mohamed. "Paul Bowles wa ʿuzlat Tanja." In *Al-Aʿmâl al Kâmila*, vol. 2 (Casablanca: Al Markaz al-Thaqafi al-ʿArabi, 2008).

Choukri, Mohamed. *For Bread Alone* (London: P. Owen, 1973).

Choukri, Mohamed. *Jean Genet in Tangier* (New York: Eco Press, 1974).

Chraibi, Driss. *Le passé simple* (Paris: Donoel, 1954).

Clifford, James. *Routes: Travel and Translation in the Late Twentieth Century* (Berkeley: University of California Press, 1997).

Cole, Jennifer, and Christian Groes. *Affective Circuits: African Migrations to Europe and the Pursuit of Social Regeneration* (Chicago: University of Chicago Press, 2016).

Comaroff, Jean. *Body of Power, Spirit of Resistance: The Culture and History of a South African People* (Chicago: University of Chicago Press, 1985).

Comaroff, Jean, and John Comaroff. "Reflections on Youth: From the Past to the Postcolony." In *Makers and Breakers: Children & Youth in Postcolonial Africa*, ed. Filip de Boeck and Alcinda Honwana (Trenton, N.J.: Africa World Press, 2005).

Combs-Schilling, Elaine. *Sacred Performance: Islam, Sexuality, and Sacrifice* (New York: Columbia University Press, 1989).

Conrad, Joseph. *Heart of Darkness and Selections from The Congo Diary* (New York: Modern Library, 1999).

Conrad, Joseph. *Lord Jim* (Edinburgh: Blackwood's Magazine, 1900).

Courcelle-Labrousse, Vincent, and Nicolas Marmié. *La guerre du Rif: Maroc (1921–1926)* (Paris: Seuil, 2008).

Coury, Ralph, and Kevin Lacey, eds. *Writing Tangier* (New York: Peter Lang, 2009).

Crapanzano, Vincent. *Imaginative Horizons: An Essay in Literary-Philosophical Anthropology* (Chicago: University of Chicago Press, 2003).

Crapanzano, Vincent. "Reflections on Hope as a Category of Social and Psychological Analysis." *Cultural Anthropology* 18, no. 1 (2003): 15.

Crawford, Michael, and Benjamin Campbell. *Causes and Consequences of Human Migration: An Evolutionary Perspective* (Cambridge: Cambridge University Press, 2012).

Crétois, Jules. "A Tanger, le racisme tue." *Tel Quel*, September 7, 2014, http://telquel.ma/2014/09/07/tanger-racisme-tue_1415366.

Cyrulnik, Boris, and Gérard Jorland, eds. *Résilience: Connaissances de base* (Paris: Odile Jacob, 2012).

Dakhlia, Jocelyne. "La symbolique du pouvoir itinérant." *Annales: Histoire et sciences sociales* 3, no. 43 (1988): 735–60.

Das, Veena, and Deborah Poole. "States and Its Margins: Comparative Ethnographies." In *Anthropology in the Margins of the State*, ed. Veena Das and Deborah Poole (Santa Fe, N.M.: School of American Research Press, 2004).

Das, Veena. "Composition of the Personal Voice: Violence and Migration." *Studies in Histories* 7, no. 1 (1991): 65–77.

de Amicis, Edmondo. *Morocco: Its Peoples and Places* (Philadelphia: Henry T. Coates & Co., 1897).

de Certeau, Michel. *La prise de la parole: Et autres écrits politiques* (Paris: Seuil, 1994).

de Foucauld, Charles. *Reconnaissance au Maroc 1883–84* (Paris: Editions d'aujourd'hui, 1888 [1985]).

de Genova, Nicholas. "The European Question: Migration, Race, and Postcoloniality in Europe." *Social Text* 3, no. 34 (2016): 75–102.

de Genova, Nicholas. "Migration Illegality and Deportability in Everyday Life." *Annual Review of Anthropology* 31 (1998): 419–47.

de Genova, Nicholas. *Working the Boundaries of Race: Race, Space, and "Illegality" in Mexican Chicago* (Durham, N.C.: Duke University Press, 2005).

de Genova, Nicholas, and Nathalie Peutz, eds. *The Deportation Regime* (Durham, N.C.: Duke University Press, 2010).

Dean, Bartholomew. "Freedom." In *Keys of Mobility: A Critical Engagement*, ed. Noel Salazar and Kiran Jayaram (New York: Berghahn, 2016).

Delatronchette, Louis. "Régularisation des migrants: où en est la deuxième campagne?" *Tel Quel*, April 17, 2017, http://telquel.ma/2017/04/17/deuxieme-campagne-regularistaion-migrants-en-on_1543585.

Deme, Aisha. "Au Maroc, Scènes de racisme ordinaire contre les noirs." *Le Monde*, January 6, 2015, http://www.lemonde.fr/afrique/article/2015/01/06/le-maroc-du-reve-a-l-amertume_4550079_3212.html.

Derrida, Jacques. *Cosmopolitans du Monde, encore un effort!* (Paris: Galilée, 1997).

Derrida, Jacques. *De l'hospitalité* (Paris: Calmann-Levy, 1997).

Desjarlais, Robert, and Jason Throop. "Phenomenological Approaches in Anthropology." *Annual Review of Anthropology* 40 (2011): 87–102.

Desroche, Henri. *The Sociology of Hope* (London: Routledge, 1979).

Di Amicis, Edmondo. *Morocco: Its Peoples and Its Places* (Philadelphia: Coates & Co., 1879).

Dickinson, Emily. "Poem 254." In *Final Harvest: Emily Dickinson's Poems*, ed. Thomas H. Johnson (New York: Little, Brown), 34.

Diome, Fatou. *Dans le ventre de l'Atlantique* (Paris: Editions Anne Carrière, 2003).

Dongala, Emmanuel. *Les petits enfants naissent aussi des ètoiles* (Paris: Editions Le Serpent à plumes, 1998).

Douglas, Mary. *Purity and Danger* (London: Routledge, 1966).

Douglas, Mary. *Risk and Blame: Essays in Cultural Theory* (New York: Routledge, 1992).

Du Bois, William Edward B. *The Souls of Black Folk* (New York: New American Library, 1995).

Ducruet, César, et al. "Maghreb Port Cities in Transitions: The Case of Tangier." *Portus Plus*, 2016, http://retedigital.com/wp-content/themes/rete/pdfs/portus_plus/1_2011/Tem%C3%A1ticas/La_ciudad_portuaria_contempor%C3%A1nea/07_C%C3%A9sarDucruet_FatimaZohraMohamedCh%C3%A9rif_NajibCherfaoui.pdf (accessed March 18, 2018).

Dumas, Alexander. *Tangier to Tunis*. Trans. A. E. Murch (London: Peter Owen, 1959).

Dupâquier, Jacques. *Histoire de la population française* (Paris: Presses Universitaires de France, 1995).

Durham, Deborah. "Disappearing Youth: Youth as a Social Shifter in Botswana." *American Ethnologist* 31, no. 4 (2004): 589–605.

Durham, Deborah. "Youth and the Social Imagination in Africa: Introduction to Parts 1 and 2." *Anthropological Quarterly* 73, no. 3 (2000): 114.

Eastman, Anthony F. "The Algeciras Conference, 1906." *Southern Quarterly* 7, no. 1 (1969): 185–205.

Edwards, Brian T. *Morocco Bound: Disorienting America's Maghreb, from Casablanca to the Marrakech Express* (Durham, N.C.: Duke University Press, 2005).

Empez Vidal, Núria. "Social Construction of Neglect: The Case of Unaccompanied Minors from Morocco to Spain" (MPIDR working paper WP 2007-007, Max Planck Institute for Demographic Research, 2007), http://www.demogr.mpg.de/papers/working/wp-2007-007.pdf.

Escher, Anton, and Sandra Petermann. "Marrakesh Medina: Neocolonial Paradise of Lifestyle Migrants." In *Contested Spatialities, Lifestyle Migration, and Residential Tourism*, ed. Michael Janoschka and Heiko Haas (London: Routledge, 2013).

Escher, Anton, and Sandra Petermann. "Neo-Colonialism or Gentrification in the Medina of Marrakesh." *ISIM Newsletter* 5, no. 1 (2000): 34.

Fanon, Frantz. *Les damnés de la terre* (Paris: Maspero, 1961).

Fanon, Frantz. *Peau noir, masques blancs* (Paris: Éditions du Seuil, 1952).

Fanon, Frantz. "Racism and Culture." In *Toward the African Revolution*, ed. Frantz Fanon, trans. Haakon Chevalier (New York: Grove, 1969).

Fanon, Frantz. *The Wretched of the Earth* (New York: Grove, 1963).

Farah, Omar Abdi. "Le rêve européen dans la litérature négro-africaine" (PhD diss., Universite de Bourgone, 2015).

Farmer, Paul. "On Suffering and Structural Violence: A View from Below." *Daedalus* 125, no. 1 (1996): 261–283.

Fassin, Didier. "The Bio-politics of Otherness: Undocumented Foreigners and Racial Discrimination in French Public Debate." *Anthropology Today* 7 (2001): 3–7.

Fassin, Didier. *Enforcing Order: An Ethnography of Urban Policing* (Cambridge: Polity, 2013).

Fassin, Didier. *Humanitarian Reason: A Moral History of the Present* (Berkeley: California University Press, 2012).

Fassin, Didier. "Policing Borders, Producing Boundaries: The Governmentality of Immigration in Dark Times." *Annual Review of Anthropology* 40 (2011): 213–26.

Fassin, Didier, and Eric Fassin, eds. *De la question sociale la question raciale* (Paris: La Découverte, 2006).

Feldman, Allen. *Formations of Violence: The Narrative of the Body and Political Terror in Northern Ireland* (Chicago: University of Chicago Press, 1991).

Ferguson, Jane. *Global Shadows: Africa in the Neoliberal World* (Durham, N.C.: Duke University Press, 2006).

Foster, Stephen. *Cosmopolitan Desire: Transcultural Dialogues and Antiterrorism in Morocco* (New York: Altamira, 2006).

Foucault, Michel. "Faire vivre et laisser mourir: La naissance du racisme." *Les Temps modernes,* February 1991, 37–61.

Foucault, Michel. *Histoire de la folie à l'age classique* (Paris: Gallimard, 1976).

Foucault, Michel. *Histoire de la sexualité* (Paris: Gallimard, 1976).

Foucault, Michel. *Il faut défendre la société* (Paris: EHESS, 1997).

Foucault, Michel. *Mental Illness and Psychology* (New York: Harper Colophon, 1976).

Foucault, Michel. *Surveiller et punir: Naissance de la prison* (Paris: Gallimard, 1975).

Freud, Sigmund. *The Freud Reader* (New York: Norton, 1989).

Frohlick, Susan. "Sex of Tourism? Bodies Under Suspicion in Paradise." In *Thinking Through Tourism,* ed. Julie Scott and Tom Selwyn (New York: Beg, 2010).

Gaibazzi, Paolo. "Visa Problem: Certification, Kinship, and the Production of 'ineligibility' in the Gambia." *Journal of the Royal Anthropological Institute* 20, no. 1 (2014): 38–55.

Gambetta, Diego, and Steffen Hertog. *Engineers of Jihad: The Curious Connection Between Violent Extremism and Education* (Princeton, N.J.: Princeton University Press, 2016).

Gaou, Stéphanie. *Capiteuses* (Casablanca: Al Manar, 2012).

Geertz, Clifford. "Deep Hanging Out." *New York Review of Books,* October 22, 1998.

Geertz, Clifford. *The Interpretation of Cultures* (New York: Basic Books, 1979).

Geertz, Clifford. *Islam Observed: Religious Development in Morocco and Indonesia* (Chicago: University of Chicago Press, 1968).

Geertz, Clifford. *Local Knowledge: Further Essays in Interpretive Anthropology* (Stanford, Calif.: Stanford University Press, 1985).

Geertz, Clifford. *Negara: The Theatre State in Nineteenth-Century Bali* (Princeton, N.J.: Princeton University Press, 1980).

Gibran, Kahlil. *The Prophet* (New York: Penguin, 2002).

Gilroy, Paul. "One Nation Under a Grove: The Cultural Politics of 'Race' and Racism in Britain." In *Anatomy of Racism,* ed. David Goldberg (Minneapolis: University of Minnesota Press, 1990).

Gilroy, Paul. *Postcolonial Melancholia* (New York: Columbia University Press, 2005).

Gilroy, Paul. *There Ain't No Black in the Union Jack: The Cultural Politics of Race and Nation* (London: Hutchinson, 1987).

Glick, Thomas. *Islamic and Christian Spain in the Early Middle Age* (Princeton, N.J.: Princeton University Press, 1979).

Glick Schiller, Nina, Tsypylma Darleva, and Sandra Gruner-Domic. "Defining Cosmopolitanism Sociability in a Transnational Age: An Introduction." *Ethnic and Racial Studies* 34, no. 3 (2011): 399–418.

Glick Schiller, Nina, and Noel Salazar. "Regimes of Mobility Across the Globe." *Journal of Ethnic and Migration Studies* 39, no. 2 (2013): 183–200.

Gobille, Boris. "L'événement Mai 68: Pour une histoire du temps court." *Annales: Histoire et sciences sociales* 2 (2008): 321–49.

Goldberg, David Theo. *Racist Culture: Philosophy and the Politics of Meaning* (Oxford: Blackwell, 1993).

Goldberg, David Theo. "Racial Europeanization." *Ethnic and Racial Studies* 29, no. 2 (2006): 331–64.

Gregory, Steven. "Men in Paradise: Sex Tourism and the Political Economy of Masculinity." In *Race, Nature, and the Politics of Difference*, ed. Donald Moore, Jake Kosek, and Anand Pandian (Durham, N.C.: Duke University Press, 2003).

Grewal, Inderpal. *Home and Harem: Nation, Gender, Empire, and the Cultures of Travel* (Durham, N.C.: Duke University Press, 1996).

Gross, Matt. "Lost in Tangier." *New York Times*, September 9, 2010, http://www.nytimes.com /2010/09/12/travel/12Lost.html.

Guess, Teresa. "The Social Construction of Whiteness: Racism by Intent, Racism by Consequence." *Critical Sociology* 32, no. 4 (2006): 652.

Hacking, Ian. *Rewriting the Soul: Multiple Personality and the Science of Memory* (Princeton, N.J.: Princeton University Press, 1995).

Hammoudi, Abdallah. *Master and Discipline* (Chicago: University of Chicago Press, 1997).

Hammoudi, Abdallah. "The Reinvention of Dar al-Mulk." In *In the Shadow of the Sultan: Culture, Power, and Politics in Morocco*, ed. Rahma Bourquia and Susan Miller (Cambridge, Mass.: Harvard University Press, 1999).

Hammoudi, Abdellah. *A Season in Mecca: Narrative of a Pilgrimage* (New York: Hill and Wang, 2006). French ed., *Une saison à la Mecque. Récit de pèlerinage* (Paris: Seuil, 2005).

Hannerz, Ulf. "Cosmopolitanism." In *A Companion to the Anthropology of Politics*, ed. David Nugent and Joan Vincent, 69–85 (Oxford: Blackwell, 2004).

Hannoum, Abdelmajid. "Memory at the Surface: Colonial Forgetting in Post-Colonial France." *Interventions: International Journal of Postcolonial Studies* 21, no. 3 (2019): 367–91.

Hannoum, Abdelmajid. "Cartoons, Secularism, and Inequality." *Anthropology Today* 5, no. 31 (2015): 21–24.

Hannoum, Abdelmajid. "Qu'est-ce qu'un Maghrébin? Notes sur l'anthropologie des noms coloniaux." *Awal: Cahiers d'études berbères* 43 (2011): 75–87.

Hannoum, Abdelmajid. "The Harraga of Tangiers." *Encounters: International Journal of the Study of Culture and Society* 1, no. 1 (2009): 231–46.

Hannoum, Abdelmajid. "Notes on the (Post)Colonial in the Maghreb." *Critique of Anthropology* 29, no. 3 (2009): 324–44.

Hannoum, Abdelmajid. "The (Re)Turn of the Native: Anthropology, Ethnography, and Nativism." In *The Anthropologist and the Native: Essays for Gananath Obeyesekere*, ed. H. L. Seneviratne, 423–70 (Firenze: Società Editrice Fiorentina, 2009).

Hannoum, Abdelmajid. "Translation and the Colonial Imaginary: Ibn Khaldun, Orientalist." *History and Theory* 42 (2003): 61–81.

Hannoum, Abdelmajid. "Colonialism and Knowledge in Algeria: The Archives of the Arab Bureau." *History and Anthropology* 12, no. 4 (2001): 343–79.

Harvey, David. *Cosmopolitanism and the Geographies of Freedom* (New York: Columbia University Press, 2009).

Harvey, David. *A Brief History of Neoliberalism* (Oxford: Oxford University Press, 2007).

Harvey, David. *The Urban Experience* (Baltimore: Johns Hopkins University Press, 1989).

Hecht, Tobias. *At Home in the Street: Street Children of Northeast Brazil* (Cambridge: Cambridge University Press, 1998).

Heidegger, Martin. *Qu'est ce que la métaphysique?* (Paris: Gallimard, 1938).

Heller, Agnes, and Sonja Puntscher Riekmann, eds. *Biopolitics: The Politics of the Body, Race and Nature* (Aldershot: Avebury, 1996).

Hilali, Mimoun. "Le cosmpolitanisme de Tanger: Mythe et realité." *Horizons maghrébins* 31–32 (1996): 11–16.

Holloway, Sarah, and Gill Valentine, eds. *Children Geographies: Playing, Living, Learning* (London: Routledge, 2000).

Hughes, Howard. "Holidays and Homosexual Identity." *Tourism Management* 18, no. 1 (1997): 5.

Hussein, Nashaat. *Street Children in Egypt: Group Dynamics and Subcultural Constituents* (Cairo: American University in Cairo Press, 2005).

Jabri, Abed Mohamed. *Al-Asabiyya ad-dawla: Ma'alim nazariyya khalduniyya fi t-tarikh al-islami* (Casablanca: Dār al-Thaqāfah, 1971).

Jacobs, Jessica. *Sex, Tourism and the Postcolonial Encounter: Landscapes of Longing in Egypt* (Farnham: Ashgate, 2010).

James, Allison, Chris Jenks, and Alan Prout. *Theorizing Childhood* (Cambridge: Polity, 1998).

James, Allison, and Alan Prout. *Constructing and Reconstructing Childhood* (New York: Falmer, 1998).

Jones, Heather. "Algeciras Revisited: European Crisis and Conference Diplomacy, 16 January–7 April 1906," EUI Working Papers, MWP 2009/01, Max Weber Programme, 2009, http://diana-n.iue.it:8080/bitstream/handle/1814/10527/MWP_2009_01.pdf?sequence=1& isAllowed=y.

Kamali Dehghan, Saeed. "Morocco's Gag on Dissent in Rif Region Fuels Exodus to Europe." *Guardian*, November 1, 2017, https://www.theguardian.com/world/2017/nov/01/moroccos -gag-on-dissent-in-rif-region-fuels-exodus-to-europe (accessed October 1, 2018).

Kant, Immanuel. *Political Writings* (Cambridge: Cambridge University Press, 1997).

Kapchan, Deborah. *Gender on the Market: Moroccan Women and the Revoicing of Tradition* (Philadelphia: University of Pennsylvania Press, 1996).

Kapchan, Deborah. "Performance." *Journal of American Folklore* 108, no. 430 (1995): 479.

Kapchan, Deborah. "The Promise of Sonic Translation: Performing the Festive Sacred in Morocco." In *Practicing Sufism: Sufi Politics and Performance in Africa*, ed. Abdelmajid Hannoum (London: Routledge, 2016).

Kempadoo, Kamala. *Sexing the Caribbean: Gender, Race, and Sexual Labor* (London: Routledge, 2004).

Kerach, Adil. *Le Tanger des peintres. De Delacroix à Matisse* (Tangier: Kerach, 2003).

Khaled, Mona. "Perceptions marocaines de la migration française au Maroc." In *La question du "chez soi" au Maroc: Les representations des migrants francais confrontées aux points de vue des Marcains-es* (Rabat: Association Marocaines d'Etudes et de Recherche sur les Migration, 2014).

Khiari, Sadri. *Pour une politique de la racaille* (Paris: Textual, 2006).

Khosravi, Shahram. *"Illegal" Traveler: An Auto-Ethnography of Borders* (New York: Palgrave Macmillan, 2011).

Kibicho, Wanjohi. *Sex Tourism in Africa: Kenya's Booming Industry* (Farnham: Ashgate, 2009).

Kierkegaard, Søren. *Fear and Trembling/Repetition* (Princeton, N.J.: Princeton University Press, 1983).

Kleinman, Arthur. "The Violence of Everyday Life: The Multiple Forms and Dynamics of Social Violence." In *Violence and Subjectivity*, ed. Veena Das, Arthur Kleinman, Mamphela Ramphele, and Pamela Reynolds (Berkeley: University of California Press, 1998).

Korbin, Jill E. "Children, Childhood, and Violence." *Annual Review of Anthropology* 32 (2003): 431–46.

Koutonin, Mawuna Remarque. "Why Are White People Expats When the Rest of Us Are Immigrants?" *Guardian*, March 13, 2015.

Lahlou, Mehdi. *Les migration irrégulières entre le Maghreb et l'Union européenne: Evolutions récent* (Florence: Institut universitaire européen, 2005).

Lahlou, Mehdi. "Morocco's Experience of Migration as a Sending, Transit, and Receiving Country" (15 Working Papers, Instituto Affari Internazionali, September 30, 2015).

Laroui, Abdallah. *Les origins du nationalisme au Maroc* (Casablanca: Cenre culturel arabe, 1993).

Lazreg, Marnia. *The Emergence of Classes in Algeria: A Study of Colonialism and Socio-political Change* (Boulder, Colo.: Westview, 1976).

Lefebvre, Henri. *La production de l'espace* (Paris: Anthropos, 2000).

"Le Maroc lance une campagne de régularization des sans-papiers." *Afrique*, January 3, 2014, http://www.rfi.fr/afrique/20140103-le-maroc-lance-une-campagne-regularisation -papiers

Lendja Ngnemzue, Bergson. *Les étrangers illégaux à la recherche de papiers* (Paris: L'Harmattan, 2008).

Lentin, Alana. "Europe and the Silence About Race." *European Journal of Social Theory* 11, no. 4 (2008): 487–503.

LeTourneau, Roger. *La vie quotidienne à Fès en 1900* (Paris: Hachette, 1965).

Leveau, Rémy. *Le fellah marocain défendeur du trône* (Paris: Presses de la Fondation Nationale des Sciences Politiques, 1985).

Lévi-Strauss, Claude. *Race et histoire* (Paris: Donell, 1952).

Lindsey, Ursula. "Morocco's Rebellious Mountains Rise Up Again," *New York Times*, June 28, 2017, https://www.nytimes.com/2017/06/28/opinion/morocco-protest-monarchy.html (accessed March 5, 2018).

"Liste von 33.293 registrierten Asylsuchenden, Geflüchteten und Migrant*innen die aufgr- und der restriktiven Politik der Festung Europas zu Tode kamen." *Der Tagesspiegel*, June 15, 2017, http://www.tagesspiegel.de/downloads/20560202/3/listeentireberlinccbanu .pdf (accessed July 1, 2018).

Lucchini, Riccardo. *Sociologie de la survie: L'enfant dans la rue* (Paris: Presses Universitaires de France, 1996).

Mace, Celian. "Colere du Rif: Le fosse se creuse entre les deux Maroc." *Libération*, May 30, 2017, http://www.liberation.fr/planete/2017/05/30/colere-du-rif-le-fosse-se-creuse-entre -les-deux-maroc_1573426 (accessed March 5, 2018).

Maghraoui, Driss. "The Dualism of Rule and the Immune Monarchy." (Paper presented at the conference "Rethinking the 'Arab Spring' in the Maghreb," Aga Khan University, April 28, 2018).

Maalouf, Amin. *Les désorientés* (Paris: Grasset, 2012).

Marcus, George. "The Uses of Complicity in the Changing Mise-en-Scène of Anthropological Fieldwork." *Representations* 59 (1997): 85–108.

"Maroc: Arrestation de Nasser Zefzafi, leader de la contestation dans le Rif." *Middle East Eye*, May 29, 2017, http://www.middleeasteye.net/fr/reportages/maroc-arrestation-de-nasser -zafzafi-leader-de-la-contestation-dans-le-rif-183852197.

"Maroc: Un sénégalais egorgé avec deux autres africains tués." *Senenews*, August 30, 2014, https://www.senenews.com/2014/08/30/maroc-un-senegalais-egorge-par-des -marocains-avec-deux-autres-africains-tues_88909.html.

"Marruecos opta por la represión en el Rif: Intenta decapitar la rebellion." *El Confidencial*, May 27, 2017, http://www.elconfidencial.com/mundo/2017-05-27/marruecos-opta-por-la -represion-intenta-decapitar-a-la-rebelion-del-rif_1389824/.

Martin-Hillali, Francine. "Images centre ville de Tanger: Pratique et perception de l'espace." *Horizons Maghrebins* 31–32 (1996): 49–57.

Marx, Karl. *The Capital, Volume I: A Critique of Political Economy* (New York: Dover, 2011).

Massad, Joseph. *Desiring Arabs* (Chicago: University of Chicago Press, 2007).

Massad, Joseph. "Re-Orienting Desire: The Gay International and the Arab World." *Public Culture* 14, no. 2 (2002): 361–85.

McClintock, Anne. *Imperial Leather: Race, Gender, and Sexuality in the Colonial Context* (New York: Routledge, 1995).

McCormick, Jared. "Transition Beirut: Gay Identities, Lived Realities: The Balancing Act in the Middle East." In *Sexuality in the Arab World*, ed. Samir Khalaf and John Gagnon (London: Saqi, 2006).

Menjívar, Cecilia. "Liminal Legality: Salvadoran and Guatemalan Immigrants' Lives in the United States." *American Journal of Sociology* 111, no. 4 (2006): 999–1037.

Menjívar, Cecilia, and Daniel Kanstroom, eds. *Constructing Immigrant "Illegality"* (Cambridge: Cambridge University Press, 2013).

Merleau-Ponty, Maurice. *Éloge de la philosophie et autres essais* (Paris: Gallimard, 1965).

Merleau-Ponty, Maurice. *Phénoménologie de la perception* (Paris: Gallimard, 1945).

"Meurtre d'un Sénégalais au Maroc: Deux personnes interpellées." *Afrik.com*, September 1, 2014, http://www.afrik.com/meurtre-d-un-senegalais-au-maroc-deux-personnes-interpellees.

Michaux-Bellaire. *Tanger et sa zone* (Paris: Ernest Leroux, 1921).

Miège, Jean-Louis, *Le Maroc et l'Europe*, 4 vols. (Paris: Presses Universitaires de France, 1961).

Miège, Jean-Louis. "Les refugies politiques a Tanger, 1796–1875." *Revue Africaine* 1–2 (1957): 129–46.

"Migrants: Plus de 10 000 morts en Méditerranée depuis 2014, selon l'ONU." *Le Monde*, June 7, 2016, http://www.lemonde.fr/international/article/2016/06/07/migrants-plus-de -10-000-morts-en-mediterranee-depuis-2014-selon-l-onu_4940967_3210.html.

Miles, Barry. *Call Me Burroughs: A Life* (New York: Twelve, 2014).

Miller, Susan Gilson. "The Beni Ider Quarter of Tangier in 1900: Hybridity as a Social Practice." In *The Architecture and Memory of the Minority Quarter in the Muslim Mediterranean City*, ed. Susan Gilson Miller and Mauro Bertagnin, 139–74 (Cambridge, Mass.: Harvard University Press, 2010).

Miller, Susan Gilson. "Crisis and Community: The People of Tangier and the French Bombardment 1844." *Middle Eastern Studies* 27, no. 4 (1991): 592.

Miller, Susan Gilson. "Watering the Garden of Tangier." In *The Walled Arab City in Literature, Architecture, and History*, ed. Susan Slyomovics (London: Routledge, 2001).

Montagne, Robert. *Les Berbères et le Makhzen dans le sud du Maroc: Essai sur les transformation sedentaires des Berbères sédentaires (groupe chleuh)* (Paris: Alcan, 1930).

Montagne, Robert. *Naissance du prolétariat marocain: Enquete collective 1848–1950* (Paris: Peyronnet, 1964)

Montagne, Robert. *Révolution au Maroc* (Paris: France Empire, 1953).

Montagne, Robert. "Perspectives marocaines." *Politique étrangère* 16, no. 3 (1951): 259–78.

Moussaoui, Rosa. "Maroc: Les rebelles du Rif dans le viseur du roi Mohammed VI." *L'Humanité*, May 30, 2017, http://www.humanite.fr/maroc-les-rebelles-du-rif-dans-le -viseur-du-roi-mohammed-vi-636710.

Munson, Henry, Jr. *Religion and Power in Morocco* (New Haven, Conn.: Yale University Press, 1993).

Myers, Garth. *African Cities: Alternative Visions of Urban Theories and Practice* (London: Zed Books, 1998).

Naamane-Guessous, Soumaya. *Au delà de toute pudeur: La sexualité féminine au Maroc* (Paris: Karthala, 1991).

Nafaa, Mohammed. "Les pauvres riches de Rabat." *Le Reporter.ma*, November 1, 2014, http://www.lereporter.ma/actualite/a-la-une/3801-reportage-les-pauvres-riches-de-rabat.

Ndiaye, Malick. *Un nègre à Tanger* (Tangier: Khbar Bladna, 2013).

Ndiaye, Pape. "Questions de coulee: Histoire, ideologie et pratiques du colorisme." In *De la question sociale a la question raciale. Representer la France*, ed. Didier Fassin and Eric Fassin (Paris: La Decouverte, 2009).

Newcomb, Rachel. *Women of Fes: Ambiguities of Urban Life in Morocco* (Philadelphia: University of Pennsylvania Press, 2010).

Ngozi Ezeilo, Joy. "Report of the Special Rapporteur on Trafficking in Persons, Especially Women and Children," April 1, 2014, http://www.ohchr.org/en/professionalinterest/pages/crc.aspx (accessed March 23, 2018).

Nietzsche, Friedrich. *Beyond Good and Evil: Prelude to a Philosophy of the Future.* Trans. Walter Kaufmann (New York: Vintage Books, 1989).

Nietzsche, Friedrich. *Thus Spoke Zarathustra.* Trans. Graham Parks (Oxford: Oxford University Press, 2005).

"Niger Says 34 Migrants Found Dead in Sahara Desert." BBC, June 16, 2016, http://www.bbc.com/news/world-africa-36545015 (accessed March 20, 2018).

Noiriel, Gérard. *Le Creuset français: Histoire de l'immigration XIXe–XXe* (Paris: Le Seuil, 1988).

Nordstrom, Carolyn. *Global Outlaws: Crime, Money, and Power in the Contemporary World* (Berkeley: University of California Press, 2005).

"Nouveaux affrontements entre Marocains et Subsahariens à Tanger." *Tel Quel*, June 23, 2014, http://telquel.ma/2014/06/23/nouveaux-affrontements-marocains-subsahariens-tanger_139883.

Nussbaum, Martha. *For Love of Country* (Boston: Beacon, 1996).

O'Connell Davidson, Julia, and Jacqueline Sanchez Taylor. "Travel and Taboo: Heterosexual Sex Tourism to the Caribbean." In *Regulating Sex: The Politics of Intimacy and Identity*, ed. Elizabeth Bernstein and Laurie Schaffner (New York: Routledge, 2005).

O'Hagan, Andrew. "The Aesthetes," *New York Times*, April 11, 2014.

Obeyesekere, Gananath. *The Apotheosis of Captain Cook: European Mythmaking in the Pacific* (Princeton, N.J.: Princeton University Press, 1992).

Ong, Aihwa. *Flexible Citizenship: The Cultural Logics of Transnationality* (Durham, N.C.: Duke University Press, 1999).

Ong, Aihwa. "(Re)Articulations of Citizenship." *Political Science and Politics* 4, no. 38 (2005): 679–99.

Ossman, Susan. *Moving Matters: Paths of Serial Migration* (Stanford, Calif.: Stanford University Press, 2013).

Ossman, Susan. *Picturing Casablanca* (Berkeley: University of California Press, 1994).

Pandolfo, Stefania. "'The Burning': Finitude and the Political-Theological of Illegal Migration." *Anthropological Theory* 7, no. 3 (2007): 329–63.

Panter-Brick, Catherine. "Street Children, Human Rights, and Public Health: A Critique and Future Directions." *Annual Review of Anthropology* 31 (2002): 163.

Péguy, Charles. *Le Porche du mystère de la deuxième vertu* (Paris: Gallimard, 1929).

Peraldi, Michel, ed. *Les mineurs migrants non accompagnes: Un défi pour les pays européens* (Paris: Karthala, 2014).

Pettman, Jan Jindy. "Sex Tourism: The Complexities of Power." In *Culture and Global Change*, ed. Tracey Skelton and Tim Allen (London: Routledge, 1999).

Pian, Anaïk. *L'aventure incertaine des Sénégalais au Maroc* (Paris: La Dispute, 2009).

Piot, Charles. *Nostalgia for the Future: West Africa after the Cold War* (Chicago: University of Chicago Press, 2010).

Piot, Olivier. "Tanger, La mille et une ville." *Le Monde*, April 27, 2010, http://www.lemonde.fr/voyage/article/2009/09/01/tanger-la-mille-et-une-ville_1339691_3546.html.

Poliakov, Léon. "Racism from the Enlightenment to the Age of Imperialism." In *Racism and Colonialism: Essays on Ideology and Social Structure*, ed. Robert Ross, 55–64 (Hague: Martinus Nijhoff, 1982).

Przybyl, Sarah, and Youssef Ben Tayeb. "Tanger-Med, un espace hautement securise mais non moins attractif." *Hommes et migrations: Revue française de référence sur les dynamiques migratoires* 1304 (2013): 41–48.

Quentel, Jean-Claude. "Penser la différence de l'enfant." *Le Débat* 132 (2004): 18.

Rabinow, Paul. *French Modern: Norms and Forms of the Social Environment* (Cambridge, Mass.: MIT Press, 1989).

Ribas-Mateos, Natalia. *The Mediterranean in the Age of Globalization. Migration, Welfare and Borders* (New Brunswick, N.J.: Transaction, 2005).

Ricœur, Paul. *La mémoire, l'histoire, l'oubli* (Paris: Seuil, 2000).

Robbins, Bruce. "Actual Existing Cosmopolitanism." In *Cosmopolitics: Thinking and Feeling Beyond the Nation*, ed. P. Cheah and B. Robbins (Minneapolis: University of Minnesota Press, 1998).

Roitman, Janet. "The Ethics of Illegality in the Chad Bassin." In *Law and Disorder in the Postcolony*, ed. Jean Comaroff and John Comaroff (Chicago: University of Chicago Press, 2006).

Roitman, Janet. "New Sovereigns? Regulatory Authority in the Chad Basin." In *Intervention and Transnationalism in Africa: Global-Local Networks of Power*, ed. T. Callagy, R. Kassimir, and R. Latham (Cambridge: Cambridge University Press, 2001).

Roitman, Janet. "A Successful Life in the Illegal Realm: Smugglers and Road Bandits in the Chad." In *Readings in Modernity in Africa*, ed. P. Geschiere, B. Meyer, and P. Pels (Bloomington: Indiana University Press, 2008).

Rubin, Robert. *Travel, Modernism, and Modernity* (New York: Ashgate, 2015).

Sabra, Adam. *Poverty and Charity in Medieval Islam: Mamluk Egypt 1250–1517* (Cambridge: Cambridge University Press, 2000).

Sager, Tore. "Freedom as Mobility: Implications of the Distinction Between Actual and Potential Traveling." *Mobilities* 1, no. 3 (2006): 465–88.

Said, Edward. *Orientalism* (New York: Vintage, 1979).

Said, Edward. *Reflections on Exile and Other Essays* (Cambridge, Mass.: Harvard University Press, 2000).

Saigh Bousta, Rachida. "New Forms of Migration: Europeans in Marrakesh." In *Going Abroad: Travel, Tourism, and Migration*, ed. Christine Geoffrey and Richard Sibley, 158–266 (Cambridge: Cambridge Scholars, 2007).

Salazar, Noel. "Keywords of Mobility: What Is in a Name?" In *Keywords of Mobility*, ed. Noel Salazar and Kiran Jayaram (New York: Berghahn, 2016).

Saleh, Tayeb. *Season of Migration to the North* (New York: New York Review of Books, 2009).

Saleh, Tayeb. *Mawsim al-hijra ila al-shamâl* (Beirut: Dâr al-maʿârif, 1981).

Sanders, Will, and Travis Hodges. "The Aesthetes: Expats in Tangier." *New York Times Magazine*, April 11, 2014, http://tmagazine.blogs.nytimes.com/2014/04/11/the-aesthetes/?mcubz=0&_r=0.

Sartre, Jean-Paul. "Introduction." In *Orphée noir* (Paris: Presses Universitaires de France, 1948).

Sassen, Saskia. *The Global City* (Princeton, N.J.: Princeton University Press, 2013).

Sassen, Saskia. *Guests and Aliens* (New York: New Press, 1999).

Sassen, Saskia. *Globalization and Its Discontents* (New York: New Press, 1998).

Sayad, Abdelmalek. *La double absence: Des illusions de l'émigré aux souffrances de l'immigré* (Paris: Seuil, 2014).

Sayad, Abdelmalek. *L'immigration ou le paradoxe de l'alterité* (Paris: De Boek, 1992).

Scheper-Hughes, Nancy, and Carolyn Sargent, eds. *Small Wars: The Cultural Politics of Childhood* (Berkeley: University of California Press, 1998).

Scheper-Hughes, Nancy. *Death Without Weeping: The Violence of Everyday Life in Brazil* (Berkeley: University of California Press, 1992).

Schloss, Mark. *The Hatchet's Blood: Separation, Power, and Gender in Ehing Social Life* (Tucson: University of Arizona Press, 1988).

Schroeter, Daniel. "Philo-Sephardism, Anti-Semitism, and Arab Nationalism." In *Nazism, the Holocaust, and the Middle East*, ed. Francis R. Nicosia and Boğaç A. Ergene, 179–241 (New York: Berghahn, 2018).

Scott, Joan W. "Gender: A Useful Category of Historical Analysis." *American Historical Review* 5, no. 91 (1986): 1053–75.

Scott, Joan W. *The Politics of the Veil* (Princeton, N.J.: Princeton University Press, 2007).

Seddiki, Abdeslam. "In Morocco Youth Unemployment Is Driving Up Inequality." *Guardian*, August 20, 2014, https://www.theguardian.com/global-development-professionals-network/2014/aug/20/youth-unemployment-interactive-abdeslam-seddiki-morocco (accessed June 4, 2017).

Seidman, Steven. "The Politics of Cosmopolitan Beirut from the Stranger to the Other." *Theory, Culture, and Society* 29 (2012): 3–36.

Shah, Tahir. *The Caliph's House* (New York: Bantam, 2006).

Shamir, Ronan. "Without Borders? Notes on Globalization as Mobility Regime." *Sociological Theory* 2, no. 23 (2005): 197–217.

"Sit-in de soutien au Hirak d'Al Hoceima dans plusieurs villes, un journaliste algérien interpellé." *Tel Quel*, May 29, 2017, http://telquel.ma/2017/05/29/journaliste-algerien-interpelle-al-hoceima_1548377.

Slyomovics, Susan, ed. *The Walled Arab City in Literature, Architecture, and History* (London: Routledge, 2001).

Smith-Spark, Laura, and Arwa Damon. "Sahara Desert Deaths: 92 Migrants Perish in Niger After Vehicle Breakdowns." CNN, October 31, 2013, http://www.cnn.com/2013/10/31/world/africa/niger-bodies

Spencer, Claire. "The Zone of International Administration of Tangier (1923–1935)" (PhD diss., University of London, SOAS, 1993).

Staudigl, Michael. "Racism: On the Phenomenology of Embodied Desocialization." *Continental Philosophical Review* 45, no. 1 (2012): 23–39.

Stephens, Sharon. "Children and the Politics of Culture." In *The Global History of Childhood Reader*, ed. Heidi Morrison (New York: Routledge, 2012).

Stoler, Ann Laura. *Duress: Imperial Durabilities in Our Times* (Durham, N.C.: Duke University Press, 2016).

Stoller, Paul. *Money Has No Smell: The Africanization of New York City* (Chicago: University of Chicago Press, 2002).

Stuart, Graham. "The Future of Tangier," *Foreign Affairs*, July 1945.

Stuart, Graham. *The International City of Tangier* (Stanford, Calif.: Stanford University Press, 1955).

Tétu-Delange, Marie-Thérèse. *Clandestins au pays des papiers: Expériences et parcours de sans-papiers algériens* (Paris: La Découverte, 2009).

Therrien, Catherine, and Chloe Pellegrini. "French Migrants in Morocco." *Journal of North African Studies* 20, no. 4 (2015): 605–21.

Therrien, Catherine, ed. *La question du « chez-soi » au Maroc: Les représentations des migrants français confrontées aux points de vue des Marocains* (Rabat: AMERM, 2014).

Torpey, John. *The Invention of the Passport: Surveillance, Citizenship, and the State* (Cambridge: Cambridge University Press, 2000).

Trouillot, Michel-Rolph. *Anthropology and the Modern World* (New York: Palgrave, 2001).

Tucker, Aviezer. "In Search of Home." *Journal of Applied Philosophy* 2, no. 2 (1994): 184.

Tucker, Hazel. *Living with Tourism: Negotiating Identities in a Turkish Village* (London: Routledge, 2003).

Turner, Bryan. "The Enclaved Society: Towards a Sociology of Immobility." *European Journal of Social Theory* 10 (2007): 287–304.

Turner, Victor. *Forest of Symbols: Aspects of Ndembu Ritual* (Ithaca, N.Y.: Cornell University Press, 1967).

Twain, Mark. *The Innocents Abroad or the New Pilgrims' Progress*, vol. 1 (New York: Harper & Brothers, 1869).

Ugor, Paul, and Lord Mawuko-Yevugah. *African Youth Cultures in a Globalized World: Challenges, Agency and Resistance* (New York: Routledge, 2015).

Vaidon, Lawdom. *Tangier: A Different Way* (London: Scarecrow, 1977).

Van Reekum, Rogier, and Willem Schinkel. "Drawing Lines, Enacting Migration: Visual Prostheses of Bordering Europe." *Public Culture* 29 (2016): 27–51.

Vigh, Henrik. *Navigating Terrains of War: Youth and Soldiering in Ginea-Bissau* (Oxford: Bergahn, 2006).

Vigil, James Diego. "Urban Violence and Street Gangs." *Annual Review of Anthropology* 32 (2003): 225.

Visweswaran, Kamala. "Race and the Culture of Anthropology." *American Anthropologist* 100, no. 1 (1998): 70–83.

Walonen, Michael. *Writing Tangier in the Postcolonial Transition* (London: Ashgate, 2011).

Waterbury, John. *The Commander of the Faithful* (New York: Columbia University Press, 1982).

Weber, Max. *Economy and Society: An Outline of Interpretive Sociology*, vol. I. (Berkeley: University of California Press, 1978).

Weil, Patrick. *La France et ses étrangers: L'aventure d'une politique de l'immigration de 1938 à nos jours* (Paris, Gallimard, 2005).

Werbner, Pnina. "Vernacular Cosmopolitanism." *Theory, Culture, and Society* 23, nos. 2–3 (1999): 496–98.

Whitehouse, Bruce. *Migrants and Strangers in an African City* (Bloomington: University of Indiana Press, 2012).

Wieviorka, Michel, ed. *Racisme et modernité* (Paris: La Découverte, 1993).

Wihtol de Wenden, Catherine. *La question migratoire au XXIe siècle: Migrants, réfugiés et relations internationales* (Paris: Presses de Sciences Po, 2010).

Williams, Erica. *Sex Tourism in Bahia: Ambiguous Entanglements* (Urbana: University of Illinois Press, 2013).

Williams, Gisella. "A Fabled City of the Dissolute Gets Shine," *New York Times*, December 19, 2008, http://www.nytimes.com/2008/12/21/travel/21next.html.

Wilson, William Julius. *The Truly Disadvantaged: The Inner City, the Underclass, and Public Policy* (Chicago: University of Chicago Press, 1987).

Wintour, Patrick. "1m African Migrants May Be En Route to Europe, Says Former UK Envoy." *Guardian*, April 2, 2017, https://www.theguardian.com/uk-news/2017/apr/02/1m-african-migrants-may-be-en-route-to-europe-says-former-uk-envoy.

Zeghal, Malika. *Les Islamistes marocains, le défi de la monarchie* (Paris: La Découverte, 2005).

Index

Acknowledgments

Writing a book is rarely a solitary endeavor. This one is the result of years of dialogue, discussion, and consultation with colleagues, students, and also with people who have nothing to do with the academic world. In its making, I accumulated many intellectual debts and took several emotional loans. The list is so long that any attempt to be exhaustive would surely risk omissions. Nevertheless, I would like to express my deep gratitude and sincere thanks to all who in some way or another helped me bring this project to fruition.

First of all, I am grateful to the hundreds of Moroccan youth and children and the dozens of West African migrants whose lives I shared from 2008 to 2016. Their generosity with information, their trust, and, in some cases, friendship were all essential for this research. I hope that, with this book, I can at least record their heroic attempts at survival and their struggle for human dignity and the realization of a decent life. I hope it will also record some part of their sufferings and the daily injustices they are subjected to. Despite my skepticism that writing can change social reality, I am reminded of the words of Mohamed Choukri: "Writing could also be a way to expose, to protest against, those who have stolen my childhood, my adolescence, and a piece of my youth." I see myself in these children and youth, as well as in many of my own generation. Writing about the first generation is also in many ways writing about the second. The predicament is similar.

Also in the field, but in its comfort zone, I benefited from the generosity of many friends. I am deeply grateful to Elena Prentice, Karla Raïss El Fenni, Michel Peraldi, Hanae Bekkari, Abdelatif Saouri, Hicham Nouri, Stéphanie Gaou, Silvia Coarelli, Mohamed Ahrazem, Marouan Assaidi, and Houria Hamouhaj. During all these years, many friends helped in many ways, beyond the intellectual. I would like to thank especially Joane Nagel, Néjat Brahmi, Daniel J. Schroeter, Heba Mostafa, Elisabeth El'Khodary, Debbie Goldberg, Mona Zaki, Nyla Branscombe, Ahmed Jebari, Carlos Nash, Jennifer Haag, Jackie Brinton, Michael Crawford, Randy David, Meryem Fati,

Jerome Levi, Jason Olenberger, Hamza Walker, Haj Mahfoudh, Hassan Essadiq, and my late friend Hachoumi Ismael. Lawrence Rosen supported this project early on. I am grateful to Thomas Glick, Deborah Kapchan, James Boon, and Gananath Obeyesekere for their enduring encouragement.

During the writing process, my colleagues Barth Dean, Bob Antonio, Barney Warf, Don Stull, and Brahim El Guabli—each in his own way—read drafts of chapters, generously engaging with aspects of the book. Charlie Hubbard read and commented on Chapter 5 several times and provided much-appreciated comments on both my ideas and well as the style of my writing. Meghan Webb generously read and commented on Chapter 2.

A shorter version of Chapter 1 was published in the *Journal of North African Studies*, and some material in Chapter 2 was published in an early essay I wrote called "The *Harraga* of Tangiers," published by *Encounters*. I gratefully acknowledge permission to reproduce this material.

This book would not have been undertaken without the financial support of several institutions. The American Institute for Maghrib Studies generously supported my research in 2010, and a Fulbright research fellowship allowed me to conduct fieldwork in the city of Tangier from December 2010 till January 2012. Successive research field trips in 2008, 2012, 2013, and 2016 were supported by grants from the General Research Fund of the College of Liberal Arts and Science at the University of Kansas. I also would like to acknowledge the International Studies Program at the University of Kansas for supporting this project, especially in its early phases. The Aga Khan University Institute for the Study of Muslim Civilizations offered me an ideal setting to revise the manuscript in 2018.

I would like to express my deep gratitude to my dearest friend Fayre Makeig for her very careful and critical editing of the entire manuscript and for her many words of advice and encouragement. Ines Miranda's editing was also very helpful. I thank Pam LeRow for her careful preparation of the index.

Alma Gottlieb and two anonymous external reviewers shared insights and criticism that improved the manuscript. I am very grateful to them. My heartfelt thanks go to Eric Halpern for his support; to Liz Hallgren for her skillful preparation of the manuscript for publication; and to Erica Ginsburg and Gillian Dickens for their thorough and meticulous copyediting. Peter Agree not only saw the potential of an early draft of the manuscript, but his advice and guidance were also instrumental in the final making of the book.